BITS N' PIECES

OF OUR LIVES

COLLEEN CHAPMAN

authorHOUSE®

AuthorHouse™
1663 Liberty Drive
Bloomington, IN 47403
www.authorhouse.com
Phone: 1 (800) 839-8640

Published by AuthorHouse 09/27/2018

ISBN: 978-1-5462-6082-0 (sc)
ISBN: 978-1-5462-6081-3 (e)

Library of Congress Control Number: 2018911127

Print information available on the last page.

Foreword

Without my family and friends, there would be no stories for this book. Here is a "cast of characters."

My husband Howard

Me, Colleen. My children: Dave, Diane, Steven, Vincent, Robert, Susan, Debra, Rusty and Loren.

My siblings: Ruby, Pearl, Dorothy, Betty, Fred, Jerry, Donny, David, Linda and Skipper.

At first, I was writing this for my kids, about my kids. Then I decided it would be more fun if other family members and friends joined in.

I thank all of you for your material for Bits N' Pieces. I LOVE YOU ALL.

A FUNNY THING HAPPENED

A TRIP TO BONITA CREEK

DARVEL GREEN

It was in July or August 1970 I think. Uncle Walter and Aunt Jesse Phillips came to visit. I worked for Safford Municipal Utilities as an Engineer Aide. One of my duties was to measure the wells at Bonita Creek monthly. I asked Walter if he would go to Bonita Creek with me. He said he would go. Bonita Creek is northeast of the Gila River in eastern Arizona. The creek is the water supply for Safford, Arizona. The water collection pipes are under the creek. The system is gravity flow from Bonita Creek to Safford. There are two sand traps in the creek. The water flows from the second sand trap into a 24" pipeline. The pipeline is suspended on the canyon wall for a few miles. The canyon is really a pleasant place. On the one side is the pipeline. On the other side are some Indian ruins. There had been a flood in the creek just before Walter and I went. The road was washed out so we took a war wagon. The war wagon was an old short Dodge four-wheel drive pickup. You know the kind, they used in the war. It would go anyplace I could drive it. Part way up the creek is a big concrete block in the road. It is about 15' square and about 5' thick. It is right next to the canyon wall. To get up the canyon you drive over the block. The day Walter and I went there was a lot of muddy water in the creek. The water was running about 1' above the block of concrete. I drove across the block and there was no road on the other side. So we fell down into the creek. The war wagon was on about a 45-degree angle in the creek. Most of the back end was under water. The water level inside the cab was above the seat on Walters's side. The water level was just below the gas pedal on the floor board. So as you can see the war wagon was really on an angle. Walter and I climbed out of the war wagon to look it over. We took a look, scratched our heads and said "O NO" among other choice words.

CAMPING OUT

COLLEEN CHAPMAN

It was too hot to go outside, so Wayne and I were playing camp-out in the house. He was about 4 years old and was in the cowboy stage. He had on his boots and hat and had a bandanna around his neck. We sat on the living room floor and went fishing in the stream which ran across the room. We made a campfire close to the stream. While I cooked the fish and made cowboy coffee, Wayne fought off some rustlers who were trying to steal our cattle that were grazing in the kitchen. We had just started to eat our fish when Sierra, my sister-in-law who lived next door, came in. She had very poor eyesight because of cataracts. She almost stepped in the stream. I said, "Watch out. You are almost in the water!" She leaned over, and squinting her eyes, looked at the floor. Seeing no water, she straightened up and watched us as we sat on the floor, holding imaginary plates and went through the motions of eating and drinking from our imaginary cups. She shrugged her shoulders and started toward a chair. Wayne said, "Look out! You almost stepped in the campfire!" She turned and left the house. Just then the rustlers returned and we had to fight them off again. We were about to lose the battle because we were outnumbered and running low on ammunition. We were saved just in time by—that's right! The Cavalry!

ELKHORN SLOUGH

Colleen Chapman

Our normal routine on Saturday was to have a cup of hot cocoa with marshmallows and then the kids changed their sheets, the older ones helping the little ones. While they did that I fixed breakfast. After breakfast they cleaned their rooms. Unless there was a job that needed to be done, they had the rest of the day off.

One Saturday morning they took longer to finish the cocoa than usual. I told them it was time to get busy and reminded them we were going fishing and picnicking. They didn't budge except to look at Dave. Dave looked at the floor and kind of shriveled up. Then he stood up as straight and tall as he could. He took a deep breath and looked at me and said, "well, ya see Mom, we don't want to do our rooms today. We don't think we're going to." Ah ha, I thought. So that's what the huddles and whispering was all about. "What do you think you are going to do instead?" I asked. "Whatever we want to." He replied, obviously feeling nervous and trying hard not to show it. "You think everyone should do as they please today? Have you given this a lot of thought? All of you agree?" They had and they did. I thought this over, or pretended to. Then I said, "OK, sounds good to me. It's a nice sunny day. Go on outside and do whatever you want to."

Very surprised and a little apprehensive, they went out but didn't go far. I made myself comfortable with a book and a cup of tea. I could see the kids through our glass front door. They stood in a circle talking and looked toward the house often. After about half an hour, they came to the door and were very surprised to find it locked. *__They had never before been locked out!__* They went to the other doors and found them locked also. They came back to the front door. Dave knocked on the plate glass door.

"Mom, it's past breakfast time."

"It sure is." I said, not looking up.

"Mom, we're hungry."

"Of course you are. That's what happens when you miss a meal."

"When will breakfast be ready?"

"Gosh, I don't know. Who do you suppose wants to fix it?"

3

"Mom, aren't you gonna fix breakfast?"

"Ya know Dave, you kids are right. We should all do as we please on Saturdays. I'm enjoying this book, and I would rather read than cook. I don't want to fix breakfast. I don't think I'm going to."

The kids walked a few yards away from the door and conferred, then came back to the door.

"Mom, if you let us in we'll go do our rooms. Then will you feed us?"

"I don't think so. This story is just getting to the good part!"

"Mom, we have reconsidered. Will you please let us in so we can do what we are suppose to?"

"Oh well, if you really want to. Are you sure? Do you all agree?" They were and they did.

As they came in and went to their bedrooms, they didn't look at me. I could hear then talking as they worked.

Steven, "who's bright idea was *that*, anyway."

Diane, "yeah, just because some other kids get away with telling their Moms they aren't gonna do something it doesn't mean we can!"

Robert, "we didn't say we arent gonna, we just said we don't want to. The only reason I went along with it, well, ya know fwhat Mom always says, don't say you can't if you haven't given it your best shot."

Dave, "yeah, well, we tried and now we know."

Vincent, "*I* knew we wouldn't get away with it".

Diane, "I think we all did"

Sue, "Ya think we are still going fishing"

I spite of the delay we were ready to load the car about 11. We always took a change of cloths, wash cloths, towels, a big jug of water, and a sheet that had a hole cut in the middle of it. That was slipped over the head to afford privacy when we were someplace where facilities were not available for changing cloths. What is now known as Kirby park was just Elkhorn Slough then. Except for Dave and Steve, the kids had not fished before. I was very busy teaching them to bait and cast and keeping an eye on the two little ones, Debra and Rusty, in the playpen. A game warden appeared and asked for my license. The only license the kids knew anything about was drivers license, and wanted to know why he wanted to see it, since I was not driving right then. He said he wanted to see my fishing license. I wanted to say I didn't want to drive the fish, wanted to eat them but instead I explained that although I was holding a pole right then, I was not fishing. I was teaching the kids to fish. He watched for a few minutes. After hearing "Mom! My hook is stuck!" "Mom, my line is tangled." "Mom, I think I've got somthin. What do I do now?" He said he was convinced. I couldn't fish if I wanted to.

One of the boys cast out and lost his grip on the pole, and it went sailing into the water. It was a few feet from shore, so I pulled off my shoes and went in after it. After retrieving the pole, I slipped on the muddy bank and fell. Got up, took two steps up and fell again. The kids found this very entertaining and were enjoying it immensely. Dave came to my rescue. Grabbing his outstretched hand, I gave a yank and pulled him in. After changing our cloths, we had lunch. The fish were not biting, so I turned on the car radio and danced to the music. Some of the kids joined in. We had the place to ourselves and made the most of it.

The next day my Dad came to visit. Susan climbed up on his lap and said, "hey Grampa! Guess what! Mom locked us out yesterday and we almost starved to death before she let us in and fed us! And then we went to Elkhorn Sloooon. We stayed a long time. Oh and ya know what? Mom danced. And Grampa, she got downright dirty and then ya know what, she pulled off her cloths. And Grampa, a cop came and..." Just then Robert passed by and yanked one of her braids. She wasn't going to let him get away with that and took off after him. Daddy asked, "is that true? What she said?" "Well, kinda, but" That's as far as I got. Daddy rammed his fists into his pockets and started pacing the floor. Oh no! I knew what he was thinking! Daddy was a mild mannered man but when he was mad or upset he could really cuss. Or rather, my siblings and I thought he was cussing when we were kids. It didn't happen very often, but when it did, it scared us half to death and I think kind of broke our hearts. Sure enough, he let loose those words I had not heard for a long time. Still pacing, there they came "DAD BLAMED THE DAD BLAMED LUCK TO THE DAD BLAMED DEVIL ANYHOW. DAD BLAME IT! I would never have believed it of you. The very idea. It's bad enough, *you* going to a **bar**! But taking the *kids!* And doing a ***STRIP TEASE?*** What the Sam Hill has gotten into you! ***Dad blame it!***"

I rounded up the kids and told them to get in the car. Daddy too. Don't ask questions. Just hush and get in, NOW! We rode in silence the 2 1/2 miles to where we had been the day before. "Susan, tell Grampa where we are." "Grampa, this is Elkhorn Sloooon." "Now tell him how I got downright dirty". She did. "Now tell him where I was when I pulled off my cloths, and where we danced." She did. "Dave, tell him who the cop was, and then tell him why you were locked out." He did. Daddy listened, then softly said, "Humph! Well I'll be dad blamed." Robert said, "Huh?" He looked at me and said, "What are you blaming him for?" "I'm not blaming him for anything." "Well, he's your dad, and he said......

My watercolor of Elkhorn Slough. It won a second-place ribbon at the Santa Cruz County fair

GET YOUR HAND READY

Colleen Chapman

Pearl and I met in Moro Bay for a fun week-end together. Really gonna live it up. Neither of us was familiar with that part of the country. We drove around sightseeing for about an hour and then decided to go to a movie. We drove to Paso Robles and checked into a motel. The first thing we needed to do was get a newspaper to see what was playing, and the name and address of the theater of our choice. If we didn't spot the theatre, we could ask directions from one of the many students in the area. From the pedestrian traffic, there must be a collage near-by. It was about three in the afternoon, lots of traffic, both pedestrians and vehicles. Pearl was driving slowly and I was looking for a newspaper rack.

We got honked at a lot. Pearl said, "Well darn those guys! If Sandra was here she would flip them off for me. One time when she was little someone honked at me and she said, 'don't worry Mom; I flipped them off for you'. I want you to get your hand ready, and if we get honked at again, you flip them off." "I haven't ever done that. I'm not sure I know how to do it properly." I said. We stopped for a red light. "Look, I'll show you. Put these three fingers and your thumb down like this. Keep this finger up. Now keep it like that. Have it ready, and the next time some jerk honks at us, you flip them off. I think doing that's also called giving them the bird or rooster or something. I wonder why."

I got my hand ready, and a few more blocks up the street, I spotted a newspaper rack on a corner, on the other side of the street. As we approached the intersection, the light turned red. Pearl asked me if I wanted to hop out and get a paper, and she would go on up the street, find a place to turn around, or go around the block and pick me up. NO WAY! She gets lost so easy, we joke about her getting lost going from the kitchen to the bathroom. As we sat there waiting for the light to change, I told her I could see a service station about the middle of the next block on our side of the street. She could pull into the station, go around the back of the station and out the other side, make a left turn, and come back. There were several parking places close to the rack. Just then the light turned green and we were on our way.

Pearl said, "Did you notice a lot of those people back there looking at us funny?" "No." "Some of them were laughing and pointing, some looked confused, some looked surprised and some looked mad."

"I didn't notice. I was trying to show you how to get turned around and back to the rack."

"I know why, want me to tell you? Look at your hand." I looked at my hand. It was still at the ready, as Pearl had instructed. As I had told Pearl about the service station, etc., I had pointed it all out to her as I talked and had flipped off a whole bunch of college students!

We went to see The Poltergeist. On the way in I got some popcorn and coke. Pearl said she didn't want popcorn, just a coke. I didn't know it was possible to see a movie without popcorn! The scarier the movie got, the faster she ate my popcorn that she didn't want any of. I had a lot of fun watching the people around me. On my right, in the next row in front of us were a man and his very pregnant wife. He had his arm around her shoulders to start with. When the movie got suspenseful or scary, he would ask, "Are you OK, Honey?" The movie got scarier. His arm was around her neck, his forearm across her throat, his left knee in her lap. Again he asked, "Are you OK Honey?" "I will be just fine if you will stop choking me and trying to get in my lap!" At one point in the movie, the kid on the bed was looking for the clown doll that was doing strange things. After panning the room very slowly, the camera was at floor level as the kid pulled the bedspread up veeerrry slooolllly. Everyone thought the clown would be under the bed and were ready to scream. I knew the clown wouldn't be there, and everyone would scream anyway. It wasn't and they did. I really enjoyed the movie. The people around me were so entertaining. Every time Pearl screamed, I laughed and she hit me. She also ate most of my popcorn that she didn't want any of.

HELP! POLICE!

DOROTHY PATTON

Yesterday Kim took Naomi and the two boys to spend the night in Walnut Creek with her sister Sarah and help celebrate Hava's birthday. Geoff stayed home because he had to work and Abby stayed because she wanted to go to a friend's birthday party here on the beach today. I went to bed here in my little cottage about 10.0'clock and for once went right to sleep. But about 10.30 Abby came knocking on my door. "Dad went out," she said, "And there's a strange car in the driveway with two weird looking guys in it."

I went out and peeped around the house and there was a car there that I didn't recognize and I could see there was someone in it. We came back to my house and she tried to call Geoff on his cell phone but it was turned off so she left him a message about the two men. "Maybe it's someone waiting for Dad to come home," she said. "It makes no difference," I said. "Nobody has any right to pull up in the driveway and sit there without letting us know what's going on." I called the police station and asked if they could send someone to check them out. The woman said she would send someone and if they got out of the car to call 911. Well, the police were here in a few minutes. They made the weird looking guys put their hands behind their heads and get out of the car.

It turned out to be Geoff and his friend; they had just been sitting there talking. Abby didn't know that the friend had picked Geoff up, and Geoff had left his pickup parked and we couldn't see it so we thought he had left in the pickup. I felt really stupid and apologized but the policeman said we had done the right thing. Kim called this morning and Abby told her about it and she thought it was funny. Geoff was not amused but he also agreed, somewhat grudgingly, that we had done the right thing.

HOBO HOT SPRINGS

Colleen Chapman

Howard's family had a cabin on the Kern River. We went there for a couple of weeks in the summer. We didn't always stay in the cabin. It was the only cabin on the far side of the river. It was more fun to stay in the campground. We had some inner tubes and air mattresses and tied them to tree trunks so the kids could play with them and we didn't have to worry about them floating down river. The river was calm and safe where we were, but I had heard some scary stories about how dangerous the river was down stream from us. One afternoon Vincent was laying on an air mattress. It came untied, probably with some help from him, and away he went down stream. He was just 9 years old, and could swim, but there was no way he could swim well enough to get out of the fix he was in. I panicked. I had not yet learned to swim. There was no one in the river close enough to help him. I didn't know where Howard was so I started into the water. Suddenly Howard was walking along the edge of the river, talking calmly to Vincent. He told Vince to scoot back until his legs were in the water from the knees on down so he could paddle with his feet. Then to use his arms and hands like oars and get himself to shore. He was safe in no time at all.

Not all of the things I'm telling about happened during one summer. Thank goodness! We did have *some* summers with no upsetting events. The summer Rusty was about 8 months old I laid him on an air mattress. He lay there holding his bottle with one hand, the other arm resting on his forhead. One leg was reating on the upraised knee of the other leg. I sat in the water beside him, my right arm resting on the mattress. I looked to the left to check on Diane and Sue who were playing a few feet away. They facing the river and suddenly looked surprised. Diane said, "Mom!" and pointed. There was Rusty in the same position he had been in on the mattress, floating in the water.

There was a café near the campground. One day we decided to take the kids there for lunch. Sierra, Howard sister and her daughter Lynn, who was working in a little town nearby, were with us. His mother was there also. Howard, his mother, sister, niece and I sat in a booth with Debra and Rusty in high chairs by the table. Dave, 11, Diane, 10, Steven, 9, Vince, 7, Robert, 6, and Susan, 4, sat in the next booth. I could see them in a mirror on the wall. I knew I didn't have to worry about the kids behavior or manners. Dave would see to that. When I couldn't be at the table at home or anywhere else, Dave took over. I never asked him to, he started this when he was only six or seven years old. He was never loud, just quietly kept an eye on the rest of the kids and corrected them if they did something wrong. None of the kids questioned his authority.

We ordered salad, chili beans, crackers and milk for everyone. Ruby, the waitress and owner, took care of the kids first. We had coffee while we waited. Ruby brought the silverware and napkins. As she placed them in front of the kids we could hear each one say thank you. Ruby said you're welcome to each thank you. Then came the milk. Again, six times we heard thank you and six times, you're welcome. Then Ruby brought the salads. After the third thank you with no response from Ruby, Robert said, "it's too bad your Mom didn't teach you very good manners." Ruby had just placed the last salad on the table. She stepped back, put her hands on her hips and said, "what? You mean because I didn't say thank you?" Robert nodded his head "yes Ma'am." Ruby said, "I have to make several more trips to this table. I tell you what. Don't say thank you any more until I'm all through. Then you can all say it one time, and that will be for everything. I will say you're welcome one time, and that will be for all of you. OK? Is it a deal?" The kids looked at each other and then they all nodded in agreement. Robert said, "it's a deal." and stuck out his hand. Ruby looked at his hand and said, "what!" "We made a deal. We have to shake on it." Robert said. As Ruby shook his hand she said, "I don't need to shake hands with all of you, do I?"

We had all just about finished eating when the cook came out of the kitchen. She said, "there's a little girl in the kitchen. She came in carrying her dishes and asked 'where's the sink, please?' I told her I would take the dishes but she won't give them to me. She said it's her job to put them in the sink." I checked the kid booth. Susan was missing. The other kids were getting their dishes ready to take to the kitchen too. I had not thought to tell them not to do that. This was their first time in a restaurant other than fast food places. As we were leaving Ruby said, "the kids are so well behaved and have such nice manners, you are welcome to come back any time. As a matter of fact, if you want to come back tomorrow afternoon I would like to give you all a treat on the house."

On the way back to the campground Susan, Vince and Robert looked back at the cafe several times. Then they stopped and stood looking at the roof. I stoped and waited. The three of them talked, their heads together. They came to me and Vince said, "it's real nice of that lady to give us a treat. What do you think it is?" I said, "I don't know, maybe some ice cream." The kids looked back at the cafe again. Then Vince said, "but Mom, why does she want to give it to us on the house?" Robert said, "yeah! And how are we suppose ta get up there?" Susan, with trembling chin said, "I don't want **anything** on the house!"

When Debra was about two years old she ended up in the deep water some how. I didn't know how to swim, and no one else was close enough to get to her in time to keep her from being carried down stream. I went in after her. After we had both gone under a couple of times, I managed to turn on my back, put her on my chest, and paddle with my feet. I wasn't getting anywhere, but we were not going down river. Another camper rescued us. We went home the next day as planned. A few days later we went to Chuck's. (Howard's ex-brother-inlaw) I got in their pool and did not come out until I could swim!

Daddy went with us the summer the kids learned to swim. We found a place where the water was shallow enough, and ran very slow. Howard showed them how to swim, then standing up, he demonstrated how to do strokes with his arms. He explained the position and movements of the feet and legs. They caught on pretty quick. When they tired of swimming they rested a short while and began to play...I think it's called chicken fight. You stand, with someone on your back, and the ones on backs try to push or pull another back rider into the water....or something like that. Steven got in some water over his head and went under. Daddy stood up and took a few steps. Steven came up, sputtering, then went under again. Daddy looked at Howard and said, "Aren't you going after him?" Howard said, "He hasn't gone down the third time yet." Steven came up and swam to safety.

We were staying in the cabin. The older kids were on the other side of the river with Howard, Sierra and Lynn. The little kids were playing around the cabin. Sierra's son Jim was visiting, and had gone for a walk. I saw Jim, holding Debra, run down to the river. He stopped at the edge, bending down to the water. When he came back, he was rather pale. Three year old Debra wasn't very happy. She told me Jim had let her new pet go. Jim explained that just as he came around the corner of the cabin, a rattlesnake about eight inches long had struck at Debra, who was sitting on the ground. She had somehow grabbed it just below it's head. Jim put his hand over hers, and holding tightly, rushed to the river and held the snake under the water until it drowned. Debra was very mad at Jim for letting her new pet go, but I was very grateful!

HOT FUDGE SUNDAE

Colleen Chapman

Dorothy, Susan and I went to Fisherman's Wharf in Monterey. After walking the length of the wharf, watching the Pelicans, Sea Lions, browsing the shops, etc., we stopped to get ice cream. As we stood in line, Dorothy read the menu on the wall. She laughed and said, you know, sodas always make me hiccup. I guess I'm not the only one. Look. That sign says Coke, 7UP, Sprite, HIC, Coffee and Tea. When Dorothy read hic, she made a hiccup sound. I looked at the menu. HIC was at an angle above the rest of the list of drinks. I said, "Dorothy, that says Hi C. A drink. We had a good laugh. We finally got up to the Counter. Susan ordered for the three of us. "Three Hot Fudge Sundays in a Waffle cone please." The young man stood and stared at her, so she repeated the order. He said, "uh–it–uh–I don't uh..." I told Sue, "he thinks you want all three Sundays in one cone, and he doesn't think he can do that!" Sue sighed, and very slowly and patiently said, "We three are together. We each want a hot fudge sundae in a waffle cone. One for her, one for her and one for me." The young man blushed and made the sundaes very fast and extra good. The first time I had a hot fudge Sundae I was living with Ruby and her family. We were on our way to Phoenix and stopped for ice cream. Carl ordered, then Ruby ordered for the kids. She said she thought she would have an ice cream Sunday. She asked if I wanted to too. Before we stopped she and Carl had been discussing their budget. I thought she didn't have enough money for all of us to have ice cream now, so she and I were going to wait until Sunday for ours. Trying to be a good sport and hide my disappointment, I said yes. What a pleasant surprise!

JUST ONE OF THOSE DAYS

COLLEEN CHAPMAN

Pearl, Sandra and I had a date to meet in Salinas for lunch. I took a bath, soaking in our huge bathtub for a long time. It was very relaxing, and it felt good to take my time instead of being in a hurry as I usually am. Just as I started to get dressed, I noticed a spot on my pants. I finished getting ready, intending to get another pair of pants from the bedroom when I went in there to get my shoes. I stopped at the Drug store to pick up some prescriptions before going on to Salinas. I was wearing black pants and looked at them as I got out of the car, checking for white hairs from my dog. (I keep a cloths brush in my car.) Then the cool air hit my legs. It felt cooler than it should have. Then I realized the black I was seeing was my pantyhose! I went back home and finished getting dressed. In the past I have left home without my purse, or my shoes, and a couple of times without my bridge, but never without my pants! I was a little late getting to Salinas. We had a nice lunch, did a little shopping, sat and talked for a while, then went our separate ways. I went to Costco's. After parking the car, I did not put the gear in park as I usually do. As I slid the seat back, the car rolled forward, bumping the car in front of me. I got out to see if any damage had been done. There was no damage, so I continued to the store. Just as I got to the door, I realized my purse was in the car. Back to the car I went. The door was locked. The keys were in the car. Out of habit, I had slid the lock with my thumb as I got out of the car. The window was down just an inch or two. I went to the tire shop to get a clothes hanger. They send their uniforms to the cleaners, so I knew they would have hangers. After explaining what I wanted it for, the nice man straightened it out, and bent it so it made a good tool to put through the window and hook the keys. In the meantime it had started to rain.

I was wet but decided to go on into the store anyway. Then I couldn't find my Costco card. The last time I had used it, I had put it in the pocket of my jacket. It was still there! I got a courtesy pass and did the shopping. I turned on the lights and wipers and started home in the very heavy rain. Shortly after getting on the freeway one wiper made a screeching sound. The rubber blade had come loose. I found a safe place to pull over and managed to fix the darn thing. Now I was really wet. When I got home the rain had stopped and the sun was shining. I hurried into the house to get into some dry cloths. It was about 2:30, and I had some time to myself before I had to go up to Camacho's to put medicine in Evie's eye. I made a cup of cocoa, got a book, and sat in my recliner. Shadow, my dog, wanted to join me He always waits for me to tell him OK before jumping up on my lap. But not today. Somehow the cup of cocoa ended up in my lap, on the book and on the dog. After cleaning up the mess I took Shadow and got in the shower. He didn't like it much. He ran in circles around my legs, trying to find a dry spot. After he was rinsed off, and as dry as I could get him with a towel, I finished drying him with my hair dryer.

Evie's eye was to be taken care of at 7: o'clock. The car wouldn't start. The battery was dead. I had not turned off the lights when I got home from Salinas. By the way, Howard was gone on a trip, so I was on my own. I thought-no problem, I will drive the lawn tractor up there. I couldn't get it out without moving the car. Of course without the motor running, there would be no power steering. Since our driveway is downhill, I decided not to even try. Not with the way things had been going. I called Evie and told her I would be late because I had to walk. Uphill. About 2000 feet. (distance, not altitude.) Paul and Evie always enjoyed seeing Shadow, so I took him with me. When we were about half way there, Butch, a big friendly dog, came trotting out to the road. Butch was big enough to eat Shadow for dinner. Did Shadow behave himself and keep quiet? Nooooo! Long ago Pomeranians were a large breed but were bred down to the size they are today. Shadow seems to think he is a big dog, not the little eleven pounder that he is. He growled as Butch approached. The dog ignored him and came to me expecting to be petted. Well, Shadow didn't like that a bit. I don't know what he disliked the most. Being ignored after growling as mean as he could or having me pet another dog. For whatever reason, maybe just plain stupidity, Shadow jumped as high as he could, and bit Butch on the neck, close to his head. Actually, all he got was a mouth full of hair. Butch jumped and swung his head, trying to shake Shadow loose. Shadow hung on and was being flung around like a rag doll and I could not grab him. A neighbor on his way home from work stopped, got out of his pickup and asked who needed saving. Shadow, Butch or me. He saved all of us and took Butch home.

After taking care of Evie's eye and visiting for a while, we started home. By this time it was dark so Paul gave me a flashlight. I didn't need it at first because he had the outside lights on, and the moon was very bright. But before we got home a big dark cloud covered the moon.

Time to use the flashlight. Do you think it would work? With the way this day had been going? Nooooo! I have night blindness, not all the time, it seems to come and go. That night it was bad. All I had to do was go straight downhill and Shadow would go up our driveway when we came to it, and on up to the house. Everything would be just fine.

Unless I stepped on a

Or in a hole and turned my ankle, or Shadow decided to take a side trip to check out a gopher hole or an interesting smell or **attracted the attention of a**

Or a

None of those things happened and we were almost home when one of the Morgans (a family that lives up the canyon and have big trucks and haul compost and fertilizer) came up the road and splashed us good. Wet and muddy, we made it to the house and into the shower again. That made one bath and two showers for me, and two showers for Shadow. Funny, he wanted nothing to do with me the rest of the night

LISTEN!

COLLEEN CHAPMAN

Mother was living in Betty and Larry's little guest house. I don't remember what the occasion was, but Dorothy, Pearl and I were there. We were having a 'hen party' and getting ready for bed. Mother took her shower, and went to bed, propped up all cozy and comfy, and pleased that she had the full attention of the three of us...or so she thought...and was telling us something we had all heard before, so we weren't paying much attention.

She was so caught up in the story; she was reliving it as she told it and didn't notice that we were talking quietly as we took turns in the bathroom. When Dorothy came out of the bathroom she said the window in there was wide open and anyone could climb in. She had just finished saying that when Pearl, who had gone into the bathroom unnoticed by Dorothy, cleared her throat or coughed. Dorothy, looking scared, gasped and said, "Listen! Someone is at that window." She was standing with her back to the short, dark hallway that went from the kitchen to the bathroom. Just then Pearl came out of the bathroom, clearing her throat, right behind Dorothy. Dorothy screamed. Pearl screamed. I, who was halfway in a sleeping bag on the floor, was trying to get up and couldn't. I was going to say help me up, but help is as far as I got. They heard help and screamed again. I screamed because if both of them were screaming, we must really be in trouble, and someone should scream loud enough to be heard for blocks.

About the time we figured out what had happened we noticed that Mother was oblivious to the whole thing and was still looking off into space and telling her story. She refused to wear her much-needed hearing aids most of the time. She liked to talk, no, she LOVED to talk, but was not fond of being talked to, especially if there was a story she wanted to tell. If she couldn't hear us, we could not interrupt her. We were cracking up already but that made it all even funnier.

Mother finished her story at last and looked at us. We could not stop laughing. She looked rather confused and after several minutes she said, "Well, I know it was a funny story but I didn't know it was that funny." That made us laugh even harder. Larry came in to see what all the noise was about. He stood watching, and then asked what was going on. Mother, who had put on her hearing aids, said, "I don't know, Larry, I think they have all lost their minds."

LOCKED OUT

A STRING OF EMAILS TAKEN FROM THE FAMILY SITE

Ruby----This morning when we started to go to Church Carl asked me if I had my keys as we started out the door. I told him, "No" He started back to the bed-room, where his were. I said, "but I don't have to go into the bed-room to get them," and started to get them from the key holder in the office. Carl just kept going to the bed-room, so I went on out to the car. After a minute or two, Carl came out to the car and held out his hand for my keys. I told him I didn't have them. He said "well, I just threw mine in the chair as I came out because I thought you had yours!" We carry all our keys on one ring. So, we were locked out.

We tried every door and then started trying to find a window unlocked through which Carl could crawl. No luck. They were all locked up tight except for a bath room window which was high off the floor. We got a ladder so he could go in feet first and drop to the floor. That might have worked if he had been 21, or even 50. But at 83 it was just too much. Our house had been broken into once. They had broken the latch on the kitchen door. So Carl thought he would try that.

In the meantime, I decided to tear the screen on the kitchen window. I had been wanting to replace it anyway. Besides it wouldn't be as bad as messing up the door. I found a large nail and a piece of pipe and got the screen unlocked. Carl hadn't made much headway with the door, so he crawled in through the window. We were both sweating so bad we needed to bathe and change clothes but Carl said "we'll just stand in front of the fan and dry off." So that is what we did.

But it was too late to go to Sacrament meeting. We waited until time for Sunday school. Carl gave the lesson in Priesthood meeting after Sunday school. He said it went pretty well. I had Relief Society meeting at the same time as Priesthood meeting. We had a time getting the dust off and our hair straighten out after our ordeal, before we could go to church. I'll bet we don't lock the keys in the house again. The kitchen door will take a little fixing.

Dorothy----Well, by now all you new cousins know Colleen is a little bit daffy. This reminds me of a time that I was traveling alone and stopped at a little country station for gas. The attendant filled the tank for me and I offered him my credit card. He said he didn't take credit cards. I looked in my purse and didn't have enough money to pay him. I said, "well, I'll have to dig a little deeper." I turned my back to him and dug into my bra for the money. When I turned back around he was looking at the ground and his face was very red. I was embarrassed too and I was thinking, "This is the kind of thing that happens to Colleen, not to me."

Colleen----From locked out to service station attendants--you never know where the conversation will go.

Ruby----Dorothy, remember when you and I went to Oklahoma that time? Coming home we thought something really bad was wrong with the car, for it just stopped running. A man stopped to see if he could help and after checking, asked, "is there any gas in the tank?" We hadn't even thought about that. He checked and the tank was empty. Then he went to the next town and got a can of gas and brought it back to us. I don't remember just how the story goes, but I remember we felt very foolish, and it was kind-of-funny.

Colleen-----And you guys call ME daffy! Quick! Someone think of something really smart that one of us did, so the cousins will think that at least one of us has a little bit of sense. When Dorothy, Pearl and I went to San Diego when Ruby, Cathy, Carla and Ruby's grand daughters were there for a vacation, we had so many things happen that Dorothy said she didn't know who we were more like, the three Musketeers or the Three Stooges. I named us the Four Bumbliers.

Dorothy----Okay, after racking my brain I thought of something smart that we did. After driving around San Diego for three hours trying to find our way and after ending up at the

19

Mexican border for the third time, we decided to call on our guardian angels for help. In about fifteen minutes after that we found where we wanted to go. Now, was that smart or what?

Colleen----It wasn't that long! Why didn't we call on them sooner? Remember you asked me if I had called on them and I said no, and we decided we should do that. We did, and I said I was going to turn right at the next intersection. I had just finished saying that when we got there and suddenly, without intending to, made a left turn. That put us right where we needed to be and we had no problems getting to Bill and Catherine place.

Ruby ----There's just no end to this. After the trouble we had Sunday, Carl went the first thing Monday morning and had some more house keys made. We will keep one set in the car's glove compartment and one set in the pickup. That way we can always get back into the house. Now, I would call that smart. But then this afternoon he took the car to have it serviced. I don't know how he got home. Anyway, the man at the garage called about 5 O'clock to tell us the car was ready. I told him we would come and get it. We started to go get the car. But guess what. We didn't have a key for the pickup. Carl's keys to the pickup are on the ring with his car keys. I don't have keys to the pickup. Carl tried to call the garage to ask if they would deliver the car, but got a recording. Well, he had to go find someone out in our trailer park to take him to the garage. Alex, a man who rents a small trailer from us, consented to take him to get the car.

Colleen -----Why don't you both wear a chain around your necks with every key you need?

Dorothy-----I wear keys around my neck at work. I drop them down inside the front of my apron to keep them from getting in my way. But if I take off my apron for some reason they are always in the way. So Ruby, if you and Carl wear your keys around your neck, I recommend you use your sewing skills to make you both some aprons.

Colleen----if you do, please don't put ruffles on Carl's aprons.

Sandra---My mom and aunts are all crazy. What they write about on the web is nothing compared to real life. So if the cousins at the reunion get the wrong ideatheyprobably right. They are not dangerous though; just a lot of laughs

LINDA PEARL COLLEEN RUBY DOROTHY BETTY

A LESSON LEARNES

C O L L E E N   C H A P M A N

F red and Hootie went hunting along the Salinas river and were spending the night camped out under the bridge. Jerry and I sneaked out after everyone was asleep. We didn plan to join them, we planed to scare them. Jerry could make good animal sounds. He did a really good cougar growl and cough. We had walked the three miles to the river many times, but never at night. Fortunately there was a big bright moon. We could see then sitting by a campfire roasting marshmallows under the bridge.

We crawled quietly through the grass and brush until we got close enough for them to hear Jerry. He did a couple of cougar coughs. That got their attention. They stopped talking. He went into his repertoire of cougar sounds. I tried not to giggle too loud as I watched the look of alarm on the guys faces. For added affect Jerry shook the tall dry grass.

The guys whispered and looked in our direction. Jerry shook the grass again and moved forward some to make them think the cougar was moving in for the kill. Fred stood up and fired. We had not planned on *that!* We lay as flat as we could as bullets flew. We snake crawled as fast and quietly as we could until we got far enough away to get up and run. We learned a valuable lesson that night.

Do not scare a person who has a loaded gun!

PICKING UP FIGS

RUSTY CHAPMAN

It was a Saturday during the late 1960's. Mom was spinning up to throw a fit because there were chores to be done, and we kids were lying around watching cartoons. Howard was expected home from work within the hour. She tried to get us moving several times, but our favorite Looney Toones kept luring us back.

No wonder! The chore for that morning was to pick up under the three fig trees. A stinky, maggot infested job. I don't remember what the last straw was that set Mom off. She didn't lose her cool very often, but when she did, she did it up right! She stormed into the living room, SLAMMED off the TV, waived the seldom used whip'n-stick over her head (which got every one's undivided attention.) She pointed the stick towards the back yard and threatened us in an ever-increasing tone/volume, "You kids get out there and FU*K UP THOSE PIGS!" At first I thought I had miss-heard Mom. But as we all exchanged glances, we realized she DID say what we ALL thought she said, and the laughter started. Of course, Mom had no idea what she had said and decided it was time to open her can of whoop-ass on all the disrespectful smart-ellicks that she had put on this here earth. And told us as much as she swung at us, missing us most of the time as we ducked and dodged. I don't remember much of what happened after that except Howard trying not to laugh as he sent us out to pick up the figs.

My side of the story

Colleen Chapman (AKA Mom)

As Rusty said, the chore for that Saturday was to clean up under the fig tree. And yes, it was a miserable job. I explained that it had to be done, and the hotter it got, the more flies and bees would appear. If all ten of them (my nine, my nephew Donny who was spending the summer with us) got out there and got busy, the job would only take a few minutes. When Howard got home from work we were supposed to be ready to go someplace. I was making jam with the last of the apricots, and the 'whop'n stick' mentioned was really a big wooden spoon. It was a huge one that Howard made for me. I don't remember hitting anyone with it. I do remember cleaning up some jam from the floor and wall. I guess it was flung there as I waived the spoon around. They had all been shooed out the back door several times and they went around the house and in the front door. When I get angry or upset I sometimes get my mix all worded up. I don't know how many times I had told them to GET OUT THERE AND PICK UP THOSE FIGS. Well, when it came out wrong I had no idea why I had wall to wall laughing kids! If I did hit them as Rusty said, it probably didn't hurt much. All but the three youngest ones were bigger than me and anyway, I wouldn't have wanted to break that big wooden spoon. It was the only one I had. Howard came home and opened the door to a house full of laughing kids, some rolling on the floor, and me standing in the middle of it all looking very confused, holding a sticky spoon. He asked what was so funny. Loren said, "We can't tell you because we would have to say a word we are not allowed to say. But Mom said it!" I said, "All I did was tell them to go pick up the figs." The laughter from the kids increased. Howard knew what had happened. He sent the kids out to…you know. Then he wanted to know why I had jam on my nose, and in my hair.

Several years later we were all at Pearl and Louon's house. I don't remember what the occasion was, but most of the family was there. Some we hadn't seen for a long time. Several conversations were going on at the same time. Donny nonchalantly joined Robert who was leaning against the wall and asked in a voice loud enough for all to hear, "Hey, Rob, have you fu**ed up any pigs lately?" Robert thought for a second or two, rubbing his chin, and then answered, "No, can't say I have. Not since Mom insisted we do it that summer." All conversation stopped. Everyone, almost in unison, turned and stared at them. Then turned to stare at me. And kept staring. If they were waiting for an explanation, they didn't get one from me! I just offered to go pot on a put of coffee and escaped into the kitchen

THE EASIEST WAY

Colleen Chapman

Many, many years ago when Tampons were relatively new on the market, I bought some while doing grocery shopping. Later that day, before putting them away, I was standing in the bathroom reading the information on the package. Howard came into the bathroom. He looked to see what I was reading. "Have you used these?" he asked. "No" I said. Howard took the package, opened it, removed one Tampon, and un-wrapped it. "The easiest way to do this is like this." he said as he put one foot up on the toilet stool. He demonstrated, but I will leave that to your imagination. "When did you start using these?" I asked. He never looked up. Just slowly put his foot on the floor, the Tampon on the sink, and walked out of the bathroom.

REJUVINATION

DOROTHY PATTON

A few years ago I bought a series of treatments from practioners at the Inner Light Ministries Church. They gave me two free tickets to a Woman's Rejuvenation weekend retreat. I offered the tickets to several family members and friends but they all declined so I went alone.

The retreat workshops consisted of lessons in healthy eating and cooking, exercises, ways to relax and relieve stress, and ways to improve self-esteem. They were all fun and informative and very upbeat. On the last day the very last session was called A Tribute to Women. We were led into a large room with lights low and soft music playing. Comfortable chair and cushions were arranged around the room. We were told to sit and relax. When we were settled the husband of the woman leading the workshop, the first man to be seen at any event since we started, came in leading a long line of men all carrying trays heaped with strawberries and chocolates. We were speechless as they stopped and bowed to us and all together said, "We come to honor Womanhood."

Then they passed among us serving the strawberries and chocolates. When we had eaten until we could eat no more the men lined up again and it was announced that every one of them was a massage therapist and that they would massage our shoulders, necks, backs and feet. We were still speechless but aware enough to start taking off our shoes. Again the men moved among us and I got three wonderful massages. I noticed one elderly man from the church standing aside with arms folded just watching. Who cares why he was there.

After this orgy was over our leader announced that we women were now going to honor the men. This was a complete surprise to them, she said. Even her husband hadn't known about it. I saw the elderly man come to attention leading me to believe he hadn't known about it either, but he made no effort to stop this determined woman. She had the women form two lines facing each other. Then she told the men to close their eyes, stretch out their arms in front of them and walk between the lines. The women would take their arms and guide them along the lines, whispering blessings into their ears as they went by. This was called an Angle

Walk, she said. The men seemed very touched by this and when they passed me I noticed that several had tears running down their faces, and two of them were sobbing as they left the room. The elderly man was standing by the door as they went out. Dry eyed, I think, since he declined to do the walk.

When I got home and told about the retreat all the ones who had refused the extra tickets said they wished they had gone. I never heard of a church retreat like that, they said.

FROM THE FAMILY SITE

COLLEEN CHAPMAN

Ruby…Our web-site has been dead lately. I'm with Sue; I think we need a poem, a story or something. Colleen, haven't you done anything crazy lately --Like the time you were in a hurry to meet Pearl and Dorothy and Sandra for lunch and got dressed in a hurry and put on your black shirt, laid out your black pants, put on your black pantyhose and ran out to the car and as you stopped at the drug store before meeting the girls, you thought the air was cold as you got out of the car. Looking down, you had forgotten to put on your pants. Another story and strings of remarks can keep us laughing for a month or more.

Colleen…If I have done something crazy lately it isn't anything I am willing to tell about! Well, I guess there is one thing that might give you a chuckle.

I was on my way to Gilroy, to the outlet stores. Wanted to go to Harry and Davids to get some sugar free goodies for a friend, who had a birthday coming up. The traffic was very heavy. Stop and go, stop and cuss and go, all the way. It took about an hour to get there. I had coffee for breakfast instead of tea, and well, you know what coffee can do to old...I mean matronly....no, don't like that either.... women my age. When I got there, there were no parking spaces anywhere near any place that has a restroom. I found a space at the far end of the parking lot, straight down from Harry and Davids. I knew the situation was desperate. As soon as I stood up, the water works would start. There was no way I could get out of the car. There was an empty, large paper cup in the cup holder that I use for a small trash container. I slid the seat back as far as it would go, scooted to the edge of the seat......to be continued.... I'm suppose to be in Soledad in an hour and I'm still sitting here in my bathrobe!

OK so I didn't finish it last night. Where was I....and looked around. The front and right side were screened by bushes. No one could see in through the rear and side windows, because they are tinted. So all I had to worry about was the driver's window. I thought about getting into the back seat, but I knew as soon as I stood up.....So, facing the driver's window, I raised up enough to slip my pants and panties down. My pants had an elastic waist, no buttons, no zipper. My blouse was a pheasant type, full, and reached past my hips. So I was well covered. Nothing showing that shouldn't. With my left thigh on the seat, I got the cup.

It was made for coffee, and had a fold out handle. Holding it in place, I let the water works begin, just in time. I had just finished when a man walked up to the car and with a big smile said "Well hello there!" I said, "Hello" still holding the cup and thinking he was going to try to sell me something or ask for money. He didn't look like the people who ask for money. He said, "You don't recognize me, do you. We went to school together. Washington Jr. High. Of course it's called middle school now. I walked you home several times and wanted you to be my girl, but you sure didn't encourage me. Broke my heart." "Jr. high...that was in 1947 or 48...and you expect me to believe you recognized me?" "I did. Really! I'm good with faces and names. Your name is Colleen. I was in the 7th grade and you were in the 8th. I'm Russel Jeffries." "Oh yes. I remember you. You had brown curly hair." I said, looking at his bald head. "Yes. One loses some things and gain others." he said as he patted his stomach. He was not slim anymore, either. Then I thought, here I am, sitting here holding a big cup full of pee, talking to an ex mayor of Salinas. It was ridicules, and it took all my self control to keep from bursting into laughter. Fortunately, he said he had better continue on to his car where his wife and grandson were waiting. I carefully set the cup on the floorboard on the passenger side, and slid my clothes into place. Got out, emptied the cup by the bushes. That ought to confuse some dogs if they came sniffing around. Sigh. Sometimes I miss our old bet up camping van. When Sue and I were into selling our arts and craft stuff at craft shows, we did a lot of our shopping for supplies in San Jose. One day we had gone to Pay and Pak, Pick and Save, and two other places with similar names I don't remember, and had been shopping most of the day, we started calling the van Park and Piss. Well Ruby, is this story crazy enough for you? And I hope it isn't too unladylike for Dorothy.

OOOPS!

RUBY GREEN

Verona is my daughter-in law. My son Eddie's wife. They live in Duncan. about 45 miles from Thatcher. They had gone to see their two sons in Texas. Verona had her teeth pulled before they had gone to see the boys. Her new teeth hurt her mouth too much. The dentist said she had a floating jaw and she would have to wait about 3 month for it to harden enough to wear her new teeth. But they desided to go to see the boys anyway. I hadn't seen them for about 5 or 6 weeks. I didn't know they were back home yet. One day as I was shopping in Safeway, I looked up and saw Verona comming toward me smiling. I threw my arms out to greet her. She threw her arme around me and we gave each other big huggs. I said "I'm so glad to see you, she said "I'm so glad to see you too." I asked her "How was the trip?" She said it was just wonderful. I asked "How are the boys?" She said "They are just really doing well." We talked for a while, then I noticed her teeth. I said "Oh. I see you have your teeth." She said yes I have my teeth.' I asked, "Do they feel good?" She said "Yes, they feel real good." After some more talking, I asked her, "Is Eddie with you?" She looked at me in a differant manner and asked in a deep,dark expression, and asked, "EDDIE WHO?" I was about to say, "Your husband, silly--But I didn't say it. then she turned and hurriedly went to the other side of the store, and every time she saw me start in her direction, she would hurry away. She finnaly left the store. It finnally dawned on me that she wasn't Verona after all. I felt really stupid. But she looked like Verona, she sounded like Verona, she acted like Verona.

IMPOSTER

Dorothy Patton

When I lived in Phoenix my friend, Marge, and I had gone to a pancake house for breakfast. As we were leaving we passed the counter where several people were sitting. In profile, one of them looked just like Uncle George. He had on a cowboy hat and western shirt just like Uncle George usually wore. It was strange to see him clear across town from where he lived and without Aunt Ada. I was so surprised I stopped and said, "Uncle George!" He turned and looked at me. "You are not Uncle George," I said. "No." he said. "Imposter!" I said. Then Marge and I went on our way. I don't believe in taking the blame for any stupid thing that you can blame on somebody else.

WHO WAS SHE?

C OLLEEN C HAPMAN

I was walking on Main Street in Salinas. I looked at a woman walking toward me at the same time she looked at me. We both smiled, and I was so happy to see her. She looked like she was happy to see me, too. When we were close enough, we hugged, and said all the usual things, and decided to have some tea and chat in a little tea room nearby. Then I realized I didn't remember her name. I could see, as we continued to chat, that she was going through the same thing. Well, after asking questions, it turns out that we had never met before that day. She was from another state, and this was her first time she had been to Salinas. She was on her way to see a son who was stationed at Fort Ord and stopped to have lunch and talk a walk, since she was ahead of schedule and couldn't see her son until evening. Weird! We were so happy to see each other!

Another weird thing....When Fred lived in Arizona, I called him and when he answered the phone I said Hi Fred, It's Colleen. He said "Oh hi! What's up? Haven't heard from you for a while." Then the usual chit chat. Then I asked how Nila and the kids were. He said he didn't know any Nila. It turns out he had a cousin named Colleen, and he said I sounded just like her. He sounded just like Fred. I had asked him if he still lived in the same place. I was planning a trip to Arizona, and wanted to see him while there. He said he did, and I asked him to tell me the best way to get there from Tuscon, since I had not gone that way before. If I hadn't asked about Nila, I would have shown up at a strangers house! I don't know how close he lived to Fred, but he lived close to Lavene, and so did our Fred!

A MOUSE IN THE HOUSE

R U B Y   G R E E N

From the family site

Ruby……I sat down in my chair to rest. I caught a movement in the corner of my eye. I looked and there was a little mouse running back and fourth on top of my toy-box. He must have seen me, for he dissapeared for a few seconds. Then he climbed up the back of the toy-box and held on with his little paws,and looked at me with his big eyes and big ears and tiny little face, looking right at me. We stared at each other -- it seemed like a long time. Then he dissappeered. I don't know where he came from or where he went. I don't want to set a trap to catch him, for he was so cute. If I see him again, I think I'll name him Marvin.

Colleen….I hope that cute little Marvin won't nibble on your ear lobes in the middle of the night. Or maybe it isn't a Marvin, but a Mable, and will get bigger, and older, and meet a Marvin and have a little Myrtle and Mary and Minnie, and Myra, and Mark and Mason and Mike and Mickey and they will all munch on your muffins and mattress and your many pretty dresses, and each have many more cute little mice, and……..

Sandra….When we lived out on the ranch, I would find mouse nest. We watched and played with them. Named the cute little pink things. About the time they were big enough to get out of the nest, they would disappear. After I grew up I realized that Dad took care of the cute little darlins before they got big enough to be a problem.

SHOPPING

COLLEEN CHAPMAN

As most of you know, I do not like shopping! But the time had come for me to buy some bras and a few other things. My bras are too big for me now and I have only one or two pair of pants, other than the ones I wear when gardening, that fit. So yesterday I went to Penny's, where everything was either too large or too small. Then went to Sears. I took two pair of pants and some bras to try on. There are only three fitting rooms in the women's department! They were all in use. After a few minutes a woman came rushing out of one. There was only one hook on the wall. There was several more things hanging from the hook than the hook was meant to hold. hangers hanging from hangers. The floor was half covered with cloths, and the little corner shelf had a couple of sweaters on it, along with a purse. The woman who had just left didn't make all that mess, because she had taken a bunch of things out with her.

I was trying on a pair of pants when I noticed the purse was open a bit and had stuff in it. Until then I thought it was a purse some one had decided not to buy and left it behind with the cloths. Neither pair of pants fit, so I took them and the purse and went looking for the woman who had left the room just before I went in. I looked in the purse for some I.D. Right on top of everything else was a check book. I looked at the name on the checks, and went to the service counter, and asked for that person to be paged. After several minutes I went walking around to see if I could find her. I went to another service desk and asked for a security person. The impatient person at the desk asked why. I said, "I found..." as I was saying that, the woman I was looking for came rushing by. She whirled around and said, "A purse?" "Yes. I had you paged, but when you didn't come to the desk, I went looking for you. I had just about given up." I handed the purse to her. She Thanked me over and over, and hugged me. She said she had left the purse close to where we now were. She said she had sat the purse and the cloths down while she looked at things for her husband, and didn't miss the purse until she went to pay for the things she still had in her arms. I told her no, she had left it in the fitting room. Then why, she asked, had I gone to the men's department looking for her? I had not noticed that, I had just been looking for her. She said, "There ARE Angles! You are an Angle, and it was not a coincidence that you are right here just at the right time. Ordinarily, you would have stayed in the woman's department, and I wouldn't have gone back there, thinking I had left it here." I said, "you are right about Angles. Maybe one guided me here at the right time." "Well," she said, "you are an Angle and I love you." It made me feel really good to have found her. I didn't care that I didn't find anything for myself and started home. I had to laugh at the thought of informing my husband and siblings that I am an Angle! My kids already know that. *DON'T YOU!*

SUSAN SAVES THE DAY

DOROTHY PATTON

Yesterday Susan and Dick came over and got Fred's Lark for Dick to use till he can walk again. Fred seldom uses it anymore. Susan brought pencils and paper for my grandkids. Soon after they left Kim and the twins arrived. The boys were really revved up, running through the house and kicking and chopping each other like out-of-control karate kids. I gave them the pencils and paper and we gave them assignments, things to write and to draw. They really settled into that and Jared drew some pictures of Colleen's dahlias that she posted to the web site. And did a pretty good job for a six-year-old. The boys spent the night and when we were ready for bed we were sitting there talking and Leif came over and closed more tightly the top of my robe. "I could almost see your bra, Gramma," he said.

"Thank you," I said. "That was a very gentlemanly thing to do." "You don't want to know what happened at the ranch today with a girl," he said in almost a whisper. Kim teaches riding at the Barlocker Ranch and the kids go with her. "Yes, I do want to know," I said. "Tell me." "I was walking past a door and I saw a girl take off her top." He shook his head and put his hand over his eyes. "It was blue," he said. "What was blue?" "Her bra," he said. "But I just walked on by and didn't look anymore. And I didn't tell her I had seen her bra. She might have been embarrassed." "You are such a gentleman," I said Today they are competing to see who can draw the most stupid looking picture of me. Not very flattering but better than all that exuberance. Thank you, Susan.

BIG OCEAN, LITTLE BOAT

Susan Aubert

Back in 1993 when Dick and I discovered fishing on the ocean, we would go out in our little 16-foot boat that we also used for duck hunting. Oh what a couple of crazies! One beautiful morning we set out with our friend John Shea, for a Rock Cod trip up the coast. We were fishing off shore from Wilder Ranch. After several cups of coffee, I realized we didn't bring the porta- potty! (A 5-gallon bucket) Well, with the sea so calm and all, Dick decided to take me into shore. He spotted a nice cove and started toward it.

We were doing just fine, maneuvering in and out of the kelp, with John standing up on the bow, holding the rope in one hand, and directing the way. We were so intent on watching what was going on in front of us; no one noticed the swell coming up from behind. The following events showed us a whole new (to us) side of Mother Nature.

The first swell came over the boat and knocked John off his feet and down on his side. The second swell swept us all out of the boat. We tried to get back in, but the swells kept knocking us out. All we could do was hang onto the boat and try to make it to shore. When we and the boat got to shore, we had to act quickly. All of our stuff—tackle boxes, life jackets, dead fish, etc., was being washed up on shore. The boat, totally swamped, was being pulled back out to sea.

We managed to get most of our stuff that floated to shore in one pile, and the boat pulled far enough on the beach to keep from being pulled back out to sea. Then we stopped to evaluate our situation. The first thing that we noticed was that on three sides of us were cliffs about three stories high. In front of us of course, was the ocean. The boat still had the motors, batteries, gas tank, anchor, life jackets and rope. So what was the plan? First we tried signaling people up on the cliffs. That was useless because we could not communicate with them. The tide was coming in and the beach was getting smaller and smaller. We needed a plan of action.

Our first step was to bail the water out of the boat and see if the motor would start. Hooray! It worked. But then what? It would take two of us to push the boat out pass the breakers. John, knowing we could not stay on the beach for long, took a look around. He found that if we timed it right, we could wade around an outcropping of rocks on the East Side of the cove. O.K. Cool. We developed a plan. We piled what was left of our stuff into the boat. John and I would push Dick and the boat out. John and I would then hike out to the highway. Dick would go to the Yacht Harbor, get the truck and pick us up. It was a good plan—in theory.

We pushed Dick out, waded around the rocks to a large stretch of beach and turned to see if Dick and the boat was O.K. Shortly after Dick got the boat passed the surf and the kelp beds, the motor died. He then switched to the electric motor. We knew it would not get him to the Harbor, but he could at least stay away from the beach and rocks. If worst came to worst, he could drop anchor and wait. So now the plan changed. We needed to get to a phone and call someone to rescue Dick.

John and I started off on our mission across the beach and sand dunes. Standing on top of the last stretch of sand, John turned to me and said, "Wait, Sue. You're gonna love this." He began pouring water out of the pockets of his rain slicker. (I'm glad a sense of humor runs in both our families.) After we laughed and rested for a while, we were off again. Across railroad tracks, down bike paths, through agricultural fields, until finally we saw the guard gate house at the entrance of the Wilder Ranch Visitor Center. Fortunately, it was a weekend and the center was open for business.

We told the lady at the gate our story and the predicament my husband was in. Not knowing what to do, she called her boss at the command center. He put out a call, which alerted the Coast Guard, Fire Department and Lifeguard. When the Fire Department showed up, we tried to explain what kind of help we needed. I guess they thought they should drive out to the cliffs anyway. And when the Lifeguard trucks showed up we tried to explain what was needed. John and I sat at the Visitor Center and watched the Lifeguards try to make it to the beach.

Fortunately, Shamrock Charters at the Santa Cruz Harbor was monitoring the airwaves and knew it was our boat that needed a tow. They got one of their customers who happened to be in the area, to come to the rescue. The lady at the gate got word that Dick was being towed in and everything would be O.K. She called a cab for us to get back to the Harbor and got that message to Dick. She told us that if Dick had not gotten a tow from a good citizen, in another 15 minutes he would have had a rescue helicopter overhead, and a Coast Guard Cutter alongside. By the time Dick got to the Harbor, a news crew was standing by for the story. The one we had agreed to tell. Not the one where he said, "My wife had to pee…" No! The one that said, "I don't know what happened. We were fishing along the kelp beds and this wave came out of nowhere and…."

Meanwhile back at the ranch, as John and I were getting into the cab, we wondered if we had enough money for cab fare. We did! When we bought bait that morning, I put the change and the truck keys in my pocket. I had about $8.00. Reaching into his pocket, John found that his wallet and money had survived. We had enough for the 4-mile ride to the Harbor. All in all it wasn't so bad. We didn't have any broken bones. John did have one heck of a bruise on his right cheek and hip. Our homeowners' insurance covered 75% of the losses for us and for John. But if you see a Mermaid with a Macy's charge card, stop her! It's mine!

MAN OVERBOARD!

SUSAN AUBERT

On a beautiful November morning, Dick and some of his buddies decided that going out of the Monterey Bay on an Albacore Tuna fishing trip was a good idea. Having things to do at home, I opted not to go. So after wishing Dick, Randy, Mike, Javier and Guy on a fond farewell, I returned home to do my chores with the instruction that they should call when they are 5 miles out of the Santa Cruz Harbor so I could meet them down there to help pull the boat out and clean the fish.

That afternoon, I got a phone call from Todd at Bayside Marine, telling me that the Salty Dog II was on its way in. I asked Todd why it was that he called instead of Dick calling on the cell phone. He said he did not exactly know, just something about the phone getting wet, just that they had radioed in and asked him to make the call.

Okay fine, jump in the truck and head on down to the harbor. Then I got to thinking-- The cell phone is wet. It was in the same case as my new digital camera. Oh man, if the cell phone is wet, how is the camera? Starting to get angry now. Then the mind switches to…Oh the camera case is in the form of a fanny pack…did someone go overboard? Settle down, it was not the Harbor Patrol that called.

Of course my arrival to the harbor is before the Salty Dog II, so I go out on the deck at Shamrock Charters and look towards the harbor entrance to see them come in. After a few minutes the Salty Dog II comes into view. As it approaches the harbor mouth, I notice that the boat is not coming in at the usual angle. Not Dick's approach. Sure enough, as they get closer, it hits me that Dick is not the one driving the boat. As the boat got closer to the dock, I can hear the guys saying things to Dick like, "Oh Bro, you are in trouble now." And, "Hey Dick, there's Momma now, how are you going to explain this?" And, "She is never going to let you go out without her again." Seeing that all the guys were okay and scared for Dick at the same time was quite humorous and a relief at the same time. I couldn't wait to hear the explanation. As we pulled the boat out of the water, did the wash down, and got the tuna to the cleaning station, the whole story came out. The bottom line is…. After some successful tuna fishing, and a lot of time piloting the boat, Dick needed to relieve himself. Being that there was nothing but men on board; going over the side would be the manly thing to do. So Randy, a boat owner himself, took the helm while Dick had a chat with Mother Nature. A thing to remember about this trip…they are 35 miles off shore, the swell is 6 – 8 feet high and 10 or 11 seconds apart. They are trolling at 8 – 10 knots, dragging six lines behind the boat that have huge hooks on them.

So, as Dick is relieving himself, Randy manages to get the boat sideways in the swell. And of course Dick is on the down side of the boat. You can probably imagine what happened next. Yep, he went overboard. The guys said he did a flip in the air and went over the side. But Dick never let go of the boat. Guy jumped up and grabbed onto Dick's arm and yelled at Randy to stop the boat. Well, Randy, in a panic, grabbed the wrong controller at first, which did nothing. Guy yelled at him to grab the upper control arm, he did, but then pushed it forward and made the boat go faster. But not for long, he pulled it back and stopped the boat.

Thank the Good Lord Guy never let go of Dick. The guys wanted to pull Dick in right away. But he would not let them. They had to pull the lines in so Dick could go around the back of the boat to the swim ladder and climb aboard. After all dagnabbit, he installed that swim ladder himself and no one has ever used it. Oh by the way, the phone was toast. It was in his pocket. The camera was okay. But he did lose his glasses and his slickers that were around his ankles when he went overboard.

IT'S RAINING

ROBERT SILVA

One summer Mom took us kids, Pee Wee (nickmane of Uncle Sterling's wife) and our cousins to Arroyo Seco. We had fun playing in the river and climbing trees. After eating a picnic lunch and resting a bit, we were back in the water. The day had turned from bright sunshine to a gloomey gray. Then a light rain began to fall. Mom yelled "get out of the water! Can't you see it's raining? You're gonna get wet!" Well, when Mom yells, we pay attention! We started to get out until we heard the last part, you're gonna get wet. We sank back down in the water. But as soon as PeeWee heard Mom yell at us, she yelled at her kids too. Then she looked at Mom and had a few choice words for her. PeeWee could cuss like a Sailor.

ANIMAL CRACKERS

AN INCH OF MY LIFE

C OLLEEN C HAPMAN

Mother told me to stay out of the chicken coop. There's lice in there she said, and if I got lice she would beat me within an inch of my life. An inch of my life? What was an inch of my life? Whatever it was, I didn't want to be beaten with it or anything else, for that matter. Never the less, a few days later I just had to see if the chicks had hatched. A quick peek in the nest shouldn't take much time. The chicks had not hatched. On the way out I noticed another hen sitting on a nest. I slid my hand under her, feeling for eggs or chicks. The hen thought I had no business doing that. She scratched my face as she flew to the top of the coop and flew in circles, squawking very loud. That stirred up all the other hens. Sitting on the floor cross-legged, I bent forward and covered my bleeding face and sat still. There was no way I could get to the door until they settled down.

A few minutes after making my escape I felt something tickling my scalp. It's probably sweat I thought, but it might be lice. I'd better not take any chances. Two or three days before, after Mother and Daddy had been talking about the chickens having lice and mites on their feet, Daddy put creosote on the roosts. My three-year-old mind reasoned that if the creosote killed the lice and mites for the chickens, it would do the same for me. I painted a board with creosote and squatted on it. After a while, still feeling the tickling, I got a stick and put creosote on my head. Five or six globs on the top and dabs all around. It didn't seem to be working. The tickling was still there but I had to get cleaned up. Mother would be calling me in soon.

I went to the faucet at the corner of the house. Next to the faucet was a bar of soap, a towel and a pan for us kids to use. I put my head underneath the faucet and turned it on. The faucet. Not my head. The water was scalding hot. I jerked my head out from under the faucet, hitting my head in the process. The cut was about an inch above my forehead, and the blood ran down my face. I let the water run until it was cool. I soaped up my wet hair and stood still, closed my eyes, praying the soap would work some magic and dissolve the gunk. It wasn't working! Then I prayed I would become invisible so Mother couldn't see me.

A loud scream scared me half to death. Mother was staring at me and yelling for Daddy so loud I was sure the whole town heard her. Daddy came running. He stopped beside Mother and they both stared at me. "Are you hurt bad?" Daddy asked. "No, not yet. But I'm gonna be." "Why?" he asked. "Cause Mother's gonna beat me with an inch of my life!" I wailed. Daddy said to Mother, "She doesn't need to be punished. She needs cleaning up. Then we'll find out what in the Sam Hills she did this time and why she did it. And what does she mean, an inch of her life?"

BIG WEEK

COLLEEN CHAPMAN

In 1961 the kids wanted to be in the Kiddy Kaper Parade. (Every year we have Big Week in Salinas, which includes the Rodeo, Chili Cook-off, Kiddy Kaper Parade, and other events.) Three of their cousins, who live near us wanted to do it too. They decided this two days before the parade! To be in the parade, you must be in costume. I was supposed to come up with ten (this was before Loren was born, and Rusty was only eight months old) costumes in a very short amount of time. None of the little darlings seemed to have any doubt that it would happen. The only thing I could think of worked well.

I had a bunch of new gunnysacks. I don't remember where they came from or why I had them. I washed them so they would be soft and more comfortable. Then I made a mouse costume for all the kids except Diane, my oldest daughter. For her I made a pied piper costume, and Howard carved a wooden flute for her. The mice looked cute with rouged noses and cheeks and painted whiskers. They won a prize and got free tickets to the Rodeo.

So to the Rodeo we went. We arrived early to get good seats. We all got sunburned, and every time it looked like an animal was getting hurt, the younger kids, four of mine and two of the cousins, cried and yelled at the cowboys to leave them alone. They wanted me to make those guys behave. The people around us thought it was funny....at first. Two of my kids decided if no one else would do anything, they would. Before I could stop them, they took off. I handed the baby to Diane, told Dave to watch the other kids, and went after Vince and Rob (6 & 7 years old) who were almost at the bottom of the bleachers. I tripped and fell. Don't know how far I might have tumbled if the legs of the peanut vender hadn't stopped me.

He fell, and all the commotion got the attention of the kids, and here they all came. The two from the bottom of the bleachers, and the nine from above. Except for some scrapes, nothing was injured except what little dignity I had left by then. I thought it would be a good idea to leave before we got thrown out. On the way home, the older kids were angry. The little kids, ages 3 to 8, were crying. Susan informed me that we had to go back because she didn't pay for the peanuts she had picked up. When I refused, she was upset because now she was a thief and would get arrested and thrown in jail, and even if she didn't, God knew about it, and her life was ruined, and I didn't seem to care! Sarah Barnhart had nothing on Susan! Debra, Susan, Vincent, Robert, Riff and Gary cried and worried about the animals. Dave, Diane, Steven and Jay fumed and griped for days. None of them ever again asked to go to the Rodeo. They didn't dare!

Several years later I took the kids to the carnival during Big Week. When we were about ready to leave, Debra had her heart set on riding on the Hammer. I think that was the name of the blasted thing. I told her no, but she managed to slip away and get in line for that ride. The kids very seldom disobeyed, and when I saw her in that line, I knew how much she wanted to ride, to dare such a thing. Remembering my disappointment when I was about her age, when I was not allowed a carnival ride, I relented. She could have a ride, but no way would I let her go alone. I sat all the other kids on a bench and told them to stay put.

I got in line with Debra. A little girl about Debra's age was in line alone. I told her to come with us. The thing we were in was an egg-shaped pod, and a metal bar was pulled up across our waists. No straps if I remember right. If there were straps, they did not hold us firmly to the seat. When the pod turned upside down, all three of us were hanging over the bar. I was afraid the girls were going to fall out. I was in the middle, and I put my legs over the girls legs and my arms across their chests and held on to the sides of the contraption. We yelled stop, let us off as loud as we could. The idiot operator just laughed and waved. When it finally stopped and we were safely on the ground, I went to the operator and read him the riot act, while bleeding from a cut on my lip and forehead. I then went looking for whoever oversaw the whole thing. I don't know if it did any good or not, as far as how the rides were managed. They listened to my complaints, probably thinking they were going to get sued, my wounds were taken care of, and we were offered passes to the carnival for the rest of the week, which I did not accept. All we wanted to do at that point was to leave. The girls, who had been scared half to death, came through it OK, but I was bruised all over.

BRILLIANT

SUE AUBERT

Why is it that we do not recognize our parent's brilliance until we ourselves are adults? Once again, one recent summer, I was reminded just exactly how brilliant my parents are. I sent out a desperate plea to my parents one day when I got home to find that my kitchen was over-run by ants. There wasn't a cabinet or drawer that was ant free. Over the phone, my Mom gave me the first brilliant piece of advice, which deserves to be passed on. She had me get a fresh bag for the vacuum cleaner and spray it with insecticide. Install it in the vacuum and suck those babies right on up. I then grabbed a large plastic garbage bag, sprayed the inside of it with insecticide, and placed all those items that were unsealed and infested with ants into the bag and seal it up. Then returned to the cabinets to vacuum up some more of those pesky little critters.

The only thing other than those items mentioned that got sprayed, was the places of entry by the ants into the house. After I cleaned up all the ants and my kitchen was restored to it almost original condition, I called my parents back. It was then that I received the second brilliant, yet strange sounding advice. My Dad told me that if I placed food and water outside for the ants, that they would have no reason to come into the house. After all, THEY do not want to be in my kitchen any more than WE want them to be in my kitchen. So after kidding Howard about his ludicrous idea, I decided it weren't so crazy, hung up the phone and did just what he said. I placed some cat food and 2 pans of water on the ground near the areas where the home invasion took place. And lo and behold, it works. We have not had any intrusions since. And one last tidbit. Do you know why anteaters rarely die of illnesses? Because they are full of ant-i-bodies.

CATS!

Colleen Chapman

I am not normally a violent person, but right now I am about ready to kill some cats! I usually push my keyboard into its compartment under the monitor when I leave the computer for any reason. Today I didn't, just went to stir something on the stove, and when I got back to the computer it was doing things I have never seen before. A cat was sitting on the keyboard, very interested in what was going on. The only way I can start and run the computer is in diagnostic mode. I might have to reformat, and that takes a long time. Besides that, the other day when I was ready to come home from Salinas, the car was so hot; I opened the windows to let it cool off some before getting in. Then decided to drive home with the with the passenger side window open instead of using the air conditioner. When I got home I forgot to close the window. I NEVER leave the windows open when the car is parked. Especially when there is a pregnant cat around. Yep, you guessed it. A cat had her kittens on the front seats, on my almost new genuine sheepskin covers. Luckily, I saw them before the gunk was dry and after moving the cats into a box, managed to wash the covers without leaving stains.

But that is not the end of the story. I carefully pinned the straps with the hooks to the lining so they wouldn't snag anything, set the temp for cool, and put the covers in the dryer and went about my business, since it would take a looooong time for them to dry. Somewhere along the way a pen opened, got caught in a hole in the lint trap cover. A hook joined it, well, when I went to check the dryer because it didn't sound right, there was a balled-up mess of straps, hooks and pens. It took a pair of needle nose pliers, a screw driver and as a last resort, scissors to undo the mess and get the covers out of the dryer. I will have to replace one strap, and Howard will need to make one new hook to repair the damage. I guess I should be thankful that was the only damage done. As for the kittens in the car, I am glad it didn't happen on the rear seat. I keep a cover on it for my dog but had taken it off to wash it. Also, I shouldn't blame the cats. But how come they had to do those things the ONE TIME I left the window open and the keyboard out? Yeah, go ahead and laugh! Maybe I will too, next week. Nah. Make that next year!

HORSE BREAD

Ruby Green

One day when Carl and Tyson were feeding the horses and admiring Star's new colt, Tyson asked "Grandpa, when you want your horse to have a colt, do you feed her bread?" Carl said, "Where did you get that idea?" To which Tyson replied, "Well, Janna said her dad is going to take Cutie down to Keith Smith's pasture with his big pinto, and get her some bread to eat, so she will have a colt that will look like Keith Smith's big pinto". Carl decided Tyson needed to learn about the birds and the bees and proceeded to give him that talk. A day or two later I passed by the family room where all the kids were hanging out and the boys were teasing Janna about feeding Cutie bread. Janna was just looking at the floor with a grin on her face. Janna, Tyson and Jeremy all 3, were 11 years old at the time.

MILK AND EGGS

Colleen Chapman

Pearl took Dave, Diane and Steven (ages 5, 4, &3) with her to milk the cow and gather the eggs. They observed a chicken laying an egg. On the way back to the house they lagged behind, talking quietly instead of rushing ahead. Pearl was pleased that they seemed to be talking about the wonderful experience they had just had.

For breakfast Pearl scrambled some of the fresh eggs while I made toast and poured milk. The kids didn't touch anything but the toast. Dave asked if the milk in the glasses came from the cow instead of the store. Pearl proudly replied that it did. Diane said, "We like milk that comes from the store." Pearl laughed and said, "All milk comes from cows or goats to start with." Dave looked at me accusingly and said, "Why didn't you tell us milk is cow pee and eggs are chicken poo! We are not never gonna eat eggs again, and not gonna ever drink milk again!

ONE SUMMER DAY

RUSTY CHAPMAN

One summer day in the early 70's, we lived in the cabin on the Tule River. Howard was still on the job in L.A., so most of the time it was just Mom and the youngest four kids. We had a busy summer clearing the land, raising rabbits and chickens. Most of the chickens turned out to be roosters, and the breed was a big one. The chickens were the size of turkeys, and they left lots of poop in the yard. A typical summer day was to work in the cool of the morning, then spend the rest of the day in the cool of the shade, or in the river. The only regular adult visitors we had were some older Jehovah's Witnesses. And us kids would do anything to get out of talking to them. From our viewpoint, we saw the VW full of old people who would talk our ears off for hours while there was good swimming and fishing to do. So we ran like hell. From their viewpoint, they were going to visit this "poor woman" who lived in a shack down by the river, with God-knows-how many un-tamed children. From what they saw of the kids before they ran off down a cliff or into the brush, the kids were usually barefoot and almost naked. A household to be saved if there ever was one!

One fateful day began with a bear trying to eat the rabbits in the wee hours of the morning. We lost a few, but most escaped when their cages were ripped open. The chore that day was to repair the cages, and round up the live rabbits, and get rid of the dead rabbit parts. Somewhere about noon we had the cages repaired and all but one rabbit back in the cages. This rabbit refused to be caught. After several attempts Vince and I decided on rabbit for dinner. We had the rabbit cornered under a car. Vince stayed put to watch the rabbit while I ran to the house to fetch a gun. At this point, parallel paths of fate began to converge…

While I was running back to where the rabbit was, with the gun…. Into the driveway came the familiar VW. But on this trip, an older couple had brought along their two granddaughters. They were about the same age as Debra and me, twelve and fourteen. While I was lying up under the car and taking aim at the rabbit's head…Mom was greeting the old couple and cursing her kids for running off again. While Mom met the granddaughters…I took final aim on the rabbit. Just as Mom started to explain where the kids got off to, they heard a gunshot and LOUD, HORRIBLE, blood gurgling scream. The greetings stopped, and as grandkids moved closer to grandparents with open mouths and big eyes…back at the car, the rabbit had jumped just as I pulled the trigger. The bullet went through the rabbit's juggler vain, the rabbit SCREAMED and ran straight at me. I ducked my head as the rabbit ran across my face and down my back. The rabbit ran a few more feet and died.

Out front by the VW there was only silence…. Out back, Vince went to hang the rabbit on the skinning hooks while I ran back to put the gun away and get the skinning knife. I was wearing only cut-offs and was covered head to toe in rabbit blood. Convergence… Just as conversation re-started by the VW, it stopped when they saw me. I trotted by, bloody, half naked, and packing a gun, and proudly announced, "Hey Ma! We finally got him!" I don't remember if the granddaughters fainted right then, or if they fainted when I came trotting back out of the cabin carrying that big knife. But I do remember the chicken poop over those "going to church" dresses as they poured the girls into the VW. That particular V W never entered our driveway again.

PLAYING WITH ANTS

RUBY GREEN

When Pearl was a little girl she liked to play with ants. She would sit on the ground near an ant hill. She picked up ants and put them in a bottle. She put a finger in the bottle so that they couldn't get out. They never bit or stung her. The rest of us tried it but always got stung. She said all we had to do was hold our breath while turning in a circle three times before touching the ants. It didn't work for us.

DRAWING BY SANDRA

RABBIT HUNTING

COLLEEN CHAPMAN

Fred, Hootie and Sonny were going rabbit hunting. I wanted to go. Fred said no. Sonny and Hootie said it was ok with them. Fred said "No! Huh uh. Never!" Fred had a bee bee gun, but one of the other boys had his Dad's shotgun. I said I would tell about the shotgun if he didn't let me go. He wouldn't get to go either. Fred said he would make a deal with me. If I could do everything he did, I could go. If I couldn't then I had to stay home and keep my mouth shut. We spit on the palm of our hands, and shook on it, so neither of us could go back on our word. It just was not done, if you did a spit hand shake. The first test was to play marbles with the three of them. No problem. I had been playing marbles with Jerry and Donny and their friends for years. After I had won most of their marbles, we went on to the next test. Fred lined up some cans on the ground. We were to take turns shooting them with Nigger Shooters. Excuse me! They are called sling shots now.

The boys took turns and did pretty good. Fred hit all but four of them. Then I took my turn. I lay on my stomach and hit all but four also. It was a tie. He said, "No fair. We stood up and did it." "You didn't say I had to do it standing up. All you said was to see if I could do as good as you did." "That's right, Fred, you didn't set any rules." Sonny said. Fred grumbled as we went on to the next test. We went to the school ground. We were to climb as high as we could in a Eucalyptus tree and get it to swaying. He didn't think I would do it. Hah! Betty Sue and I did it all the time. I was smaller and could get higher than they could. The limbs up top were more limber and easier to get to swaying. Fred unhappily told me I won, and to stop and get down before the limb broke and I killed my stupid self.

We went back home. Fred sat thinking up something to do next. He tried to sneak some chewing tobacco out of the café. I was soooo glad he got caught. Then he had a great idea, he said. He got an empty coke bottle. He said, "You know I could pee in this if I wanted too. Right? Well, I want to see you do it. Standing up." I took the bottle. "I'll go in the bathroom and do it."

"No. You have to do it here." I had a dress on, so I turned my back to them, held the bottle strategically placed, and peed in it. They were amazed. He gave up and said I could tag along, but try not to get in the way and be a pest.

We left as soon as we could slip away the next morning. We went to the river. We sat under the bridge and rested. Fred said it was time to hunt. Hootie was the first to spot a rabbit. We all lay down, waiting for it to come closer. He shot and missed. Fred was the next to fire the gun. He almost got one. Then I saw a rabbit. I wanted the gun. Fred said, "No! That wasn't part of the deal." "What's the matter, Fred, afraid she'll hit it?" Sonny asked. Fred gave me the shotgun. I had never fired a real gun. I really had no intention of even trying to hit a poor little rabbit. I just wanted to fire the gun. As I pulled the trigger, without aiming, the rabbit jumped and ran right into the path of the bullet! It shrieked and fell dead. I threw the gun and started crying. Fred was furious. We went home.

SALLY

Colleen Chapman

Howards niece Lynn and her husband Curt lived in Alabama and use to drive annually to New Jersey for Thanksgiving with Curts mother. The ducks would be migrating in giant vee formations. The kids would watch them so fascinated from the car windows. They would talk non-stop like kids do, and Curt would try to keep up with them and drive at the same time. They passed a dead duck on the highway and Curt said, "Oh, there's a dead duck". Sally jumped up to the window and studied two vee formations she could see and asked him, "How can you tell which one is dead?" So for the next fifty miles or so, Curt had her going. Couldn't she see the little stretcher two other ducks had in their little bills? How could she miss it, etc.

Another time, picnicking, A fly kept buzzing around her lunch. Very sticky. She would shoo it away and it would move only an inch or two. Finally she announced, "I can read that fly mind. He thinks he will have some of my sandwich." We still use that phrase when something is obvious, like a jerk about to cut you off on the freeway-I can read that fly's mind.

SKUNK!

SANDRA JOHNSON

Frank and I went on a camping and fishing vacation at Burney Falls. One night I got out of bed to go to the bathroom. I was gone 15 minutes at the most. Since I was gone such a short time and Frank was asleep in the tent I didn't zip the bottm zipper to the tent. When I came back I heard this noise like something trying to get in the side of the tent. I said "what the hell is that?" I turned on the light and there on the INSIDE of the tent is a skunk. I let out a femanine EEK. and since I didn't know if Frank had zipped up the bottom of the door yet I started for the door. So did the skunk. I froze in the spot. I didn't want the skunk to think I was going for IT! Frank said "don't move. Don't scare it." Like I was stupid enough to get it more excited than it was. Luckily the zipper was still open and the skunk left without anything but a slight lingering smell. Frank and I just layed in our sleeping bags and giggled for awhile. We are very grateful to the skunk for its calm retreat. Just goes to show Frank will sleep with anything the minute my back is turned.

SO, WHAT'S THE PROBLEM?

DAVE SILVA

(bleeps by Mom)

I went to a friend's house and he was in the barn yelling when I drove up, so I went to the barn and asked what was wrong. Ron pointed and said, "There is a (bleeped) snake at the ladder!" I looked over at the ladder and said "Yep, so what's the problem?" He stared at me and said, "Get rid of it!" "Oh, I guess I can do that." Soooo, I went and got a trash can and a rake. I slowly pulled the snake into the can. It was a four-foot Timber Rattler.

Ron called the Ranger and he came out and wanted to shoot it so I opened my big mouth and said, *"no (bleeped) way!"* The idiot told me he was the Ranger and he was the boss, so but out. I said (bleeped) "George lives here." Ron said, "(bleeped) you already named it! We are gunna have a problem!" The Ranger looked at Ron and said, "Huh?" Ron is 6'5" and 245 lbs. Ron said, "Dave is **mad**! If I were you I would let Dave take care of George!" "Who is George?" the Ranger asked. Ron said, "That snake. I don't mess with Dave when he takes off his hat and coat 'cause he's pissed. When he gets this way he usually gets a little crazy." I said, "Thanks, Ron." Ron said, "Well, I warned him. It's his funeral." By this time there are several people around and thanks to Ron, they all got going on how much I like critters. Ron's friends finally convinced the Ranger to let me take George out to Ron's back pasture and let him go. Ron says he sees the snake on a rock by the pond every now and then. Ron lives over on Mount Jefferson at about 2100 feet.

THE GOPHER SNAKE

COLLEEN CHAPMAN

Howard came rushing into the kitchen and said, "Here! Hold this!" I turned from the stove and looked to see what he was so excited about, and what he wanted me to hold. He was holding a big gopher snake! And he actually expected me to hold it for some dang fool reason. Well! I was taught to be afraid of snakes. I just about made a new door in the wall next to the stove. Howard said, "Oh, it's just a gopher snake. It couldn't hurt you if it wanted to. Stop acting stupid and hold it while I tape it up. It got run over by a car and its side is split open." It took some doing, but he convinced me to hold the snake while he taped it up. He got a wooden box, put in some dirt and grass, and made a little shelter in one corner for it to curl up in. The poor thing didn't even try to get out. Would you, with all those strange beings running around? After several days it seemed to understand we would not hurt it. The kids caught grasshoppers and whatever else they thought it would eat, and the snake allowed them to pet it. We kept it until it was healed, removed the tape, and released it outside.

While it was recuperating we kept the box in the living room. One day I was sitting with my feet resting on the edge of the box while Rusty nursed. Mother came to visit. The kids told her to come see their new pet and pointed to the box. Expecting to see a puppy, kitten or perhaps an injured bird, she bent over the box and saw the snake. She let out a very loud scream and ran into the kitchen, on into the playroom, into the hallway, dashed past the kids' bedrooms, clear to the back of the house. A long way to run for someone who had claimed just a few minutes ago that they could hardly move!

We could hear her yelling at me from the back door. I told one of the kids to go tell her if she wanted to talk to me she had to come closer. She did, after ten or fifteen minutes. She ventured as far as the kitchen and asked, "What in the world do you mean, sitting there with that baby so close to a snake, for God's sake!" "Don't worry about it, Mother." I said, "Rusty isn't going to bother the snake." She was not amused. She left, using the back door. Before she got in the car she came to the front door but didn't open it. In a loud voice she informed us that she would not be back as long as we had a snake. Howard said, "Hummmm! Maybe we should keep the snake."

YOU'RE BRINGING HOME A WHAT?

COLLEEN CHAPMAN

"*You're bringing home a what?*" I was used to the kids and Howard bringing home injured lizards, birds, frogs, gopher snakes, and things like that. But if he said what I think he said, it was going too far! "A Rattle Snake." Yep, that's what I thought he said! I was speechless for a few seconds, and then croaked into the phone, "WHY?" Howard explained they had answered a call to remove the snake from a yard in their district. "How did you get it?" I asked. "I pinned it to the ground with a shovel, then I grabbed it right behind its head. The Cap drove the truck back to the station for me, and I held the snake." After getting to the station he put the snake in a garbage can.

We went camping often and the kids could come across one. He wanted them to see and hear one first hand. With his assurance it would be perfectly safe, I agreed. I might as well. He was going to do it anyway. I had been taught to be afraid of snakes. Part of my early childhood was spent in rattlesnake country.

So bring it home he did. He sat the can on the front porch. The kids gathered around. When the lid was lifted, the snake coiled and hissed. It was the biggest snake I had ever seen. It had shed its skin recently and was shinny and pretty. After the kids had seen and heard the snake several times, the lid was secured. Our house was a favorite place with the kids in the neighborhood, and it was not unusual to have several of them in our yard. Of course the news got around and kids who wanted to see the snake kept me busy a good part of the day. Then we put the can in the garage and locked the door.

One of the kids told me Mr. Cooperman wanted to talk to me. I went outside and saw him standing on his side of the fence between his yard and ours. Mr. Cooperman asked, "Is it true that you have a huge rattle snake?" "Yes. We don't intend to keep it of course. In the morning I will call one of the places that make serum from the venom. In the meantime, the snake is in a garbage can, the can is in the garage and the door is locked." Mr. Cooperman demanded, "Get rid of it now! I don't want to take any chances of my kid being bitten by that thing!" "Mr. Cooperman, if Gary is stupid enough to go into my house, find the key, unlock the garage door, take the lid off of the garbage can and stick his hand in, knowing what is in there, then you should keep him at home tied to a chair!"

Howard was on duty the next day, so it was up to me to get rid of the darn thing. I called two labs that make the serum. They had enough and didn't want it. I called the Zoo. They had enough and didn't want it. I called Howard. I'd had enough. I didn't want it. Mr. Cooperman called the cops. They didn't want it. They sent a man from Animal Control. Howard arranged to get the rest of the day off, and got home right after the Animal Control officer arrived. I had taken the can out of the garage, thinking he, the Deputy, was going to take the snake and leave. Instead, he removed the lid and aimed a gun at the snake just as Howard walked through the gate.

Howard…. "What the hell are you doing?"

Deputy….Killing that snake."

Howard…."No you are not!"

Deputy…."Yes I am. It is against the law for it to be inside L.A. City limits."

Howard…."Tell that to the snake. It was born inside the city limits."

The Deputy looked puzzled.

Howard…."Besides, that can belongs to the L.A. City Fire Department. You can't shoot the snake without putting a whole in the can. It's against the law to damage Fire Department property."

The Deputy looked more puzzled.

Howard…."Put that gun away. How dare you draw a loaded weapon with all these kids here? You and that gun are more dangerous than the snake."

The officer looked around to see more than a dozen kids in the yard, and my mother looking out the window of her bedroom. (She had not left her room since the snake had arrived the day before, except to scurry to the bathroom and back to her room as fast as she could. She had her meals in her room.) The officer holstered the gun. Howard said, "Look. I know you are just trying to do your job. I intend to take the snake out into the country and release it. Outside the city limits of course."

Deputy…."I can't give you permission to do that."

Howard…."How about we go into the house and you call your boss or whoever has the authority to give me permission and see what he says" The Deputy agreed. Good. Because I knew Howard was going to do it with or without permission. I put the can back in the garage and followed them into the house.

The Deputy talked to his boss then gave the phone to Howard. He explained how he came to have the snake, and why he had brought it home. Howard…."That snake did not get as old as it is by posing a threat to humans. It had been living under that house for years, from the looks of things. No one knew it was there. It's a big, beautiful, healthy creature and it deserves to live. I intend to take it far away from any inhabited area and let it go." He smiled, said thank you, and gave the phone to the Deputy. The Deputy listened, a look of disbelief on his face, then hung up and left muttering "I don't believe it!"

Howard put the can in the back of the station wagon. Leaving the kids with my mother, who agreed to come out of her room as soon as we were gone, Howard and I set out to find a place to release the snake. We went to the mountains between L.A. and Bakersfield. We stopped several times but saw signs of people or animals. We found a fire break road and went a good distance off of the highway. We got out and examined the area for signs of man or domestic animals. We saw none. There was a small stream of water at the base of the sloping hillside. Perfect. Howard took the can from the car, removed the lid and dumped the snake on the ground. While he was doing that I climbed up on top of the car.

When the snake hit the ground, it coiled and rattled. Howard sat on the open tailgate. The snake would not turn its back to us. Look at it from his point of view. After all, it had been minding its own business, and along came these strange beings that captured him, took him for a ride on a contraption of some sort that made a lot of noise. Then put him in a cold dark place. Periodically, there would be a flash of bright light and strange beings looking down at him. Then it would be dark again. And now this! It just wouldn't be wise to turn his back to these beings. No telling what they were up to now.

We didn't want to leave until the snake had crawled off into the brush. There wasn't much chance that anyone would come along any time soon, but we didn't want to take any chances. We sat on the tailgate looking at the snake. The snake was still coiled and rattled occasionally. Howard got up, found a long stick and sat back down. He began to stroke the snake on the top of its head, and down its body. I was going to say neck, but how do you tell where its neck ends? At first the snake ducked and dodged, trying to get away from the stick. It soon decided that felt good. When Howard stopped and held the stick still, the snake would lean toward it. It reminded me of a cat rubbing itself against a leg or something. This went on for quite a while. You could see the snake relaxing and enjoying the scratching. Howard stopped, and eventually the snake gave up. It went off through the grass toward the stream. If that snake was ever exposed to humans again, I hope he didn't try to get them to scratch him!

VERDA'S COUSINS

COLLEEN CHAPMAN

My cousin Verda and her husband Bert were driving across Texas. Verda told Bert she had cousins who lived in that part of Texas. They raised cattle and sheep. Verda went on and on, about her cousins. They rounded a curve and in the middle of the road were about 10 sheep. Verda yelled, "Look out! Don't hit them! They might be my cousins!" After maneuvering safely around the sheep, Bert went on and on about what funny looking cousins Verda has.

Drawings by Colleen

DO THE RIGHT THING

C O L L E E N   C H A P M A N

Dan was getting old. His eyesight and hearing were bad and getting worse. His bones ached. He couldn't eat much anymore. But he'd had a good life on the farm where he had been born and raised by a loving family. When he was a youngster he loved to run. Oh! How he could run! He would chase everything that moved and pee on everything that didn't. When he was old enough to be turned loose on the farm, he explored every nook and cranny. He then went looking for someone to play with. He saw a creature with a long tail and barked a hello. The darn thing ran up a tree! What fun! No matter how hard he tried, he couldn't climb the tree. Well, he decided the next best thing would be to see what else he could get to climb a tree. He came across another creature, not quite like the other one, it also had long hair and a long tail. He remembered his humans calling it a cat. He barked and the cat ran up the tree. The old barn cat didn't. No matter how he barked, the old barn cat ignored him. So he went looking for something else to chase. Chickens! A whole lot of them! So that's what Pa was talking about going to feed.

Wow! This was even more fun! How they ran, flapping their wings and squawking! But Ma didn't like that, and he knew it wasn't nice to upset Ma, so he didn't do it anymore. Well, not very often and not for very long. He learned that chasing cars was not allowed, and tractors go too slow to chase. He wandered out to the pasture. Three horses were standing under a big Oak tree. He went closer and barked. Nothing happened. He looked at the horses, barked, looked at the tree, barked again, but the horses just didn't get it. Neither did the cows. He was ignored by all. Other animals were added to the farm from time to time. Some were taken away, too. But somehow Dan knew he was here to stay. He was different. He was the only animal allowed in the house and in the car when it took Ma and Pa for a ride.

One day a human female they called Colleen was added to the family. She called Ma Aunt Doris and called Pa Uncle Buddy. Colleen became a very good playmate. She and Dan were constant companions. She loved to run as much as Dan did. Wrestling was fun too. Dan taught her to throw a stick for him to retrieve. Dan tried throwing the stick for her, but that didn't work out very well. Dan took Colleen to all his favorite places and showed her some of his favorite things to do. Dan loved to roll in the horse and cow patties, but she wouldn't even try it, and tried to make him stop!

But now Colleen was 11 years old in human years and Dan was a very old man in dog years. She was away at school most of the day now. It was just as well, seeing as how Old Dan wasn't up to entertaining her. Pa gently explained to Colleen that Dan was not enjoying life anymore, and the right thing, the merciful thing to do, because they loved him and didn't want him to go on suffering, would be to have the Vet put him to sleep in the morning when he came out to the farm to care for an injured cow. Colleen cried, but agreed it was the right thing to do. Dan died peacefully with his head on her lap and was buried under a tree in the back yard.

A month or so later, the family went to visit Pa's sister and her husband. No one paid much attention to Aunt Pearl's complaints of aches and pains. They had heard it all before, and anyway, according to her Doctor, Aunt Pearl was in good health. All the family knew Pearl had always been a complainer. If you wanted to make her happy, give her something to grip about. But Colleen didn't know all this. She hadn't seen Aunt Pearl since she was two or three years old, since she lived too far away to visit often. So Colleen felt very sorry for her. She sat on the floor and listened to her describe the aches and pains. "I don't know why the good Lord doesn't just take me to Heaven." she said. "But no, he just lets me linger and suffer!" With tears in her eyes, Colleen laid a hand on Aunt Pearl's knee and said, "I love you Aunt Pearl. I know Aunt Doris and Uncle Buddy love you too. I think the right thing for us to do is have you put to sleep and end your suffering. We did that for Ole Dan. If you want, you can be buried next to him under that big beautiful tree out back."

BIG BIRDS

Debra Littler

We went on a new adventure of raising birds. Not little ones. Nooooo. We spent time on 14 ft. fences. I thought birds would be easy to care for but nature will teach you better. Birds like to peck on shiny things such as earrings, keys and belt buckles. Emus run really fast and like to beat you with their necks and feet.

When the Rheas get your keys and run, they also attack you, knock you over and then sit on you to pick your brains out. It is funny to watch but we went through this every time we went to feed or water them. We did good for a while. The Rheas laid very large green eggs. One egg was the equivalent of a dozen extra-large chicken eggs. The Emus laid white eggs the size of a small football.

One time an Emu got loose. We chased it through Springville and all the way to the lake. We finally caught the Emu, and to get it home Ken had to sit on it in the back of the truck. As we drove through town we got many different looks. Later that day a lot of people came up to see the birds. After that we started selling the eggs for $5.00 each. We had the birds for about five years until Coyotes killed all of them.

CAGE DIVING WITH THE SHARKS

COLLEEN CHAPMAN

My granddaughter wanted to go cage diving with the sharks. She needed someone to go with her to share the expense of the sleeping quarters. No one was interested. I was keeping track of the conversation about it on Facebook. Just joking, I asked what about me? I thought she would laugh and say something like "Oh Grandma! Act your age!" But to my great surprise, she thought it was a great idea. She seemed so excited, I didn't want to tell her I was just kidding. I couldn't go, I thought, Howard is not well enough to leave him that long. But the more I thought about it, the more I wanted to go. If I didn't go, Jennifer wouldn't get to go. And she wanted to so much. I decided to find a way. Howard's nephews lived a very short distance up the road. I asked if they could look in on him every day. I fixed meals and put them in the freezer and fridge. I also arranged for a friend to spend a few nights with him. Yes! I was getting away for a little over a week.

I drove to Porterville. Jennifer drove us to San Diago where we boarded the boat. Shortly after we got underway Jennifer was sea sick. She went to bed and I handed her the waste basket to throw up in and gave her a wet wash cloth and water to sip. After she went to sleep I went out to explore the boat. As I was climbing the ladder to the upper deck, I heard the Captain telling a couple of men that they had an eighty-year-old woman on board and they should look after her. I hopped upon the deck just as he finished. The Captain let me go into the pilots cabin. What a view from there! It didn't take long to explore the boat. It wasn't very large. I spent a lot of time in the bow of the boar, hanging onto a rope and a cable. It was my favorite spot. I felt sorry for Jennifer and hoped she would recover soon. But I had to smile as I remembered several people tell her to take care of Grandma.

Recover she did in time to go cage diving with the Sharks. We were anchored off ....I think it was Guadalupe Island In Mexican waters. There were two cages which held four people each. So eight people went down for an hour, and then eight more went down. I spent my time relaxing and enjoyed not having to do anything at all. No cooking, no housework, no dishes, just resting and enjoying everything. I knew I would go down in the cage before we left. Jennifer went down every time it was her turn. She said she was sorry I wasn't having fun. But I was! I had always been afraid of being in water over my head. I don't like being afraid of anything and was working up my courage to do it.

On the last day, as a cage was going down for the last time, I went. I popped right back up. Went back down and stayed a bit longer. I was terrified but went down and stayed down. I soon calmed down. I wasn't as interested in looking at sharks as I was looking up and seeing the sun shine down on the seaweeds and making patterns. The fish were beautiful when the sun hit them. Jennifer tapped me on my shoulder and pointed at a huge shark who was checking us out. It came close enough to pet, but that wouldn't be a good idea. I enjoyed that trip so very much!

On our way back to Porterville we were talking about the experience and how some people would be shocked that I had gone cage diving with the sharks. I don't know where it came from, but I heard myself say, "Well, why not shock them more and get a tattoo of a shark?" Me? A tattoo? What am I thinking? Oh well, what the heck! Why not. When we got back to Porterville James said he knew a good tattoo artist who had done work for him and arranged for him to come to the house. I chose a picture of a shark that I liked. He worked the number 80 into the picture. Before I started home, I talked to some of my kids on the phone and told them I had gotten something I had always been against women having. They were relieved I had a tattoo and not a nose piercing!

Today is September 25th, 2014 and Dolores Colleen Chapman has just received her 1st Tattoo! She had previously gone on an ocean voyage to participate in the very singular and exciting underwater experience of "Swimming With Great White Sharks", and was then inspired to commemorate and immortalize that occasion with a GREAT WHITE SHARK TATTOO!!!

If that wasn't already Incredible, she did all of this while celebrating her 80th Birthday! In doing so, Colleen has also become the oldest person that I have ever personally given a Tattoo!! And the oldest person that I have ever heard of getting a tattoo locally! It was my honor and my pleasure to work on such an Amazing Person! *It just goes to show that YOU'RE NEVER TOO OLD TO TRY SOMETHING NEW! & IT'S NEVER TOO LATE TO GET A TATTOO!!!

Tattoo Artist,
Travis Fiori

On September 20th 2014 aboard the vessel Islander Dolores Colleen Chapman entered into an elite group of the world's population, as she overcame her fears of the water and dove with great white sharks. At the age of eighty she has to be one of no more than 10 people in the world to have done what she did. As captain of the vessel my hat goes off to her as she is an inspiration for us all.

captain

AROUND THE KITCHEN TABLE

A LITTLE BLACK CLOUD

COLLEEN CHAPMAN

Several years ago, my son Rusty was having a run of bad luck. He said it seemed like a little black cloud followed him around and dumped on him all too often. Well, I think his little black cloud found me! This is what has happened since we got home from our trip to the reunion. The day after I got home I went out to check my garden. Mildew had started on the Dahlias. It didn't look very bad, so I thought spraying could wait for a day or two while I got caught up on some other things. While I was getting caught up on those other things, I got careless and lost my footing coming down a hill. I had gone up there to get an empty trashcan. When the can and I got to the bottom of the hill, it was in better shape than I was. I had a twisted knee, ankle, and wrist. No, the empty trashcans will not be kept up there in the future. I had to take it easy for a few days, and when I went to spray the Dahlias, it was too late. Spraying would do no good at this point. All the leaves, except the very small new ones, had to be stripped from the plants, and then the stalks and new leaves had to be sprayed. Since I had never had a mildew problem, I didn't know what to use. I went to 5 or 6 nurseries and they all said the same thing. All the sprays for mildew that they had were too strong for Dahlias. I bought some stuff and mixed it half strength, and it worked. The Dahlias are looking good. All 400 or so pots of the danged things. Then the terrorist attacked.

I, like most of us, was stunned, and forgot our little problems. Just in case something happened, like an attack on our power plants, I checked our water supply, etc. We needed gas for our generator. I put our empty gas cans in our beat-up old camper van (it thinks it's a pick-up now) and went to fill them up. I had the trip all planed. First I would go to Salinas, do my grocery shopping, fill the cans, go to Little Baja, a place close to Moss Landing, that sells pots, statues and other interesting thing, to pick up a gift for a friend, have lunch in a little restaurant that overlooks the ocean, and then home. All went well until I was approaching Moss Landing. A Highway Patrolman stopped me. When he asked for my driver's license, I couldn't find it! The last thing I had done before leaving home was to balance my checkbook. I keep my license in a pocket in the checkbook. It was at home on the desk. I did remember all but the last two numbers of my license number. That helped, but there was still a problem.

The officer had misunderstood and thought I had said my last name was Chatman instead of Chapman. Here I was just a mile from a big power plant, just days after the terrorist bombings, in an old van with three five-gallon cans, four two-gallon cans and five one gallon can of gas, and no driver's license, and according to the officer, the wrong last name.

He called for backup. Seems the service station where I got the gas had called to report it. I had never been to that station before. I thought I was going to jail for sure. These guys were so on edge, all six of them, that I made sure I kept my hands where they could always see them. Even when the poison oak on my hip was itching like crazy. (Got the poison oak when I rolled down the hill.) I explained over and over that we use a lot of gas because we have a generator that we use during power outages, a tractor, a riding lawn mower with a spray tank on it, another riding lawn mower, weed eaters, and chain saws. I told them that if one of them would just look in my purse they would find all kinds of identification and explained why my driver's license was not with me. They did, at long last, and let me go. I think they were disappointed that all they had was a forgetful old lady instead of a terrorist in disguise.

The next thing that happened is we learned that a very dear friend does not have much longer to live. Then my dog disappeared. He had been on his rope out front. There is a metal ring on the end of his rope. Howard had put the ring over the gearshift on the riding lawn mower that has the tank on it, while he was putting a longer hose on the tank. He came in the house for something, was in here about ten minutes, and when he went back out, Shadow was gone. The only way he could have gotten loose was to jump up on the seat of the mower and lift the ring off. I started looking for him right away. Two neighbors took their cars and went looking, while I searched with the riding lawn mower. He loves to ride on it in a box we attached for him. He always comes running when he hears it start up. But not this time. There was no sign of him.

A neighbor said he saw a little white dog go up a driveway about an eighth of a mile from us. Was not sure it was Shadow. I went all the way up that driveway, stopping at all four homes. No one had seen him. I spent the rest of the day looking for him. Some kids on our road joined the hunt. After dark, I gave up for the night. I sat outside most of the night listening for his bark or whine. His rope could be tangled up in the brush someplace on the hills on both sides of the road. We have mountain lions here. I didn't sleep a wink.

The next day I was up early and combing the hillsides again. No sight or sound of him. After dark I made up some fliers to put on all the mail boxes in our area. Did that early the next morning. Susan called the animal shelters and vets offices where he might have been taken. I continued the search. I kept being drawn to the first house on the driveway where he had, maybe, been seen. I just stood and listened. The man who lives there saw me but didn't come out. I thought I heard Shadow bark when I called him but wasn't sure. The third time I went there, the man came out and asked if I was still looking for my dog. I felt like telling him, no, I just like to stand in the middle of the driveway staring at houses.

Instead, I told him my dog had last been seen going up this way, and I felt he was still here someplace. He said he didn't like me standing in front of his place, and not to do it anymore. I informed him that I was not on his property, this property belongs to the Clarks, and he is a tenant. I had permission from the Clarks to go anyplace I wanted to in my search. I had not stepped foot on the property he rented. He could not stop me from looking and listening for my dog. He was not happy about that. I climbed the hillside enough so I could see down into his yard and could see both the front and back doors to his mobile home. I spent a lot of time there.

On Saturday, I spent the morning looking for him, and then I needed to go get a prescription refilled and do some other errands. It would take at least 1 1/2 hours. I didn't get far from home when I got an overwhelming feeling that I should go back home. So I did. When I got home Howard was on the other side of the road looking for Shadow. I started retracing my steps, looking in places we had looked a dozen times. I felt that Shadow was nearby, and asked for guidance, to be led to him. As I was going toward the rear of the house, I heard a noise and looked up. A bird was in a bush at the edge of the hill where the hill had been cut back when the house was built. The bird was about even with my head and just a few feet away. I started on past it, and it hopped to another bush and made a lot of noise. When I looked up at it, just about a foot below it, I saw something white. I called Shadow, and he jumped up and tried to get to me. He had gotten tangled up and knowing I would come to his rescue as usual, had lain down to take a nap. I made my way to him up the hill and through the brush and got him untangled and saw that he was OK. I looked at the area, to see if I could tell how long he had been there. He had not been there very long. There was no sign of him having a BM or where he had made himself a bed like animals do.

After I got him into the house he was not very hungry or thirsty and had not lost any weight. The only thing I can think of that could have happened is the guy whose place I had spent so much time observing, with him knowing I was doing so, took advantage of Howard and I being gone at the same time, and went along the top of the hill from his place to ours, and let Shadow go. It is easy to do, next to the fence line up there. He had to know that Shadow would get tangled before he made it to the bottom of the hill. But he almost made it. Shadow seemed none the worst for the experience.

Can't say the same for me. I had not thought of the part the bird played in this until Sue asked what kind of bird it was. It was just an ordinary bird, but it is strange that it didn't fly away when I was so close to it, and very unusual for it to go that close to a dog. Looks like my prayer was answered and I was led to Shadow. It brought to mind other times birds have played a role in the lives of other members of our family. And I recall my grandmother Sullivan admitting, after denying it for years, that she is part Indian. She said she could remember visiting some Indian relatives when she was a young child. The clan or tribe she belonged to was called The Bird Clan! Grandma, like Mother, had a big imagination, and I never knew if their stories were fact or fiction. But it is a fact that birds have played a part in our lives.

There is a young red-tailed Hawk that followed me around. It was hatched in a tree near where I grow

Dahlias and Iris for sale. From the time it could see over the edge of the nest I could see it watching me. When it could fly, it would perch nearby and watch me work. The Parent Hawks flew in circles overhead squawking up a storm. It paid no attention. When I go into the house it flies to a tree outside the kitchen window and watch me until I go back outside.

A FIREMAN'S LIFE LESSON

COLLEEN CHAPMAN

Howard's Captain is a fun guy to be around. He's always ready to pull a prank or tell a joke. There is a more serious side to him, however. The following is a letter I received from him after I asked him to write something for Bit N' Pieces.

After reading your letter, something came to mind about what is important. The following is the most outstanding event that has ever happened to me on or off the job.

On a very hot day, July 16, 1959, I was an Auto Fireman at engine 69 in the Pacific Palisades community of the City of Los Angeles, CA. We were working on a brush fire. We came to a part that had just been extinguished when Fireman Gladen yelled, "It's coming down!" I looked up and the hillside was coming down on me, and at the same time it was slipping from under me. I made a dive sideways to get out of the way and covered my face with my folded arms. The slide hit me and threw me ten feet or so. I landed face down and could not move. I thought I was buried 20 feet under. Actually, it was three feet of dirt and hot ashes. I said, "God save me!" I yelled, "Help" at intervals to save air. I thought "I will wake up and my firemen buddies will have the resuscitator on me." The air I had was full of steam and dust. My back and legs started to burn. I thought, "This is a hell of a way to die." My life did not pass in front of me, and I was not scared of dying. I wondered when I would pass out.

After several minutes I managed to move my left arm to get more air space. I broke open a hole and could see light. I made the hole a little larger and they heard me yelling. It took two firemen pulling and three pushing to get me out. I had 20% burn, first, second and third degrees. I was in the hospital two and a half weeks and off duty four months. Now back to what is important. I was 32 years old at the time, and every day after that has been bonus time. I get a great feeling just to see the sunrise or the sunset. It is hard for me to see why someone wants to commit suicide when they could eventually work things out or change themselves. It has made me do the things I want, as long as I don't hurt anybody. I know it does not pay to put off what you want to do. Tomorrow may not come.

FUN AT THE STATION HOUSE

COLLEEN CHAPMAN

Firemen are famous for their jokes and pranks. They test newly assigned firemen to see what they are made of. They not only spend as much time with each other as they do with their family, at times their lives depend on each other. They also like to pull jokes on the wives of firemen. Howard's brother-in-law was a Battalion Chief and his sister warned me about them, so I was prepared when I visited Howard's station for the first time. Howard called and asked me to bring his tool box to the station for him. He said he would be on top of the building working on the air conditioner. One of the guys would be watching for me and would yell for him when I got there.

Howard had described the layout: from the back-parking lot, I could enter through an open door of the hose tower. That's where the wet hoses are hung to dry. Exit the hose tower into the apparatus floor.

On the left side is a door to the kitchen, a few feet further, a door to the TV room, and up front is the office. Before I reached the kitchen a fireman, pretending he didn't know who I was, and said, "Hello. Looking for someone?" I said, "Yes. Howard Chapman." He said, "Oh. He's in the office talking to his girlfriend. I'll get him for you." I said, "No, don't interrupt them. I see him more than she does. Can I go in the kitchen and have a cup of coffee while I wait? When he's free will you tell him his wife is here?"

After Howard was transferred to another station, he called and asked me to bring him something again. I knew the guys would be ready to pull something on me, it being my first visit to that station. I was ready. We had a friend and neighbor who was the editor for the want ads in our local paper. He printed out one page with this add for me: WANTED–LIVE IN COOK FOR FIREHOUSE. FEMALE PREFERED. GOOD PAY. INQUIRE AT FIREHOUSE 86, (and then the address and phone number.)

I parked on the street instead of in the parking lot as a family member would do. I went into the office. The captain was there. He asked, "Can I help you?" "Yes, I'm here to apply for the position of live in cook." He sat in silence, staring at me. "That position is still open, I hope." "You must have the wrong place, ma'am." He stammered. "No, I don't believe so." I said, looking at the paper. "The ad says, wanted; live in cook for this station. See? The ad is circled. I really do want this job. I'm a good cook and I'm used to cooking for large groups." He took the paper and read the ad. He said the ad was somebody's idea of a joke. The department does not hire cooks. He apologized to me and said he would get to the bottom of this. I left, drove around the block, went in the parking lot and left what I had brought for Howard in his car. The captain demanded to know who had put the ad in the paper. Howard asked him to describe the woman. He called to ask if I had done it. He then informed the captain he had been had.

On April 1st one year, I called Howard and said I had made a sponge cake and was bringing it to the station. The sponge cake was made of two huge sponges I bought at a janitor supply store, and was covered with chocolate icing. Looked real and looked good. I also made a real cake. I arrived after dinner, after I knew all the dishes would be done. Herb was the cook, and the guys played cards after dinner. The looser had to do the dishes. The guys cheated and passed cards under the table so Herb always lost. He hated to do dishes. This was before they had dishwashers. I put the cake on the table. It was admired by all. Captain Hinkle got a knife and attempted to cut the cake. He put it in the sink and got a bigger, sharper knife. He again attempted to cut the cake. All the men except Howard, Captain Hinkle and Herb left the kitchen. Leo, Captain Hinkle, scraped some icing aside and saw the sponge. He grinned, covered the sponge, and winked at me.

While this was going on, Herb was getting small plates out of the cabinet. Leo put the knife down and said he wanted big plates. He put the small ones back and got the largest plates they had. He said he wanted plenty of room for ice cream to go with the cake. Herb took the big plates, put them away, and got the little plates, insisting the small ones were big enough.

Howard, who had seen the sponge, got in on the act. He took the cake and put it in the trash can, upside down, the plate covering the sponge. "My wife goes to the trouble of making a beautiful cake, brings it all the way over here, and that's the thanks she gets! You guys have to argue over plates! Well, no one is eating cake!" And with that he put his foot on the plate and pushed. All the guys, who were in the tv room next to the kitchen heard all this and were very apologetic, and probably very relieved they didn't have to eat a cake that was so hard to cut. All the commotion brought the other guys back into the kitchen. I had my head on my arms on the table and was laughing. They thought I was crying. Herb picked up the plate, saw the sponges and laughing, said, "Did you see this cake?" One of the firemen came unglued. He was reading poor ole Herb the riot act. Don't make fun of her cake, it was the thought that counted, not all cakes turn out good, Etc. He was so mad, I was afraid he would hit Herb. Herb picked up one of the sponges and turned it so Stocky could see it. Then I was afraid Stocky would hit me instead! I was afraid to bring in the real cake after all the commotion. I really didn't think anyone would be fooled by a sponge cake on April Fool Day!

Howard had four days off and had taken his mother to Salinas to take care of some property business. I took advantage of his absence. The first morning he was gone, which would have been an of duty shift for him, I called the station and asked for him.

This conversation took place:

"He isn't here."

"Was he sent to another station?" (They sometimes are, to fill in for someone else)

"UH, I don't know. Let me get the Cap."

"Hello, you're looking for Howard?"

"Yes. Something very important has come up and I have to talk to him."

"He left for work this morning?"

"Of course he did!"

"Well, I've been out of the station on business. Maybe he is out on fire inspection. Let me check and I'll call you back."

"OK, thanks, but hurry!"

Half an hour later.

"Hi, this is Chief Berteaux (aka the mama hen) I haven't located him yet. Are you sure he doesn't have a dental appointment or something you have forgotten about?"

"I don't think so. Just a minute, I'll look at the calendar. No, there's nothing there."

"I'll keep looking. Is there anything I can do for you?"

"Thanks, but no, I have GOT to talk to Howard! It's really urgent. I know you can find him no matter where he might have been sent or what errand he may be on."

"Yes, but it might take some time. I'll call as soon as I find out where he is or get a message to him to call you. Are you sure I can't help? If you tell me what the problem is...?"

"I appreciate the offer, but it's personal. I need to talk to my husband." (tears in my voice.)

"OK dear. I'll find him for you."

Captain Berteaux called Jim, Howard's nephew, also a fireman. Jim came to the house. I told him Howard had told me he was working straight through the week because there was a shortage of men, and we could use the money, too. Jim left, puzzled and worried. He went back to his station. Five or six guys got on the phones and called the off-duty firemen to see if they knew anything. Did he have a girl friend? Did he go off on a fishing trip with some of the guys? Did anyone know of any reason at all he would lie to his wife and disappear? If they knew anything, now was the time to speak up or contact him. Of course no one knew anything. About every three hours I called the station and sounded more distraught with each call.

On the second day Captain Berteaux came to the house. I told him I was worried that Howard had been in an accident. He could be in a hospital or lying dead somewhere. He promised he would personally check all the hospitals and morgue.

On the third day Howard's brother-in-law, a battalion chief, came to see me. I told him I knew how firemen covered for each other, and someone had to know where Howard was. It was obvious to me that Howard was not at work and was not in a hospital or morgue. I didn't know what was going on, but it was too late now, too late to do anything. I ran into the bedroom and locked the door and pretended to cry like my poor little heart was broken. Loud enough for Chuck to hear me of course. The kids were at school, so I didn't have to worry about them hearing all this. I made sure they knew nothing about what was going on.

Howard got home late that evening. He reported for duty early the next morning, completely unaware what had taken place while he was gone. The guys jumped all over him: where had he been...how could he treat his wife like that...

He called and asked me to come to the station and tell the guys it was all a prank. The guys realized they had REALLY been had. They promised they wouldn't try to pull anything else on me if I promised not to do anything else to them. And, they could speak for the whole battalion!

Word spread that I loved chicken enchiladas, and I was very often invited to a firehouse when that was on the menu, even if Howard wasn't and never had been assigned there. Just one of the benefits of being a fireman's wife? Or were they being nice so I would behave?

Herb loved to "debate." He also liked to lecture on many subjects. No matter what he started on, I would pretend to have the opposite view. With some careful maneuvering, and a little help from Les, I could manage to slowly turn things around so he would end up opposite of where he started. Somewhere along the way he would say he knew what he was talking about. He graduated from collage Magna Cum something or other. Did I know what that meant? Yes, I did. My formal education ended with the 8th grade, but yes, I did know what that meant, but…. It would end up with Les saying, "Herb, I'm glad you agree with her at last." "WHAT DO YOU MEAN?" "Herb, you are saying what she said in the first place. I'm glad to see she has straightened out your thinking." I was able to do that to Herb only three times. The last time, later that evening he and Howard were in the locker room. Herb looked at his Phi Beta Kappa key and said, "You know, somehow this doesn't seem to mean much anymore."

Herb is Jewish. I put a bumper sticker on his car that said HONK IF YOU BELIEVE IN JESUS. He was very puzzled because he was getting honked at by all kinds of people. When he got out of his car in a grocery store parking lot a couple of little old ladies who had honked at him a few minutes before, patted him on the back and said, "God bless you, son." It was a week or so before he saw the bumper sticker.

HEROES

A FELLOW FIREMAN

Howard became my hero when fighting a brushfire. We found ourselves trapped. Howard took charge and ordered us all to get on the engine. Les was the engineer assigned to that engine. Howard told him to drive through a wall of flames to a burned-out area on the other side. Les refused. Howard said, "Then get out of the way and let a man do it!" Howard drove us to safety.

Colleen became a hero of sorts to us firefighters. We could never figure out how she did all that she did. Besides taking care of a large family, she had time for her "extra kids." We saw the wonders that she worked with some of them. Her own kids, well, I never saw a better bunch. They were a pleasure to be around.

Firemen are known for their jokes and pranks but we never could put one over on her, but she got us more than once. She is the only person in the history of this department to fool not only us; she had the whole battalion in an uproar. I hope those events are in her book.

A NEW SINK

COLLEEN CHAPMAN

When we moved to Van Nuys we rented Howard's sister's house. The kitchen sink was a big single one. It was stained and chipped. A few months after we got settled in I told Howard I would like to have a new double sink. He didn't think it was important, but I DID! sooooo

Day 1--told Howard it was time to buy a new sink. He shrugged his shoulders.

Day 2-Howard is at work. I bought a sink. Dave and Steve sat it on kitchen floor (small kitchen)

Day 3--Howard came home from work, looked at sink, and went flying.

Day 4--Howard looked at sink, fixed airplane he crashed on day 3.

Day 5--Howard looked at sink, went flying.

Day 6-- Howard looked at sink, worked on a new airplane, fixed washing machine.

Day 7--Howard was back on duty. I looked at sink. Was tired of walking around it.

Day 8--Got up early. Howard would be home about 8 am.

1. Placed chair in front of sink.
2. Grasp very large cast iron frying pan by handle. Carefully stand on chair, raise frying pan as high as possible.
3. Drop frying pan into sink. If sink does not crack or chip, stand on drain board, raise pan to ceiling, drop as before.
4. Repeat steps 2 and 3 as many times as necessary until crack or holes appear in sink.

Do not look at children in pj's and nightgowns who appear and stare at you in wide eyed wander.

(Dave calmly asks what's for breakfast) Howard calls. Says he is working an extra shift. Manpower shortage. Will not be home for 2 days. I bought paper plates, bowls and eating utensils.

Day 10. --It is Thanksgiving. I look at broken sink. The kids and I went to a nice restaurant for dinner that evening.

Day 11--Howard came home, looked at dirty dishes, looks at broken sink, shakes head, and asks no questions, reads paper while having coffee. His Mother called. Said Howard must go to Salinas with her on business. Oh, good Lord! What has she done now. They leave that day and Howard gets home the evening of fourth day. I asked him what the business was about. He said he didn't want to talk about it. That night Howard passed out in the bathroom. I call paramedics at nearest fire station. I got a neighbor to stay with the kids. I followed the ambulance. One of the paramedics told me to turn on my flashing lights and I could stay right behind the ambulance and I would not be stopped for speeding. Howard was admitted to hospital in down town L.A. I stayed until time to go home and get kids off to school.

Day13 I get kids off to school, go to hospital. Howard is undiagnosed. Tests are being taken. Stay until time to get home before kids get out of school. Count kids, give them snack, arrange for neighbors to keep an eye on them, go back to hospital. I laid down on the bed next to Howard. I was almost asleep when a nurse came in. She started to say something. Howard said, "don't you dare wake her up!" Had a short nap. And then back home to fix dinner, etc.

Day 14, 15, 16, Repeat day 13. Nurses glad to see me each day. Howard is not a good patient.

Day17. Howard is diagnosed with mitral valve prolapsed. Not serious, apparently. (never happened again)

While Howard was in hospital, a fireman he worked with came over and installed the sink. If I had known how easy it is, Dave and Steve could have done it. But I had never seen it done, so how was I to know. Now I want a dishwasher. No problem. I can install it myself.

MY FIRST CAR

C OLLEEN C HAPMAN

In 1959 Daddy watched the kids for me and I walked to a car lot and bought my first car. I paid one hundred dollars down and would make payments of twenty-five dollars a month until it was paid off. I then drove to the DMV and took a driving test. The only driving I had done before that day was to drive my brother's car around the block once or twice. I didn't know there were booklets to study before taking the test. I passed it none the less. I remember one question I missed. It went something like this: If a vehicle in front of you loses something on the road, you should, 1. stop immediately and remove it, 2. -Go around it. I don't remember what the other choice was, but none of them made sense to me. If you stopped immediately a car behind you could hit you. And you should not stop in the road. I thought there should be a choice that said to safely pull to the side of the road and stop. Then remove the object if traffic allowed. Or something like that. I didn't see what I considered a correct answer, so I left it unanswered. When it was counted as a wrong answer, I stated my opinion of the choices given, and what the correct answer was, in my opinion. The man grading my paper just looked at me for a moment, then told me not to read so much into a question or answer. I informed him that what I read is what was there. He ignored me.

Then it was time to take the driving test. I was doing OK until I had to do a three-point turnaround. Since I had just gotten the car and was not familiar with it yet, I figured the safest way to do that was to let the rear tires rest against the curb while I shifted gears. The stick shift made a grinding noise as I tried to find reverse for the first time and again when I put it back in 1st. gear. Points were taken off. I asked why. He said the tires were not supposed to touch the curb, and I should be able to shift gears better than that. I told him that as far as the tires touching the curb was concerned, that was the safest way since this was the first time I ever drove the car, and I thought I did pretty good, finding reverse for the first time. The instructor was a little upset. He wouldn't give me back the points. I was a little upset. When we came to a stop sign, I did as I had seen everybody else do. Since there was no traffic and no pedestrians, I didn't come to a complete stop. The guy said, "That is going to cost you some points! You didn't come to a complete stop. You did what is called a rocking chair stop. I could not have gotten out of this car at all!" I slammed on the brakes and said, "You want out of this car? OK, get out!" He started to get out, and then changed his mind. I guess he didn't want to walk back to the DMV. He told me we would continue with the test. I passed, but just barely.

The next day I followed Pearl and Louon's car, and we drove to San Jose to visit someone, then to Santa Cruz, then home. Louon came close to having an accident a couple of times because he nervously kept an eye on me in his rear-view mirror. Since I started driving, I have had one speeding ticket, one for going through a red light (Rusty was a baby and tossed his bottle on the floor, it lodged under the brake pedal, and I cruised through a red light at ten miles an hour, with a policeman sitting right across the intersection.) and two parking tickets. I have had no accidents. Not bad for over fifty years of driving.

I had a lot to learn about cars! There was a service station two blocks from our house. The first time I needed gas, I went there. Bob, that was the name on his pocket, walked up to my car window, smiled at me and said, "Ethyl?" I said, "No. Will you fill the tank please?" "Ethyl" I said, "My name is Colleen. Not Ethyl and I need some gas." Bob said, "You live just up the street, don't you? I haven't seen this car there though. Your first car?" "Yes. Just got it a few days ago." "How long have you been driving?" "Since I got the car." "Good grief! O.K. there's a few things you need to know. Not all gas is the same. When you get gas, ask for regular. See that pump there? That one is regular. This one is for ethyl. Says so on the pump. So you want the tank filled with regular?" "Yes please." My face felt very hot. "Do you want the oil checked?" "Oil?" My face got hotter. "Good grief! I don't suppose you know about lube jobs or anything else!" "All I know is you put gas in the tank and water in the radiator and air in the tires." "Tell you what. If you are going to be a regular customer, I will take care of the car for you. Bring it in tomorrow and I will check it out for you. When and if something needs to be done, I will tell you what and why. If you want to, you can watch. That way you will learn about car care."

One morning I had a flat tire. I called Bob to see if he had one that would fit my car. He asked what size it was. I didn't know. I told him I would go see and would call him back. I got my tape measure and went out and looked at a tire, wondering how it should be measured. Deciding to measure every way possible so I would have any measurement he wanted, I measured across the tread, the diameter of the whole tire, the circumference, and the distance across the part that goes on the rim and from one edge of the tire from the center, across the tread and down to the edge on the other side. Any way it could be measured, I measured. I called Bob. I read off the measurements, telling him what each one was. He listened in total silence. Then he asked if I needed the tire right away. I didn't. He said he would come take a look at lunch time. Which he did and showed me the numbers on the tire. On his way home from work that evening, he changed the tire. All this happened before I met Howard. After we were married, Howard became a Los Angeles City fireman and had to pass a two-year probationary period. The kids and I stayed here until he had passed probation. He commuted. By trading shifts, he could work four 24 hour shifts in a row, with no time off, and get seven days off. Two of those days were pretty well taken up by travel, so he had five full days at home. He taught me how to take care of the carburetor; fuel pump and whatever else might get plugged up with oak leaves. That happened pretty often out here in the country. I got pretty good at basic car care.

Howard use to race hot rods, and he had two old cars that Bob was buying from him. When he came to get one of them, I was getting ready to clean the carburetor and fuel pump. I had a table set up outside. As I took things apart, I put them on the table in a row. That way I would be sure to put them back on in the correct order. I had a pan of water, a bar of soap and a towel on the table for cleaning my hands in case I had to do something else before I got through. I had put a can of gas and a pan for cleaning the parts under the table out of the sun. After saying hello, how are you and all that stuff while eyeing the things on the table, he asked what I was doing. "Cleaning this doohickey and that thingamabob." Bob looked at the pan of water and said, "Good grief! You go on in the house and I'll take care of this. I thought, "Gee, isn't that nice of him." He came in to tell me the parts were clean and back on the car. "Car parts are not washed in water. Don't ever do that" he said. "I know." I said, "That's what the gas under the table was for." "I thought that is what the water was for." "No. That was for my hands." "You've done that before?" "Yes. Living so far out in the country, I had to learn more than what you taught me." "You've come a long way from 'no, my name isn't Ethyl', haven't you." Bob told me his teenage son was working for him, and needed to learn how to handle difficult customers, and would like my help. The car I was driving at the time wouldn't start when the engine was hot. The first time I went to the gas station after Devin (the son) started working there, I told him to check the oil, transmission fluid, radiator, windshield washer water, the air pressure in the tires, including the spare tire, and anything else that needed to be checked and wash the windows. I had Okayed doing all this with Bob and went when I knew they would not be very busy. I also knew that the battery needed water. Devin looked a little confused, and went to discuss all this with Bob. Devin returned to the car and did all that he was asked to do. Every thing was fine, he said, except the battery needed water. I asked him if he was sure, it could be a dry cell battery. He assured me that it must have water. He put the water in, and when I attempted to start the car, it wouldn't start. I acted very upset, and told him it must be the battery, putting water in it probably ruined a perfectly good dry cell battery, and my husband was going to have a fit. Bob came out to the car, and told Devin to go inside and he would take care of the situation. Bob replaced the battery and coil-which caused the starting problem (also pre arranged,) and filled the gas tank. He told Devin he had to give me a free battery and tank of gas to keep me from raising a fuss. The next time I was there when Devin was working, I was taking the car in to have some mechanical stuff done. I parked the car near the garage, and walked over to the restroom. Just as I put my hand on the door knob, Devin came rolling out from under a car, and asked if he could help me. As I opened the door, I told him I thought I could manage, but if I needed help, I would call him. Devin told Bob that if he had to deal with me any more, he would go find another job.

MY FIRST WASHING MACHINE

Colleen Chapman

My seventh child was a baby when I got my first washing machine. I don't remember where it came from, but I was so glad to have it! Until then, I had to do the wash by hand on the rub board, or go to a Laundromat, or to Pearl's. The washing machine was an old wringer washer. One leg was badly bent, and the washer had to be pushed up against the walls in a corner to keep it from falling over. The wringer didn't work right either. The routine went like this: the washer leaned against a wall. I filled it, using a hose. When the cloths were ready to be taken from the washer, I pulled it to the cement laundry tub attached to the wall, put a towel between the washer and me and leaned against the washer to prop it up. If I forgot to use the towel, I got shocked when I touched the wringer. If I didn't hang on to the wringer, it would not stay in position, and would whirl around and around. So I leaned on the washer, hung onto to the wringer with one hand and poked the cloths between the rollers with the other hand, hoping I didn't get my fingers caught, that I didn't get shocked, and that the machine didn't fall over, and that I didn't lose my grip on the wringer and get hit by it if it spun around.

MY FIRST KISS FROM A BOY

COLLEEN CHAPMAN

I was about eight or nine when we first moved to Chualar, a tiny town in California. Chualar at one time was a stagecoach stop, and there were two rows of two room cabins facing each other. There was a wash house at one end, and showers which had been added some time later when the cabins were rented out. The space between the cabins was large enough to have held horses and coaches.

There wasn't much for the teen-ager to do in Chualar. The nearest town of any size was Salinas, about 16 or 18 miles away. So until someone in the group was old enough to get their drivers license, they were pretty well stuck. One thing they liked to do was to gather in front of the wash house and play games. One game, I don't remember what it was called, the kids sat on a long bench in front. A boy would stand up, face the others, and ask a girl a question. If she gave a wrong answer, she had to walk around the wash house with him. I noticed some couples went around pretty fast, but others took a bit longer. I mentioned this to a friend; I think his name was Stanley. He suggested we hide and watch them. Since there was no place to hide; we climbed a tree which had a branch hanging over the building. We dropped onto the top of the building. We were in place before the kids gathered. As the couples walked around the building, Stanley and I crawled along the edge and watched. When the couples got half way, some of them stopped, hugged and kissed. Stanley and I wondered why they did that. We decided to give it a try. After a quick kiss, we, at the same time, wiped our mouths and said, "Ugh! Pew" Our curiosity satisfied, we jumped down and went in search of something more interesting to do.

NO MORE BIRTHDAYS

Colleen Chapman

When Ruby and her daughters Cathy and Carla went to see Betty it was the first time they had been together for a long time. Betty hadn't seen the girls since they were very small, so they had a lot of catching up to do. After dinner they settled down in the living room and began filling each other in on all the things that had happened and were happening in our lives.

One of the first things Ruby said was, "Betty, you had a birthday just last month, didn't you?" Betty said, "oh no, Ruby, I don't have birthdays anymore. I stopped having birthdays a long time ago." "Well" Ruby said, "I have been trying to figure out how old you are. Isn't Dorothy about two or two and a half years older than you are?" Betty said "Ruby, if Dorothy kept on having birthdays after I stopped, then she's a lot more than two and a half years older than me."

Ruby didn't say anything else for a long time. She sat quietly with a puzzled look on her face while Larry, the girls and Betty talked and talked. After about an hour as Larry and Betty talked about the problems they had building their house, Ruby suddenly said, "I know you were still just a baby, about thirteen months old, when Fred was born but I can't remember the year *he* was born either. They were bent over with laughter at that, to think that after all this time she was still trying to figure out Betty's age instead of listening to the conversations.

They sat up until about mid-night. Cathy and Carla filled Larry and Betty in on their families and experiences, and Larry and Betty did the same on our part. Periodically Ruby would say something like this: "Dorothy is about four or five years younger than me, but I just can't remember how old she was when you were born." They had a good time that night, getting to know each other and said none of them had laughed so much in years over Ruby's interest and confusion about Betty's age. That is all of them laughed except Ruby.

The next day, while Ruby and the girls were on their way to visit with the rest of us, Betty called and told me about Ruby trying to figure out Betty's age. I told everyone else. Shortly after they arrived and we had all settled down to talk and enjoy our lunch, Ruby said, "Colleen, I know Betty is older than you, and Fred is between you, but I can't remember when you two were born, and so I can't figure out how old Betty is!" She looked very confused when all of us cracked up. I promised her I would write down all our birthdates and ages for her before they left. Which I did. For Betty I put: Betty Jo Born 1931. Stopped having birthdays when she was 30. Therefore, remains 30 years old.

Betty said, "I am the only one in the family who stopped having birthdays and I feel sorry for them as they keep adding years to their age on a regular basis."

NOT A TYPICAL WOMAN

COLLEEN CHAPMAN

When it comes to shopping I am not a typical female! If I could do it all by phone, catalogue or on line, I would. Here is an example of why I do not enjoy shopping: I needed some new Cuddle Duds. I wear thermals under my denims, but they are not good under everything. Cuddle Duds are also great to sleep in. I feel the cold more than ever this year. Yeah, I know, the older you get....They are for sale on line, but Gottschalks had them on sale, buy two, get one free, send in a coupon and six dollars to cover shipping and handling, and get a fourth one free. Too good to pass up.

This was a day or two after Thanksgiving, and soooooo many people out shopping. I found what I wanted. The line at the service counter was very long. I HATE STANDING IN LINE! But I did, for 20 minutes. Two kids were running around, bumping into people, making noise, and everyone ignored them, acting as if this was normal, acceptable behavior. The second time the boy, about six years old, bumped into me from behind, I grabbed his arm and gave him the meanest look I could muster, and growled. He ran to his mother who was in line ahead of me and grabbed her arm. He called his sister and whispered in her ear. They turned and looked at me. I gave them both a mean look. The girl grabbed the mother's other arm. She kept telling them to let go, to leave her alone, but they didn't.

When I got home I discovered I had gotten the wrong size. Actually, I think the sales girl made a mistake and gave me the wrong ones. Three other women were buying the same thing at the same time. I think the very large woman standing next to me at the counter went home with a size medium. I like mine roomy and comfy, but this was ridiculous.

Two days later I went back. I told the sales girl I had the wrong size and wanted to exchange them for the right size. I found the size I needed and went back to the counter. So far so good. Then the sales girl said I would have to pay sales tax. I asked why. She said it was store policy. I asked her to explain why tax would be charged on a transaction that should be an even exchange. She couldn't. Then another sales girl said I had bought them on a day when they don't charge sales tax, so I would have to pay it now. At first I said Oh all right, just to get out of there, but changed my mind. It was the principal of the thing. It just was not right. I refused to pay the tax. I was not buying them that day. I was just trying to exchange. The sales girl said she would call her manager, and I would see that she was telling me the truth. I said I was not calling her a liar, but either she was miss-informed, poorly trained, or the store had recently adopted a very poor policy. But please, by all means, call the manager. The manager agreed with me and said it would be an even exchange.

NOT THROUGH WITH HER MEN

THIS IS A STRING OF POSTING ON THE FAMILY SITE

Ruby----I am feeling better, but I won't be through with my men until the 16th, then the Dr. wants me to come back to see if I am over it. I would like to be there for Colleen's birthday. I really do want to come out soon. How is Pearl doing by now?

Colleen----You won't be through your MEN? until the 16th. My gosh! How many do you have? Well, I sure do hope the Dr. says you are over IT. At your age I thought you were probably over IT a long time ago! Won't be through with your men....I just can't get over the thought! Poor thing, you'll be too tired to go anywhere. If you don't come to visit us we'll know why. All those men to take care of!

Dorothy-----I guess a little old birthday party can't compete.

Ruby-----I meant to say Med. - medicine. But your reply made me laugh so hard, I forgot about my sick stomach and pains. I'll watch my language from now on

Sandra----Sorry it was a mistake. Meds are safer but I don't think as much fun. I guess it depends on the meds and the men.

Dorothy-----Well, her men must be something special since they get priority over a visit to her dear sisters. Too late to watch your language now, Ruby. The cat is out of the bag and he is not about to go back in.

Colleen----Well, Ruby, today is the 16th. Did you get all your men taken care of? How are you feeling? When do you go back to the Dr. to see if you are "over it"? Sure hope you don't have to go through it all again. Sandra says Pearl is okay now but was tired out over the weekend because she overdid it on Friday. You two just don't know when to quit.

BLACKEYED PEA

COLLEEN CHAPMAN

I sat in a high chair in the kitchen. Several women were in the kitchen picking beans. That probably needs to be explained to some of you younger people. No, the beans were not growing in the kitchen. These were dried beans. To "pick beans" you get a handful of dried beans, look them over and remove pieces of dirt and anything else that isn't beans. Mother spotted one black eyed pea among the beans in her hand. She started to discard it, and then changed her mind. With a big smile she said, "Let's have some fun. Let's put this pea in with the beans and see who gets it. Now keep it a secret. No one is to know but us." She made it sound like so much fun. The other women laughed and agreed to keep the secret. All afternoon I would think of that black-eyed pea and wonder who would get it. Perhaps the fact that I was the only one of the kids to be in on the secret made it seems more fun and exciting.

When it was at last time to eat dinner, I watched each time the ladle went into the pot and beans were served. What else we had for that meal has been long forgotten, but I can still remember the anticipation –who would get that black-eyed pea, and when! Dinner was almost over. The men had gone out on the front porch. The women were beginning to clear the dishes from the table. I could feel the disappointment growing stronger. I wanted to cry. Some of the kids were not finished, so maybe there was still a chance one of them would want more beans. My too full stomach told me I had eaten more than my share! Fred asked for more beans!! Mother dipped up some beans and there, right on top was that black-eyed pea! At last! Mother saw the black-eyed pea, and with a straight face she said, "Fred, you wantta pea Son?" Fred's face turned red and he slid down in his chair and said, "No Ma'am."

PAUL AND EVIE

COLLEEN CHAPMAN

Paul had a motorcycle and would often give the kids a ride. One day he had a pocket full of suckers and each one of the kids were given one when they got off at the end of their turn. Paul and Evie had an air horn which she used when she wanted him to come home. We had heard the horn several times. Paul would look towards home and grin every time. All the kids except Rusty, who was about a year old, had taken a turn. Rusty was insisting on a turn, his first. But he had no intention of going anywhere without his bottle. I strapped him on behind Paul and he clamped his teeth on the nipple and held on to Paul, and away they went. The air horn was sounding about every five minutes now. After Rusty's ride, Paul said he had one sucker left. I handed Rusty to Diane, grabbed the sucker and jumped on behind Paul. I really didn't intend on going for a ride, but Paul took off and I almost fell off. It was my first motorcycle ride, and he made it one to remember! After scaring me half to death, instead of taking me home, he took me up the road to his house. Evie was standing in the yard. Paul took one look, chucked and said, "I think I'm in trouble." I took a look and said, "Well, if you brought me up here for protection, it isn't going to work. I think I'm in trouble too." I popped the sucker back in my mouth and walked home.

THE PLANT SALE

COLLEEN CHAPMAN

The plant sale went pretty well, considering I put up only a few posters. I could never make a living as a sales person! A woman asked why some pots of Dahlias cost more than other pots the same size. I explained that the ones that cost more have more than one Dahlia in it, and the less expensive pots have only one. She said I couldn't do that, that all pots of the same size had to have the same price. I did not see things her way. After several minutes of her yapping, I got tired of biting my tongue and trying to be nice. I told her that this is my property, my plants, my time, work and money and I would and could do as I dang well pleased with it. If she didn't like it, that is her problem and I refuse to let her make it mine, so would she like help getting into her car to leave? She said she was going to report me. I asked her who she was going to report me to. Didn't get an answer.

The pots are sunk into the ground about six inches so if the roots grow out of the pots, they can go into the ground. When the pots that have roots into the ground are picked up and roots are exposed, the Dahlia will droop. If they are not taken care of, they droop more and more. A woman who apparently has a problem with making decisions (I was busy with someone else) would pick up a pot, put it down and pick up another one. When I could turn my attention to her, and saw what she was doing, I asked her not to do it. She said she couldn't make up her mind what to get, and would come back with her daughter to help her. A little later I noticed about three dozen drooping Dahlias! My first thought was--If her daughter comes with her, am I going to have two people doing as she had done? That evening her daughter called and said they will be here in a few days, and the way to make a quick easy sale to her mother, is to put sold signs on a dozen or so pots, and let her talk me into letting her have them.

Most of my customers, and the most pleasant ones, are men. I am surprised by that. They also buy the most. One guy was the type who seems to think he is suppose to come on to any and all females he comes into contact with. He kept getting a little too close, and getting a little too friendly. He said he had been by and admired the plants several times, but had not seen me anyplace. (BULL!) He said he started to come up to the house, but was afraid there might be a big bad watch dog up there. I told him that with a husband like mine I didn't need a watch dog. He backed off real quick, completed his purchase and left.

RUBY

COLLEEN CHAPMAN

I don't remember much about Ruby before she got married. She and Carl took me in twice when I was between 11 and 13. I learned the importance of truthfulness, self respect, respect for others, honesty, cleanness, not only as in grooming, but also in thought and every other way. And of course, the importance of having our Heavenly Father in our life. From her example I learned to set high goals for myself. To work always to improve myself in every way. But no matter how hard I try, I still can not carry a tune! I don't know if Ruby was naieve or gulible, but she was sooooo easy to tease. And I was a big tease. Looking back, I admire her self controll. Sometimes I went too far. For instance: Ruby was suppose to stay in bed for some reason. She said she was so bored she didn't know if she could stand it. Well, I decided to liven things up for her. I asked if I could bake a cake. She picked out a reciepe for me. I took the book and went back to the kitchen. After a few minutes I went back in the bedroom and asked where I could find the ingredience. She looked puzzled, and said, "You know where everything is in the kitchen, if there's something---well, honey, just hunt for it." I got everything I needed and went back to the bed room and told her I found everything except the ingreadience, and asked if that was a spice or what. I can still see the look on her face. She patiently explained. It was all I could do to keep a straight face. I began to put the cake together, and had another idea. Returning to the bedroom I told her the reciepe said to cream the butter and sugar, but it didn't say how much cream to use. Again that priceless look. Again she patiently explained. I don't remember all the things I pulled before she caught on. I think she just about lost her composure when I asked how far apart the eggs were suppose to be seperated, and why and what do I do with them then. The cake was pretty good.

Ruby......I have learned a lot of things from Colleen too. She had some very chalenging trials to go through when she was growing up. Also in her first marriage. But she handeld them really well. She is very strong woman spiritually. She always has a positive outlook and keeps a smile on her face. She has lots of talentes and uses them well. I try to be strong like her.

SUNDAY

DOROTHY PATTON

We were waiting for a table in the First Awakenings restaurant in Salinas. There were four of us sisters: Pearl, Betty, Colleen and I, along with Betty's husband, Larry. We were sitting at a table outside the restaurant while waiting for a table inside. It was a nice, sunny day. A stretch limousine stopped at the stop sign near our table. As we admired the vehicle, a man's head appeared through the sun roof. "Pardon me," he said. "Does anyone have any Gray Poupon?"

Well, we finally got a table inside the restaurant. I ordered the Popeye salad. When it came, I couldn't believe my eyes. It was HUGE! I had assumed it was called the Popeye salad because it was made of spinach. But now I think it gets its name from the way people look at it when it is served. It was on the kind of platter you would use to serve a thanksgiving turkey. It was very good but I hardly made a dent in it. I told the waitress that next time we would order one salad and five forks. We had a really good time talking about silly things that happened in the past. We lingered at the table, drinking coffee and talking long after we finished eating. I noticed that the tables around us were empty and was sure that we weren't causing anybody to have to wait by taking our time. But as we left we noticed that we were the only customers. We looked at the sign on the door and found that we had stayed an hour past closing time. I'm sure the staff was anxious to close up and go home but nobody had tried to hurry us and they were very nice. We will go there again but next time we will leave before closing time.

We also visited the Steinbeck Center on Sunday. It was the second time for Colleen and I but I think I could enjoy a visit every week or so. I decided during the visit on Sunday that I will read all of Steinbeck's work again.

I enjoyed the day very much. I hope that we can all get together again soon.

THE BEDROOM MAKEOVER

COLLEEN CHAPMAN

At long last I had the time and energy at the same time to fix up our bedroom. It was not just a simple matter of painting and papering. The roof was damaged by a storm a few years ago and our ceiling had gotten soaked. We had to wait several months for a new roof to be put on and got rained on many times. The leaks were so bad; Howard got a roll of thick plastic, cut some strips, taped it to the ceiling, and funneled the water into the shower. Very clever. The ceiling, after it dried, was a stained, sagging mess. When we first moved back here, the house had been rented out for 21 years. The place was overrun with mice. At night we could hear them running from one end of the house to the other and jumping over the rafters. It sounded like they were having a great time. There were several feral cats here, so Howard made an entrance for them by cutting a door in the wall of the washroom so they could get into the attic. He tossed a couple of cats in, and in no time, we no longer had the nightly speed races.

One of the cats had her kittens up there. When she moved them out, she left two of them. Howard put her up there but she wouldn't get her kittens. Two days later I held a flashlight in the opening and the kittens came to the light. I put them with the other kittens but that darn cat put them back up there! I got them out again and found homes for them. So what has that got to do with fixing the bedroom? The cat did it again the next time she had kittens. I was gone for the week end. Howard didn't know how I had gotten kittens out before. Being a man, the first thing he thought of was to cut a hole in the ceiling. So he did but couldn't reach the kitten and couldn't coax it to come to him. So he cut another hole. He cut the edges at a slant so the pieces would not fall through when he slid them back into place. And yes, he did close the cat door to the attic. But he did not repair the ceiling. So now we had a dry but stained and sagging ceiling with two big round scars where the holes had been cut.

I asked Howard to put our motor home next to the house and remove enough of the airplane stuff he had stored in it, so we could sleep in there while the bed room was being done. He wouldn't. Then we got a call from a friend who lives in Georgia and was being sent to the LA area by his company. He wanted to come up for the week end. Howard got the motor home ready for him to use. We had a nice visit, and his car had just barely cleared the driveway on Sunday afternoon when I started clearing out the bedroom. The cloths went in my workroom, the furniture in the living room, and the mattress stood on end in the washroom.

The first thing I had to do was to scrape all the loose paint off the ceiling, sand it and wash it. The whole thing. The room is eleven feet by eleven feet six inches. Then I got a box of Fix All to repair it. I learned the hard way that one should not wait for the Fix All to dry before sanding it smooth. It sets like concrete. It took two boxes of Fix All to fill all the cracks. Then I applied the sealer, stain blocker, then two coats of paint. It looked awful! I bought more paint and two boxes of texturizer, went home and went to work. After about half an hour I got very dizzy. This was a heck of a time for my inner ear thing to act up. It hadn't bothered me for a long time. Every time I looked up, I would go backward and almost fall. I got the cushions that make up the bed in our old camping van and put them on the floor all around me. Then I took the handle off of my broom and screwed it into the handle of the paint roller. It fit perfectly and I didn't have to climb the ladder. I could reach the ceiling from the floor. I moved the cushions around with my feet. I fell only twice and got sick to my tummy once. I applied two coats of the textured paint. It isn't perfect, but it will do.

Then, after the cleanup, it was time to tackle the walls. They were in really bad condition. It took a big can of wood filler, a lot of scraping and sanding and washing to get it ready. I decided to put up wall paper, thinking it would cover the flaws better than paint. I was told that papering is a two-man job. I figured if it WAS a two MAN job, I should be able to do it by myself. Just kidding, guys. I had some paper I really like, left over from another papering job I did years ago. There wasn't enough to do the whole room, so back to Home Depot I went. They didn't have that pattern anymore, so I had to find something that would match. I would do one paper on the lower walls, and the other on the upper walls. I had a piece of the paper with me so I could get a good match. I needed a solid color that matched the pattern on the paper I already had. The paper I chose looked OK in the store under the fluorescent lights but looked awful at home. Took it back. I found another paper that looked good and got several rolls. The paper didn't have a lot number because it was SUPPOSEDLY all the same. IT WAS NOT! I was papering in the evening and didn't notice the difference until the next day, in the daylight. I had used three rolls of paper and had three different shades on the walls. There was no way I was going to remove all the paper. There was enough paper left that matched the first wall, to put over the other miss-matched strips. I applied the wall sizing, which goes on the wall before the paper does, to the wall paper, hoping it would work. It didn't.

Back to Home Depot to get some vinyl to vinyl adhesive or glue or paste. I could not make them understand what I wanted. I explained, but he just didn't get it. I practically drug the guy to the wall paper display, showed him I was putting vinyl coated wall paper over vinyl coated wall paper, and needed vinyl to vinyl glue. He insisted I couldn't do that. The old wall paper had to be removed, he said. I know better but gave up and used wall paper paste. The paper was pre-pasted but didn't want to stick without something more. I took a different pattern and ended up with the strips you see in the pictures. I like it that way, and so far the paper has not fallen off.

When you start a papering job, you are supposed to start at a straight edge, like a corner or door jamb. I discovered there is not a straight wall in the room. One earthquake too many I guess. So how do you hang wall paper straight on walls that are not? Verrrry carefully. This is the first papering job I have done where the seams are not invisible. Try as I might, they were visible. Some 1/4 inch painted wooden sticks took care of that.

I had torn out the closet and built a larger one on the opposite wall. To save space, I put our chest of drawers in the closet. I needed a new cloths rod. The strongest thing you can get for that is conduit. Back to Home Depot. Just inside the door, a very frail little elderly Mexican man asked if he could help me. I told him I wanted some conduit. He said," Sorry I don't know conduit. What is conduit please?" "It is pipe for running wire through." "No, No. Water and gas go through pipe. Not wire." he laughed. "Yes, wire." "Yes? Why wire? I don't understand why wire in pipe." "When you put wire underground, you put it inside pipe to protect it from the elements and gophers." "Ah yes. Gophers I know. Very good idea. Look in the electrical department. Is that way. I remember seeing some pipe on rear wall. Must be it." and away he went.

I looked on the back walls in the electrical department. Didn't see conduit. I wandered around and found some on one of the isles. It was standing on a shelf and was all long pieces, and I didn't dare try to get it myself and couldn't find anyone to help me. Went back to the end of the isle and sat on a big tool box, waiting for someone to pass by. After a while the little man walked by. I stopped him and showed him the pipe. He said he couldn't get it for me, but he would get someone. I was tired and didn't mind sitting and waiting some, but this was getting ridiculous. Another half hour, and a young, strong looking guy comes to help me. I showed him the conduit I wanted and told him I wanted a six-foot length. He said it wasn't sold that way, the whole piece had to be bought and started to walk away. I stopped him, told him I would buy the whole thing, but wanted him to cut it for me. He took the pipe down and asked what I was going to use it for. I told him it was going to be a closet pole. He didn't understand. To hang cloths on, I told him. He put the pipe back and started to walk away telling me where the closet poles are. I grabbed his shirt tail and told him I knew where they were and I did not want to pay over twenty dollars for a pole that was not as strong as the less expensive conduit. He said the closet poles were a lot better looking. I said I didn't care. I did not plan to take people in my bed room, open the closet and show off my pretty cloths rod. He took the pipe down again.

He picked up some big pipe cutters and said they were not big enough and took off. I tried to tell him that is not what is used to cut it, but he wouldn't listen. Twenty minutes later he came back. Said he couldn't find bigger cutters and couldn't find anyone who knew where they are kept. I told him to look for a hack saw. There should be one in this area, because that is what is used to cut pipe that size. The pipe cutter would smash the end of the pipe. I found the hack saw and handed it to him. He started sawing. He was trying to saw all the way through and it wasn't working. I told him to turn the pipe. When he got it sawed through in that place, turn the pipe again, and do that all the way around. He made a very jagged cut. He then took the two pieces of pipe to the checkout for me, and then on to my car.

He looked at the car, looked at the pipe, and said it wouldn't fit. I unlocked the passenger side door and reclined the passenger seat explaining it would fit. He started to put the pipe in through the window, the jagged edge headed toward the seat. I yelled STOP! He did. I tossed my purse, with my keys attached, on the driver's seat. I got the plastic grocery bags I had brought for that purpose and wrapped the ends of the pipe. He put the pipe in, one end on the back seat behind the driver's seat, and the other end across the passenger front seat. He rolled up the window and slid the lock on the door and shut the door while I yelled STOP! He smiled and said it was OK. His sister has a car just like mine, and he knew how to lock the door. Then he realized what he had done. He had not only locked the passenger door, he had locked ALL the doors! I said, "OK. Where is the camera?" "Camera? What camera?" "You mean this is not for Candid Camera? This is for real?" He told me not to worry. We would go get someone to open the door. We went inside the store and I asked to see the manager. The young man said the manager was out to lunch. I said he was not the only one who was out to lunch. The young man said as a matter of fact several guys are on their lunch break. I asked him to go get whoever was in charge. Another half hour or so went by. He came back with an assistant manager. I explained the situation. He said he would get one of the employees to get a cloths hanger and ---I told him no, he would not. The windows are closed all the way. The young man said there was a guy who worked there who could get the door open. I asked the assistant manager if he was sure this whole thing was for real. Not for Candid Camera. He assured me he knew nothing about any camera. In view of all that had happened I did not want anyone working here to touch my car.

He said I could use his cell phone to call my insurance company to send someone---I said no, he could call a locksmith. I was not paying and neither was my insurance. Home Depot, or this store, or he or the young man, or whoever hired the young man was going to pay for it. He looked surprised, then laughed and said I had a lot of spunk for such a short little thing. I told him I tend to get that way when I am pi–ah--ticked off. He called someone and then said it would be at least 45 minutes to an hour before they could send someone. I said, "OK. I am hungry. I will have lunch while I wait." and held out my hand. He looked at my hand and said "What." I said, "My money is in my purse. My purse is in the car. My car is locked with the keys inside, thanks to one of your employees. I have been here for two and a half miserable hours. I am hungry. I am diabetic. My blood sugar is too low from not eating. I have a blood pressure problem. Right now it is probably dangerously high. I need money. *NOW!*" He gave me ten dollars. I walked to Jack in the box and walked back to stand in the shade next to my car. The locksmith showed up soon after I got to the car. So much for a quick trip to Home Depot.

The rod worked out fine after Howard smoothed the edges and installed it for me. Things went smoothly and we got the furniture moved back in. We put the box springs and mattress on some shelves so we can store our shoes there. After hanging the quilt I made last year on the wall I told Howard the bed is not centered and we need to move it over a little. That means taking the whole thing apart and putting it back together again. The mattress weighs a ton. The look he gave me said I had better get used to it the way it is---for now. It will get moved over. Oh yeah, the rod the quilt is on. When I bought it, I told the guy I wanted a plain wooden rod, 80 inches long. After I got home we found it to be 79 inches. Howard had already made and put up the holders for it. Back to Home Depot. The next day I discovered the mini blinds I had bought are one inch too narrow. Decided to make shades with some pink material instead of using the mini blinds. Now I need to finish up the bathroom. I think I have everything I need for that but if I do need anything I will NOT go to Home depot. Wish me luck.

Forgot to mention the windows. They had to be removed; the old paint stripped off, sanded and re-glazed. The weather was nice so I took them outside to work on them. After putting the coat of primer on them I went into the house for lunch. When I returned to put the first coat of paint on, found a cat had walked on two of the windows and left sandy foot prints in the primer. Got that cleaned up, took them inside before painting them.

During all this renovation of the bed room I had to be careful not to get too tired because that could cause me to have a recurrence of some MS symptoms. And y'all wonder why it was taking so long to get it done! Home Depot has a new manager now, and the service is very good.

THE PERFECT LEMON PIE

COLLEEN CHAPMAN

Back in 1960 something I wanted to make the perfect lemon meringue pie. Something was always wrong. If the crust was good, the meringue was weepy. If the meringue was good, the lemon filling...you get the idea. I made a pie every week, adjusting the recipe over and over. The fifth pie looked very good. I just knew it was going to be the perfect pie at last. When the meringue was a golden brown, I sat this perfect pie on the cooling rack. While it cooled I cleaned up and mopped the floor. After the pie cooled it still looked perfect. I had done it at last. The perfect pie, if it tasted as good as it looked. I picked it up and started into the living room to show it to Howard and the kids. Just then a marble came rolling into the kitchen from the living room. I stepped on it and fell. The pie hit the floor upside down. I sat on the floor looking at the pie. I looked up to see all the kids holding their breaths and looking at the pie, then me, back and forth. I got up, got a handful of forks, laid on the floor on my tummy, put all the forks but one on the floor, and started eating pie. Without a word, the kids lay down, got a fork and joined me. It tasted perfect although it didn't look as good as it had a few minutes ago.

THEY DON'T LIVE HERE

Colleen Chapman

When Vincent and Robert were little we called them Tuckey and Mickey. A nurse gave Vincent the nickname of Tuckey. I don't remember why. Anyway, it stuck. Robert's first name is Michael. I called him Mikey. All too often when I said Mikey, one of the kids, thinking it was very funny, would say, "What key? Your House key or the car key?" So I changed it to Mickey. When Mickey started high school he decided he wanted to be called Robert. Somewhere along the way he changed it to Bob. Tuckey wanted to be called Vincent by the time he was about 10. But at the time the following happened they were Mickey and Tuckey to the family.

Shortly after the two of them became Cub Scouts, all the kids had the measles. All 8 of them! (We didn't have Loren yet.) They must have been exposed at the same time, because for three days they were coming down with the measles, one after the other. Taking care of 8 feverish, itchy, cranky unhappy kids is not an easy job. Then I got the measles too! Or was it a nervous rash? I took the mattress off of their beds and put them up on the floor of the living room and I lay on the couch when I could. That made it a lot easier for me to take care of them. I closed the drapes and hung a quilt on the glass front door because the light hurt our eyes.

One day the scoutmaster (who I had not met) came by to introduce himself and meet the new cubs. I opened the door just a crack. He said he had come to see Vincent and Robert. I told him he had the wrong house. He looked at the card in his hand, read off the address, and asked if this was that address. I said it was, but there was no one here by those names. He said Joan, their Den Mother, had given him those names and this address. He looked very confused and asked if I was sure Vincent and Robert didn't live here. Miffed and miserable, I told him I guess by golly I know my own kid's names and shut the door. As I made my back to the couch over and around kids and mattress, the giggles started. For years I was teased about not knowing my own kids' names.

One day Joan told me they had an election that day at the troop meeting. Mikey –Mickey– Robert– Bob lost by one vote. She told him he would have won if he had voted for himself and asked why he had not done so. He told her it was against his "princables

DAVE WILL SET YOU STRAIGHT

C OLLEEN C HAPMAN

I was teaching my three kids to play ball. Dave was four, Diane, three, and Steven was two. A boy who lived a few doors down the street came to help. He would often show up when we were outside. I was 19, and he was a child of 17. It was getting cold, and as the kids and I started to go in the house, the boy asked if I would like to go to the movies with him on Saturday. Dave said, "You'll have to take us too. My Mom doesn't go anyplace without us kids." The boy turned as red as a beet. He thought I was the baby sitter, he explained. A car stopped in front of our house. We watched as a very angry man prepared to change a flat tire. He began to swear as he worked. Dave got up from the steps where we sat and walked to the man. He said, "Sir, that's my mother and my little sisters and brothers over there. I don't allow that kind of words in front of them." The man straightened up, looked at Dave and then at us. He shook his head and said, "I'm sorry. I didn't see them." He walked over to us and said, "I'm sorry. How old is that boy?" he asked nodding toward Dave. "He's nine, going on thirty." I answered. "First time I have been taken to task by a child." He said as he returned to the car. He didn't swear as he finished.

WHY IS THE SKY BLUE?

Susan Aubert

A while back I sent a message to Mom asking a lot of questions. At the end was the question, why is the sky blue? I did not expect an answer to that, but got one. The following messge was sent to me by Mom and I think it needs to be shared amongst us all. So enjoy!

When one of my children ask a question I try hard to give them an answer. A while back Sue, you asked a question and I just realized you did not get an answer. With all the many other things on your mind I am so sorry I have neglected to answer your question. I do hope it has not caused any worry or concern. So now to answer the question...why is the sky blue?

When sunlight travels through the atmosphere, blue light scatters more than the other colors, leaving a dominate yellow orange hue to the transmitted light. The scattered light makes the sky blue. The transmitted light makes the sunset reddish orange. So now you not only know why the sky is blue, you also know why the sunsets are mostly reddish orange. Oh don't ask me about the other colors some sunsets have! I will have to go into clouds, cloud formations, cloud density, cloud content, cloud distance, not to mention atmospheric conditions. If there are no clouds and the air is not polluted with smoke or something, the sunset is reddish orange! OK?

A STRANGE FEELING

DOROTHY PATTON

I woke up after ten o'clock this morning feeling strange. Something was wrong. looked out the window and things seemed normal out there. Someone hobbled across the parking lot with a cane. Someone else drove in and parked and walked toward the building as if nothing was wrong. But still, I felt something strange, a kind of nothingness. No weird feelings in by body, no weird noises in my head. Couldn't feel my heart racing or skipping beats, but it must be in there beating or I wouldn't be up walking around. But I've seen movies where people walked around not realizing that they were dead. Could dead people feed fish? I tried it and the fish seemed happy. But it wouldn't make any difference to them if a dead person fed them. Could a dead person eat? I saw a movie where a dead man ate an apple and when he stood in front of a mirror all he saw was the apple (a fully formed apple) hanging in the air where his stomach would have been. That was probably a cartoon. But I've read about real people who died for a short time and looked back at their dead body. There is no dead body in my bed. Of course, they could have taken it away and I'm haunting the place where I used to live. The last thing I remember when I was alive was looking at the clock from my bed and thinking: Well, it's midnight. I guess that new sleep potion I took two hours ago isn't working. Now it is ten hour later...I must have slept ten hours! This strange new thing I'm feeling is...RESTED!

GOOD NIGHT'S SLEEP

COLLEEN CHAPMAN

Dorothy was on her way from Arizona to Salinas. She stopped at our place on the Tule River. She was looking forward to a swim in the river, and a few days of some much needed rest and relaxation. More than anything, she needed some sleep. Debra took her sleeping bag and settled down on the couch, giving Dorothy the use of her bedroom.

About midnight a bushy haired man at the window awakened her. As sternly as she could, she ordered him to leave. He told her it was Steven. She informed him he could not fool her, she knew that none of Colleen's sons had long hair. (Steve's hair was very curly. He wanted straight hair. When it got a little bit long it was straight next to his scalp. He decided to let it get long, and when it was long enough to be the length he wanted it, he would get a haircut, and would have straight hair. Or so he thought!) He was in his twenties and living in Van Nuys. He had not told us he was coming. Not wanting to wake everyone, he had gone to Debra's window to wake her to let him in.

Kenny always came to pick Debra up for school. When he came the next morning Debra was in the bathroom. Her bedroom door was open and thinking Debra was in bed, he went in and kissed her cheek, rubbed her back and told her to get up, and to hurry or they would be late for school. He left the room.

The next night she and Debra changed places. Dorothy said she sometimes had to get up and walk some to relieve leg cramps. And Deb's bed was too soft. She needed something firm for her back.

Early the next morning she was awakened again by a shake and was told to get up and get ready for school. I don't know who was more surprised, her or Debra's boyfriend. Ken came to take Debra to school as usual. He knew she had slept in the living room the night before, and of course didn't know about the change. He almost gave Dorothy a kiss before discovering it was not Debra.

About 2 o'clock the next night, we were awakened by thunder and lightning. (When my kids were little and were scared by thunder and lightning, I convinced them that God was putting on a show for us. I explained what caused them, and they learned to love the nighttime

110

storms. We turned off the lights, and when we tired of watching, we made popcorn and hot cocoa, and told ghost stories.) There was no rain, and it was a warm night, so again we went outside to watch. We could see the lightening going from the mountaintop to the sky. We saw this often during hot weather, when there was no storm. The kids thought it had something to do with UFO's. I was not about to spoil their fun and explain that lightening usually goes from the earth to the sky. When it does go from sky to earth, it is caused by reverse polarity. When they observed lightening going from cloud to cloud, (heat lightening) they just KNEW there were UFO's hiding in the clouds. Dorothy's sleep was interrupted once again. She might not have minded a kiss on the cheek and hot cocoa, but the other things! The bushy haired man at her window, the shaking and being ordered to school, thunder, lightning, talk about UFO's, she could do without! All she wanted was a good night's sleep!

NAP TIME

COLLEEN CHAPMAN

When grandson Howard was a baby I was taking care of him at the cabin on the Tule River. He was not walking yet but was a very good and fast crawler. The property had two levels. The cabin was on the top level, and a big area where we could put up a tent, on the second level. Then it sloped down to the river. I put an old set of box springs and mattress on the lower level for his afternoon nap, in the shade of trees. He loved watching the breeze gently move the leaves. I read while he napped.

One day I was sewing and lost track of the time. Howard jabbered at me several times. Just wanting my attention, I thought. I was almost finished and told him to wait just a minute. I finished and looked at the clock. It was about 45 minutes past naptime. Howard was not in the cabin.

The door had been left open for fresh air, and he had crawled out. He could not have been gone more than two minutes, and I found him crawling down the path. He had made good time! The path leads to the lower level, then on to the swimming hole in the river. I usually took him to play in the river before naptime.

Would he stop at the mattress or would he try to make it to the river? I didn't think he could make it to the river but thought it would be a good idea to find out. There was a little hill and a lot of rocks to go over. It would not be an easy thing for him to do. But then I was surprised to see how far he *had* gotten. I followed, not letting him see me. He crawled, rolled and tumbled, but he made it downhill to the mattress. He managed to pull himself up onto the mattress. With a big sigh he put his thumb in his mouth and was asleep almost immediately. After that, I set the alarm clock to go off at naptime. He soon learned that when the alarm went off it was time to go to sleep. I hoped that it would not mess him up when he got older and was supposed to *wake up* when the alarm went off!

PICK UP YOUR TRASH!

Debra Littler

Well you know we like to go camping. In 1991 we went up to Camp Nelson. We had a nice campfire that night before we went to bed. When we were walking to the restroom the next morning, there was trash very where. We yelled at the other campers to clean up their trash. Arguing started among the campers and fights almost broke out. As we walked back to our campsite, some of the trash looked familiar. It was our own trash! During the night a bear had torn everything up. We loaded up our stuff very fast and left. As we were going home we didn't talk about it. We just laughed. It was a fun trip.

MY DAD

Vincent Silva

This is a story that should have been told in person. This is about my Father, Howard Chapman, the wises man I have ever known. This person did something not many men would do. He married a woman with seven kids. Now most men won't do this, but he did. He helped raise us, taught us morals, how to show respect. Here are a few rules he drilled into our heads. Never talk back to your Mother. Always show respect to your elders. Never hit a woman. All that proves is that you are a sissy. He taught us to think, use our heads to figure things out. He taught us to work on our own cars to help save on repair bills. He had a saying, you break it you fix it.

I remember Dave borrowed one of the cars and as he left he scraped the other car and broke the handles on the cars. Then there was Steve changing the oil in the red and white station wagon. He forgot to put the drain plug back in and started putting oil in the engine until he noticed oil on the ground. I thought it was funny. But guess what. I got to put a complete exhaust system on the same wagon for being a smartass. Never did that again. This man taught us kids more than you will ever know. He had two main goals, family and work. He put in a lot of overtime. At first I didn't know why, until school was out. He got us up early and said we were going camping. We packed up, loaded up the African Queen, our boat, and off to Lake Havasu Arizona we went with Howard's best friend, Bill Duncan and his four kids. There we learned to water ski. When we were good enough on two skies, we learned to ski on one ski. What I didn't realize is that if you stay in the water all day you will be the color of a lobster. I got backed. Mom warned me but I didn't listen. That vacation turned into a four-week vacation. This man taught me more things that I will never forget. I still to this day go by what I was taught.

Here are a few things I remember about our family. Deb and Sue chopping wood. Somebody missed the wood and got a couple fingers. When the well was being drilled they kept drilling until given the O.K. on the water. While they were drilling us kids played in the water and made a big mud hole. When it was time to go in the house, we got rinsed off with a water hose.

Not many people will tear down a building and use the material to build a home for his family using only hand tools. Then there is the ditch for the water pipe. We played army in the ditch. We got to re-dig the ditch. We filled it, we re-dug it. We spent most of our time running in the woods. That is how we kept ourselves busy. When we were younger we didn't have cell phones, Ipods, video games or any of those other electronic gadgets. I was taught to use my brain. Think before you act. It might save you some trouble. This man has my complete respect. He is not my step-father. He is my only father. I should have said this to him face to face. But I was too wrapped up in my own business. That is no excuse. You have only one set of parents. You must keep close to family. Don't be like me. I walked away from my family for stupid reasons. I was gone for close to thirty years. That was a mistake. That is time lost I can never get back or make up. To me, family is important. Never walk away from family even if you disagree. Talk it out. Get back to being on the same page. Howard Chapman is the only man I am proud to call my Father.

BARBER SHOP

OH! WHAT HAVE I DONE!

COLLEEN CHAPMAN

I woke up standing in the bathroom. A finger on my left hand was bleeding. In my right hand was a pair of barber scissors. Hair was in the sink, on the floor and on my cloths. I had been wanting a hair cut for a couple of months, but there just never seemed to be time to go to the beauty salon. I certainly did not want to do it myself in my sleep! What I had done to myself was beyond repair, so I cut short what little hair I had left. I went online and ordered a wig. It was delivered within a week. Until it arrived, I wore a bandana on my head.

GERALDINE ALLRED

COLLEEN CHAPMAN

We lived next door to the Allred's in Safford Arizona when I was about five or six years old. They had a girl my age. I was very envious of Geraldine's long brown hair. My hair was short, white, and straight. When I sweat it smelled like wet chicken feathers. I hated it! One day Geraldine's hair was in long curls. She said, "Doesn't my hair look pretty? Momma took me with her to the beauty parlor. She got a haircut and a perm, but I just got mine washed and curled because it's too pretty to cut or perm."

She pranced around patting her hair and looking at mine while she talked. The old Devil got a real good hold on me. I had a strong urge to pull her hair out. But I exercised what was for me, great self-control and started to walk away. She said, "where are you going, white chicken feather head?" Well! That was the last straw! The Devil won. I didn't get physical, but got what was for me, cunning.

I said, "You do have pretty hair. I wish I had a whole lot just like it. Hey! Let's play beauty parlor. I'll be the beauty parlor lady and you're a rich lady that came in to get a new hair-do." She thought that would be fun and went to get her play dress-up cloths on. While she did that, I managed to sneak some scissors out of the house. I got my old lard bucket that I used for a sand pail. If things went right, that bucket would hold something other than sand today! Geraldine came back wearing a long dress, high heels 10 sizes too big for her, gloves, a shawl, and carrying an umbrella. I greeted her at the door of the beauty parlor (a shady spot under a grape arbor) and seated her on my "very best chair", an old wooden box. I said, "good morning, Miss Allred, what can I do for you today?" She said, "Oh, I don't know. I'm tired of the same old hair do. Can you do something different with it?" I'm thinking to myself, *hee hee hee!* You bet I can!

As I caressed her long silky hair I said, "Oh Miss Allred! Your hair is soooooo pretty. Are you sure you want to change it?" She replied with a toss of her head, "everyone tells me not to change a thing, but I really would like to try something new." I walked around her, stroking my chin and looking at her hair thoughtfully.

I finally said, "Ya know what? I saw a picture of a movie star in a magazine. Her hair was short, and I think you would look just like her if you had a hairdo like hers. I'll go get the magazine!" I was back in a flash. Geraldine agreed that she was every bit as pretty as the movie star, and I should do her hair like that. She leafed through the magazine as I explained what I was going to do. Taking hold of one long beautiful curl, I held it out so she could see that I had laid the scissors on top of it and pressed down a little as I worked the scissors. It felt like I was cutting but was not. Not yet, anyway. As I worked on her hair we talked about the people in the magazine, our children, husbands, the weather, and the high price of jewelry.

Soon the scissors were no longer on top of her hair. The lard bucket was holding long, beautiful, brown curls. Her hair was not long anymore. It now reached the middle of her neck instead of the middle of her shoulders. I had cut all the curls except one on each side of her head in front of her ears. I had saved those for last because I didn't think I could do them without her seeing what I was doing. I carefully took the curl in front of her left ear and tried to cut it. She did see and ran home screaming before I could get it cut. She looked so funny, running and screaming with those two curls flopping. I had to laugh, even while I was dreading the spanking I was sure to get. It was a mean thing for me to do, and an apology is way over do. So, Geraldine, where ever you are, I'm really…I'm really… really…. OOOhhhhh!!! I just can't say it!!!

IF SHE WANTS TO BE A BOY

COLLEEN CHAPMAN

I put the three youngest kids on the bed with me to take a nap. (Vincent 5, Robert 4 and Susan 2). Dave, Diane and Steven were at school. I usually read while they napped. It was not a good idea for me to nap too. They might wake up before I did and no telling what mischief they would get into. But one afternoon I dozed off. When I woke up, the kids weren't on the bed. I found them in the kitchen. Suzi's braids had been undone, and Vincent was holding the hair on top of her head straight up. Robert was on the other side of her with the barber scissors. There was hair on the floor. I gasped and froze. I didn't want to startle Robert, with those scissors in his hand. Robert saw me, and pointing at Suzi with his pinkie finger said, "Well, if she wants ta be a boy, we are gonna make her a boy!" If that is what it takes, they had a pretty good start.

LONG HAIR

Colleen Chapman

All my boys got a haircut every month. The high school boys were in ROTC. Long hair for boys was just coming into style and was still unusual enough to draw stares. I was so glad I didn't have to worry about my sons wanting long hair! About a month before school was out, Vincent said, "I'm going to let my hair grow all summer. You'll have one less haircut to do." I expressed my feelings about that, and Vince said, "It's my hair. I have a right to let it grow if I want to." "You do not have the right to embarrass the rest of the family. Your hair is very oily and would always look awful." I said. He replied, "If my long hair bothers someone, that is their problem. They should examine their views and feelings to see what their problem is."

While this conversation took place, I was standing in the living room in front of the mirror, combing my hair. I was always complaining about my unmanageable mess. I stopped combing and looked at myself. Vince and the other kids were waiting for me to continue the conversation. I said nothing, just stared at myself in the mirror. Vince shifted from one foot to the other, waiting for the confrontation he was sure would take place. All the other kids had stopped whatever they were doing and waited expectantly. I went into the bathroom and got the hair clippers and cape. Vincent's eyes got big, and he said, "You don't intend to cut my hair now, do you?" I walked past him to the mirror and while putting the cape on, I said. "No, you're right. It's nobody's business how a person wears their hair. All these years I've hated my hair, and hate trying to make it look nice. It's been a real hassle. My life would be so much easier if I didn't have any hair at all. I'm going to cut it clear to the scalp. If you have enough courage to wear your hair long and get made fun of, or called a punk, rebel and all the other things you'll get called, then I will try to be as strong and brave as you are. I won't care what people say about me. Thank you so much for opening my eyes! Oh, it will be such a relief!"

By this time I had the cape on; the clippers oiled, plugged in, and ready to cut. Vincent grabbed the clippers and yanked the plug out of the wall. (Just as I thought he would, thank goodness!) "You wouldn't really, would you?" he asked. "Has she *ever* said she would do something she wouldn't do?" Robert said excitedly. "Do you know what it's going to be like when she shows up at the ROTC awards, or PTA meetings, all that stuff? Do you know what you have done? Do you know anyone with a bald mother? Well, you're going to now, *US!*" All the other kids were in tears, even the kids from next door. Vince begged me not to do it and promised he would get his regular haircuts. After five or ten minutes of everyone begging, I reluctantly promised, for my children's sake, I wouldn't do it. Oh the sacrifices we Mothers make for our families!

STEVEN'S FIRST HAIRCUT

COLLEEN CHAPMAN

Steven watched as I cut Dave's hair, and then trimmed Diane's hair. Then it was his turn for his very first haircut. I put him in the chair, put the cloth around his neck, combed his hair, and began to cut. Up to this point he had been very still and quiet. But now he put both hands on his head screaming, "My hair! My hair!" over and over. I was getting nowhere. Pearl came by just then and said she would help me.

We decided the best way to get it done, was for me to hold him on my lap while she cut his hair. It was too dangerous to use scissors, so she used the clippers. It ended up with Pearl lying on her stomach on the floor. Steven's head was on the floor and I hung onto his legs. He was almost standing on his head. We gave up. He was a funny looking little boy. A day or so later while he was sleeping, I managed to cut his hair with the scissors. That was how he got his hair cuts for several years.

STEVEN'S HAIR

Susan Aubert

Back in 1976, Steve was thinking of getting a "natural" because his hair was like wire and very curly, no matter what length. Diane and I thought he should get a straightening perm. But before committing to that, he should try it out. So after a trip to the store to get supplies, he sat down and I began to roll his hair on perm rods. About the time I was finishing up, Steve saw his friend Carl and another fella walking up the steps to the house. Boy, did he move fast. He ran to the bathroom and pulled the rods from his hair. Several weeks later I consented to do it again. As it turned out, he liked it.

THE VERY IDEA

COLLEEN CHAPMAN

When Susan was about five and Debra three, I asked Dorothy to trim their hair. Their hair was waist length, and I usually kept it braided. There must have been a lack of communication, because Dorothy didn't TRIM their hair, she CUT it. She held the braids in her hand and cut it even with their earlobes. Sue put her hands over her eyes and cried. They both had curly hair and when the haircuts were finished and their hair shampooed, they were really cute. Howard had never seen them with short hair. He thought I had not only given them haircuts but had given them permanents. He was so mad he wouldn't speak to me for three days. When he did, he said, "The very idea. Giving those two babies perms!" I told him, "If that is what you have been stewing about all this time, you got all steamed up for nothing. Those curls are natural."

Their hair was allowed to grow out, and when Sue was a young teen-ager, decided she wanted short hair. I told her to think about it some more, and in three or four days if she still wanted it cut, I would do it. She did. She sat on a chair outside, and I cut her hair. I told her that before I finished, to shampoo her hair and let it dry so I could see the curls and know how to finish. She looked in the mirror, put her hands over her eyes and cried. I told her again that I wasn't finished, but she was not listening. She wouldn't wash her hair. She announced that she had been ruined and put on a bandanna. She would wear it until her hair grew out, she said. And apparently cry all the while.

For three days no one saw her without that bandanna or with dry eyes. After three days enough was enough! I told her, like it or not, I was going to finish her haircut. She had a choice. She could sit down and let me finish or I would get the boys to help me tie her to the chair. She shampooed her hair and let it dry in the sun. She sat down, sobbing. It took just a few minutes of trimming and I was finished. She looked in the mirror and squealed with delight. "I love it!" Ahh yes! Teen-age girls are soooooo much fun!

CORKSCREW HAIR

COLLEEN CHAPMAN

I was getting ready to go to Az. for Ruby's 90th birthday celebration. I got a manicure, pedicure, and a perm. I drew a sketch of the hairdo I wanted. I wanted it short enough on top so there would be fullness. I wanted to be able to pull the rest of my hair into a bun, or roll, or pulled back and up and held with combs or hair pins. The Vietnamese woman said she understood. I was very tired and rested with my eyes closed while she worked. The only time I opened them was when I had to move from the chair to the sink and back again. Even if my eyes had been open I couldn't have seen what was happening without my glasses on.

After removing the rollers, she said, "Ok. You all finished now." As I put my glasses on I said, "but you haven't dried or styled my hair." I looked in the mirror and saw what looked like wet corkscrews sticking out of my head! As I sat starring, open mouthed, she said, "Yes, you all done now. In morning just pull hair back likes this. No comb." She pulled each side back just a couple of inches. When I recovered from the shock, I told her she had not done what I wanted. I did not ask for corkscrew hair. She said, "It called spiral. You no like?" "I NO LIKE!" I am not leaving here looking like this, and with wet hair. It's cold out there." She said, "If dry hair, it be ruined." I asked how can something that looks that bad be ruined. She said if she dried and styled my hair it would cost more. I informed her I would pay for the shampoo and that is all. She had not cut my hair except for the sides in front, and about an inch of the rest, according to what I saw on the floor. The sides were now too short to pull back as I'd wanted, and the back too long. She said, "you no leave without pay! I call Police!" I said, "OK, you call Police. I call newspaper and TV station. While we wait for them to get here, I'll go next door to the Dollar store and buy poster board and a big black marking pen. I will write enter at your own risk! Look what they did to me!" "You no can do that!" she said. "Oh no? You just watch me!"

At this point the manager who had been in the back came in. I told him this could be resolved by letting me dry my hair and leave. He told the woman to dry and style my hair. She was so mad; I didn't want her to touch me. I would do it myself. She said I couldn't use her tools. I didn't care whose tools I used. After doing the best I could with the mess, I left and didn't pay for anything. Now my hair is a frizzy mess. Oh well, I still have the wig.

CHURCH CHAT

CORN FED MORMONS

RUBY GREEN

While we were going to school in San Simone, Arizona, the kids there were always talking about "Those terrible corn-fed Mormons over in the Gila Valley." We thought, from the way they talked about them, that they must be a different breed of people which we had never heard of before. We asked, "What are they like?" One boy said, "Well, I've never seen one, but I hear tell they have horns which they hide in their bushy hair. Otherwise they look pretty much the same as anybody. But you should never let them look you in the eye, for they will get you to be one of them. Then you are lost for sure!" When we told them our Daddy was going over to Safford to find work, they told us, "Tell him to look out for them corn-fed Mormons and to stay away from them." Needless to say, we were really worried when Daddy went over to the Gila valley where all those terrible corn-fed Mormons were.

GRANDMA'S BOARDING HOUSE

COLLEEN CHAPMAN

At one time Grandma Sullivan had a boarding house in Safford. It had a big front porch, a good place to sit and watch the world go by. Safford was a very small town at the time and there really wasn't a lot of world going by. Anything out of the ordinary caught our attention. One day there was a lot of activity on the vacant lot across the street from the rooming house. A big tent was being set up. We asked Grandma if it was a circus tent. She just grinned and said, "Some people might call it that." We waited and watched impatiently. Would we be allowed to go to the circus? Well, even if we weren't, we would be able to see what was going on anyway, because the sides of the tent were being rolled up to let the air in. We could sit right there on the porch and see and hear everything!

The night after the set up was finished, people began to arrive. The music started and people sang. The preacher preached. At first we were disappointed, but were soon fascinated by the goings on. People began to act very strange. They sang, they shouted, they trembled all over, they jumped, yelled, they talked gibberish; they scared me half to death. They were "Getting the Holy Ghost" someone said.

Fred thought it was just about the funniest thing he had ever seen when a rather large woman got the Holy Ghost, fell flat on the ground, and flopped around "Like a chicken with its neck wrung." according to Fred. The woman's husband tried to keep her dress down. He kept reaching over to tug on it when it crept up too far. He got kicked several times but that didn't stop him. The more she flopped, the more he tugged, the more Fred laughed, slapping his leg. We both decided if the Holy Ghost made a person act like that, we didn't want any. Grandma, who was standing behind us, decided it was time for us to join the people in the tent.

The next night when the revival started, she said it was time for us to join them. We tried to tell her we didn't need to, 'cause we could see and hear from the porch. She insisted, and we knew better than to disobey her. I don't remember where the rest of the family was, but even if Mother or Daddy were there they wouldn't have gone against Grandma. So we went to the revival. Things were even livelier than they had been the night before. A man got the Holy Ghost and ran around and around. Up one side of the tent and down the other side, up the middle, onto the stage, then ran and tried to jump over two or three rows of kids sitting on the ground in front of the rows of adults. He almost made it. He kicked Fred's forehead, and went sprawling over a bunch of people in the first two rows of chairs. I was crying by this time, and I think Fred might have been. The man untangled himself from people and chairs, and, I think to take attention away from himself, drug me, Fred and a couple of other kids up to the bench in front. He plopped us down amongst the others there and declared that we were on the verge of salvation. He prayed for us real hard and loud. Some women came to help with our salvation. They prayed, cried, and kept slapping us on the back, and asking, "Are you saved?" I cried and shook my head no, wishing with all my might that someone would save us before they beat us to death. It was very confusing. Why were they beating us, and asking if we were saved? What did we need to be saved from, if not them? They must be insane, I thought. As the women were beating and asking if I was saved, Fred said in my ear, "Say yes, you idiot, before they beat us to death!" We both yelled "YES! YES!" They let us up, and we pushed our way through and made double time getting across the street and into the house. Grandma came in from the porch. She was still laughing. Said she hadn't seen anything so funny in years. For a long time after that if we misbehaved she would say, "Hummm. Looks to me like you need to go get saved again."

HOLY ROLLERS

DOROTHY PATTON

This story in not meant to put down the so-called Holy Rollers. I believe everyone has the right to worship and express themselves in their own way and I would not dare to judge. This is just what happened.

I must have been six or seven years old when a neighbor invited us to a revival meeting. All chairs were taken and a row of us children were sitting on the floor. A man jumped up on the stage and started shaking a tambourine and dancing. Then he ran down the middle isle and back up the side isle and jumped over us kids, stepping on my finger in the process. I was sitting there holding my finger and wondering what was going on when a girl I didn't like leaned over someone between us and said: "My mother is shouting and yours isn't." I looked and indeed her mother, along with other people, was shouting and dancing up and down the aisle, excess flesh flapping with every step. I leaned over to her and said: "Well, my mother doesn't act like that in church." "Oh! God heard that!" she said. "You're going to get it!" That scared me a little and I sat there wondering if she was right and didn't dare say another word. The shouting and praising God wasn't bad but when they went to the mourning bench and started crying and begging God's forgiveness I was sure something terrible was about to happen. I started crying and Mother had Ruby take me out to the car. It sounded worse out there. I had never heard such mournful and desperate sounds. Ruby just sat there at the car window looking toward the church like she didn't know what to think. But I knew that we were all doomed.

The next day the neighbor woman that had invited us to the meeting came over and she and mother went into the bedroom and soon I heard the same mournful sounds that I had heard the night before. Pearl was washing dishes and I was drying. I started crying and Pearl said: "Don't be such a baby."

I went out the back door and started running. When I got to the barn I looked out over the countryside and wondered where I could go. A rain barrel was at the corner of the barn and I stopped and leaned against it. It was warm from the sun. I remembered something a Sunday school teacher had said about the warmth of God's love. Suddenly all my fear was gone. I guess that was the moment of my salvation because I have never doubted since then that my soul is safe in God's hands no matter what terrible things may happen. The body may suffer, but alive or dead, the real me is safe in God's hands. I went back to the house and sat on the steps and listened to the sounds inside and felt at peace.

HOLY ROLLERS

Ruby Green

When Pearl, Dorothy Gentry and I were just little girls, Dorothy Gentry and I were probably about 7 or 8 years old and Pearl was between 5 and ½ to 6. We had been to Grandma's house and were walking home. We happened by a revival of the "Holy Rollers." We had learned that was a good place to watch a good show. So we went inside. They were making such a noise and dancing around, that Pearl got frightened. She started to cry. Some fat woman saw her and shouted "This little girl is- a- getin- the "Holy Ghost!!!" Then a whole bunch of fat women gathered around her and took her up to the mourner's bench and started pounding her on the back and shouting "HALALUYAH!!' Pearl was scared half to death and the harder they pounded and shouted, the more Pearl cried. Dorothy and I would try to get to Pearl to take her away, but they wouldn't let us near her.

They would say "leave her alone honey, She's -a-get-in the Holy Ghost." I shouted to Dorothy, "GO GET DADDY, I'LL STAY WITH PEARL!!" Dorothy broke for the door in a dead run. I couldn't get near Pearl. The circle of shouting people around her was impenetrable. Pearl was crying louder. The louder she cried, the harder they pounded her on the back and shouted "HALALUYAH!!! I thought they would kill her. I was so frightened. After what seemed like hours, Daddy appeared with Dorothy behind him.

He was FURIOUS!! He walked right up to the mourner's bench pushing those silly women aside and picked Pearl up who clung to him for dear life. Those women stood and looked at him with their mouths open not daring to interfere with a man as angry as Daddy was. He took her right out of that place with Dorothy and me following. I sure was glad Dorothy Gentry was with us that day and I told her she saved Pearl's life by going and getting Dad.

YET ANOTHER H.R. STORY

Dorothy Patton

Again I want to say that I am not putting down the H. R. people. Honest. I have great affection and respect for some of them. When my kids were small we were in the front yard one evening enjoying the nice weather. We lived in the tiny town of Chualar. My husband, Jack, was a volunteer fireman and had gone to a meeting at the firehouse. It was just getting dark when we heard singing and saw the church people marching up the street carrying lanterns and singing hymns. I thought it was a clever way to advertise their revival. The kids saw friends and cousins marching and wanted to join them. I thought, why not? So we did.

We had a fine time marching around the little town and singing with gusto. After awhile I was surprised when Jack showed up and insisted on taking us home. Someone had gone to the firehouse and told him that his family was marching with the church people who had vowed to march and sing until the sinful walls of Chualar came tumbling down like the walls of Jericho did when God's people marched around it. In this case, the particular walls they wanted to fall down were the walls of the bar owned by W.R. Patton, my husband's uncle. Jack insisted that he wasn't worried about the walls falling down, he just didn't want us mixed up in the effort. But if he hadn't pulled us out, who knows, it might have worked.

MY MANY BAPTISMS

DOROTHY PATTON

I have been immersed ten times and sprinkled twice. This is how it happened. My parents were believers but not consistent churchgoers so when I was growing up I would go to church with friends. I was going to a Baptist church when I reached the age of twelve which is considered the age of reason by some churches. I was asked if I was ready to accept Jesus as my personal savior. I had always accepted Jesus so of course I said yes. They obtained my parent's consent and I was baptized. Immersed, of course.

Soon after that my oldest sister, Ruby, started going to the Mormon Church and the missionaries came and taught our parents and it was decided that the whole family would join that church. I told Mother that I had already been baptized and couldn't be again because it would be illegal, like getting married again. Besides, I had heard some awful things from the Baptists about the Mormons. But Mother insisted that all the family that was old enough would be baptized in the Mormon Church. I was scared half to death but I had no choice, I was baptized a second time.

Once I got in the church I began to suspect that most of the things I had heard from the Baptists about the Mormons was not true. When Ruby's first daughter, Catherine, was born I examined her head carefully and decided that Mormon babies are not born with horns which are surgically removed at birth. And I learned not to talk about the fact that I had been a Baptist.

I enjoyed going to the Mormon church and the young people's meetings and became such a faithful Mormon that I discovered one day that I was scheduled, along with several of the other young people, to go to the temple in Phoenix and be baptized for the dead. Now this was one Mormon belief that I had not come to terms with and tried to refuse. But Mother said that it was an honor and that I was going. I was terrified. I thought about running away but decided to wait until we got to the temple then get lost on the grounds and not be found till time to go home.

It didn't work. We were driven right up to a side door, hustled into a room and into our baptismal garments. I felt like I was going to my doom as we entered the room where the deed was to be done. But when I saw the huge baptismal basin resting on the backs of twelve life-size oxen just like in the bible, my fear vanished and I felt like I was in a sacred place. I still didn't believe that this would save those souls but I thought that they were probably appreciating all the effort in their behalf. And it was certainly being done out of love and concern. So I felt peaceful as I was immersed six times in the name of six people who had died. That made eight immersions.

About three years after that our family moved to California. I went to the Mormon church a few times but my family had lost their interest in going to church and didn't care where I went. Without family and friends there the church didn't seem the same. I ended up going back to the Baptists. I joined the Southern Baptist Church in Salinas and found that I must be baptized again. I couldn't remember the brand of Baptists that had baptized me the first time and besides, I had been a Mormon. So under I went for the ninth time.

I went to that church for many years. I married and had two sons. When they were nine and twelve years old my husband died in an accident. His family, who were farmers in Oklahoma, was so devastated that I thought it would help them if I moved out there with the boys. And I thought it would help the boys to live in the country. In Oklahoma there was no Baptist church in the area where the family lived. My mother-in-law was a member of a Methodist Church so naturally I joined the Methodists and they sprinkled me. When the time approached for my oldest son to graduate from high school he announced his intention of moving back to California to find work. There wasn't much opportunity where we were so I decided that we would all move back to California. I went back to the same Southern Baptist Church. I didn't tell them that I had been sprinkled by the Methodists.

After a couple of years I remarried. He belonged to a Missionary Baptist Church and I agreed to change my membership to his church. But it wasn't that simple. Southern Baptists believe that The Lord's Supper must be shared only with the immediate church family while the Missionary Baptists believe that any repentant Christian, if visiting while this sacrament is being observed, may partake. Or is it the other way around? If I am wrong in this may God and all Baptists forgive me. The point is that this difference in beliefs made it necessary for me to be baptized, immersed of course, a tenth time. That marriage didn't last and after a number of years I moved back to Arizona. Being a glutton for punishment, I married again. This time to a Methodist and was sprinkled a second time.

At the present time I am back in California, single and without church membership. I go to various churches sometime but never ask for membership. I am spiritual but not religious. I am seventy-three years old. I work part time at the Boys And Girl's Club of Monterey County and enjoy my grand children and writing on my computer. It is much better than a type writer in spite of the tricks It likes to play.

STRANGE LITTLE GIRLS

Ruby Green

Pearl and I were fascinated with funerals when we were little. When we would be going to or from Grandma's and happened to pass a house where they were holding a funeral (they held funerals in homes quite a lot those days) we would go in as if we knew the person and were sad he or she had passed on. One day the funeral was for a pretty little girl. It was the custom for the coffin to be open and the people would file by and view the dead person. When we saw the sweet, pretty little girl in the coffin, we cried real tears. We indeed were very sad.

There was a Mortician in Walters. He was tall and skinny and his skin was ashen. He always wore a black suit like the pictures of the ones President Abraham Lincoln wore, and the tall, black Top hat. Pearl and I called him 'the dead man.' He would go to a home where someone had died to "Lay them out."

We kept an eye out for him. When we saw him going somewhere with his black bag, we would follow him. We sometimes were able to see through a window, or crack. He would put money on the eyes so they would stay shut. (Mother used to tell us not to put coins in our mouths, for it may have been on a dead person's eyes.) He would straighten their arms and legs. I don't know why we were so fascinated with that kind of stuff. My kids would say we were weird.

THE BARN LOFT FUNERALS

Ruby Green

When we were growing up girls didn't wear jeans or slacks like they do now. When we played cowboys and outlaws we stuffed our dresses inside our bloomers when we rode our broomstick horses. Carroll strips from old rubber inner tubes for bullets. The rubber band was stretched from the front of the gun to the cloths pin, which held them until we wanted to shoot. We shot by squeezing the cloths pin. When one of those bullets hit you, it really hurt! I was usually the Sheriffs sweetheart and ran a café in an empty pig pen. I would gather green onions and radishes from the garden and get bread and butter from the house. I served it to the Sheriff, the good guys and the bad guys.

After a battle there would be a lot of dead guys. Sometimes I got killed too. We had funerals in Gentry's barn loft. Mr. Gentry made a big cotton seed bin and bought cotton seed to fill it up. I don't remember who thought it would make a good grave in which to bury the kids who died each week. The cotton seeds stuck together so it was easy to make a hole for the dead guys to breathe through.

We had two preachers of funerals. Pearl and Carroll Gentry. I don't know how they decided which one would preach a coming funeral. I think they drew straws or something. Any way it was decided between Pearl and Carrel. They would decide who's turn it was to die and send out word to all the neighborhood kids that so-n-so had died and the funeral would be in the Gentry's barn loft at 3: O'clock on Tuesday. None of the kids in the neighborhood would miss a funeral in the barn loft for anything. We had a make-shift pulpit and the dead person was laid out on a board in front of the pulpit. The kids brought their own buckets or boxes to sit on. As word of the wonderful funerals held in the barn loft spread, the audience grew bigger.

I loved it when I had died and Carroll was to preach my funeral. Carroll would start out, "This sweet soul is going to heaven." Then he would tell how good I had been all my life, doing good to others and helping my mother and carrying my little baby brothers and sisters around sitting on my hip, until he thought I would grow crooked. I would lie still with my hands folded across my chest with a smile on my face. Carroll's sermons were tearjerkers and by the time it came to lay me in the cotton seed grave, the kids would actually be crying.

Pearl preached a different kind of sermon. If she was preaching my funeral, she would start out, "This poor old soul is going to hell. She always made her younger sister (Pearl) do all the work. When her sister was washing the dishes, she would hand the dishes back and yell "THIS IS NOT CLEAN!" Then her poooorrrr little sister would have to wash it all over again." I couldn't listen to her telling how mean I was, so I would sit up and begin to protest. Pearl would say "You're dead! Lay down!" I would lie back down, but soon I couldn't stand it anymore and I would rise up and start to protest. "I did not!" Pearl would tell me again that I was dead and to lie down. By this time, all the kids were holding their tummies and rolling on the floor with laughter. She would finish her sermon with "OH, she was MEAN, I tell you. MEEEAAAANNNN! Hell is where she's going. It's too bad, but she *deserves* to go to hell." *SO WHEN I DIE, PLEASE DON'T LET PEARL PREACH MY FUNERAL!*

DRAWING by SANDRA

THEY'S A GOIN TA HELL

C OLLEEN C HAPMAN

We could hear them in the morning when we left for church, and we could hear them still going strong when we got home. Those colored folks didn't have a regular time for stopping. They went on and on until the preacher ran out of breath and the small congregation didn't have a praise the Lord or a glory hallelujah amen left amongst them. Their services were much livelier than ours. They sang, danced, clapped their hands, jumped up and down, and "got the Holy Ghost." I know because Fred and I would sometimes watch them. We would crawl up the irrigation ditch that ran near their little settlement, then crawl through the brush, getting as close as we dared. One hot Sunday afternoon we had gotten closer than usual. Fred sat leaning against a tree, and I was crouched behind a bush next to the tree. Fred wasn't watching, but thought the Preacher said some pretty funny things, and put his hands over his mouth and laughed. I didn't think the things I heard was anything to laugh about. The Preacher was talking about the Devil and how he just loved to come and get sinners and take them right down to Hell, the bottomless pit where you burned forever and ever. That didn't sound funny to me.

It was a very hot day, and a shade had been rigged up for the Preacher, but most of the people were in the sun. A few had chairs or boxes to sit on, and they used newspapers or anything they could find for a little shade. An awful lot of energy went into fanning themselves. An old man who always had a lot of halleluiahs, glory to Gods, praise the Lord, went to a faucet at the corner of a cabin to get a drink of water, and wet his face and head. The Preacher noticed him and was not pleased. He pointed at the man and yelled, "That man isa gowin ta Hell. He done left the ceremony! Yes sir, the Devil gonna get em fo sho!" Fred burst out laughing. I jumped up, expecting to see the Devil coming to get that poor old man. The Preacher saw me and heard Fred laughing. "And so is them chillens! Come here you sinners!" he said pointing at us. We took off for home. "The Devil's gonna get you, you'll see, yes sir, he's afta ya'll rat now!" I was sure I could hear the Devil's foot steps behind me and feel his breath on my neck. If I ever had the Devil in me, I didn't any longer. He had been scared plumb out of me

It seemed like it took hours to run the short distance home. We stayed outside until we caught our breaths. Fred gave me THAT LOOK and said, "Don't you tell. Don't you DARE tell!" We casually entered the house and went into the kitchen to get a drink of water. Mother took one look at us and asked, "Where have you two been and what have you been up to?" Fred gave me THE LOOK and said, "Oh, nuthin much. Just went to the ditch for a while like you said we could." Just then there was a knock on the door. I dropped my glass and screamed and dove under the table. Does the Devil knock? Can you hide from the Devil? Mother and Daddy stared at me in surprise. Fred stared at me with THAT LOOK. "Dad blame!" Daddy said, "What in the world?" Another knock. Another scream. Daddy looked at me, then at the door. He started to the door. I grabbed his pants leg and whispered as loud as I could. "Don't open the door. It might be the Devil!" Another knock, another scream, another dad blame, then silence. Daddy looked out the window and informed me I had scared off whoever it was, and I could come out now.

Mother said, "Alright Fred, I want to know right now where you have been and what happened, and I want the truth!" Fred, trying to sound casual and truthful, said we had been at the ditch and had overheard the Preacher talking about the Devil. That's all. Mother didn't buy it and ordered Fred to go get a switch. We were going to be punished for going where we didn't belong. Daddy rammed his hands in his pockets and paced the floor saying, "Dad blame the dad-blamed luck to the dad-blamed devil anyhow! Dad blame it!" When he cussed like that we knew things were really bad. This time I didn't know if he was real mad at us, or upset because the Devil was after us, or what! Fred came back in with a switch and handed it to Mother. Daddy said, "Well now, I don't know about a woman who would whip her kids just for going to church!" Mother had drawn back the switch to hit Fred but stopped half way there. "What? They have been told to stay away from there and you know it! The whipping is for not minding me! They went to church this morning. They didn't need to go to the Negro church." "A church is a church." Daddy said, "No child should be whipped for going to church. Any church" Mother threw down the switch, put her hands on her hips and said accusingly, "You just don't want me to whip them!" Daddy said," If you whip them for going to church the old Devil just might come after you!" Just then there was a knock at the door. I ran to open it.

TOMMY

COLLEEN CHAPMAN

There was a small church three or four blocks from our house which some of our neighbors went to. One little boy who lived near us was referred to as that mean little devil Tommy, by most of the people in the neighborhood. Actually,he was not mean, just full of mischief. Anyway, his mother invited us to go to church with them. Tommy was going to be baptized. It was his 12th birthday, and there would be ice cream and cake after the services. At our church there was a nursery for the babies and toddlers, and classes for the other kids while the parents attended the service. This church did not do it that way. Everyone stayed together. I didn't realize that and had not explained to the kids what would be going on. They had never seen a baptism. Their ages at the time were 5, 4, 3, 16 months and 4 months.

We arrived a bit late and got seated just as the services began. Everything went smoothly until time to begin the baptism. A curtain was opened and there was a large glass or plastic container, filled half way with water. Two wooden step ladders, one on the outside and one on the inside were used to enter and exit the water. That got the kids attention. The preacher entered the water. Then Tommy, in a long white robe, entered the water. As the preacher lowered Tommy into the water, Dave, Diane and Steven gasped. Dave yelled, "No! No! Don't do that!" He went running up the aisle. "I know he's a mean little devil, but please don't drown him! Mom! Come quick! Can't ya see the preacher is gonna drown Tommy?" Diane and Steven were standing in the aisle crying and screaming. When Dave first yelled at the preacher, it startled him to say the least. Tommy, holding onto the preacher's arm, tried to pull himself up to see what was going on. Tommy and the preacher fell. All this commotion scared most of the other little kids, and they cried too. All the adults were laughing. All except the preacher, that is. The baptism was postponed until the next Sunday. We were not invited.

WHO IS GOING TO DO IT?

COLLEEN CHAPMAN

After the Sunday School session, we were all together in the church. The preacher was telling of all the things that needed to be done for the church. After telling of a job that needed to be done, he would say, "Who is going to do it?" He would pause and look all around the room as if expecting volunteers. Then with a sigh he would go on to the next item on his list.

Dave would look around the room each time the preacher did. He was getting rather upset. He whispered to Steven and Steven nodded his head. Before I could stop them, those two little guys, seven and five years old, stood in the aisle and raised their hands. When the preacher saw them and asked what they wanted, Dave said, "Looks like all these men are lazy sons-a-guns! Me and my brother here, we'll help you!" "Yes we will!" said Steven as the two of them glared at the men.

Every man there signed up for a job or two on the paper that had been provided for that purpose on the Bulletin board.

FAMILY HISTORY

This is not a book on genealogy, but I am including some facts and stories I find interesting. I hope you do.

BETTY JO

RUBY GREEN

After Betty Jo was born, it was a struggle to keep her alive. I remember we had to put lime in a gallon jar with water in it and after it sat a while, pour the water into a baby bottle and give it to her. She had to drink (from the baby bottle), pure grape juice, alternating with tomatoes juice. She had to have special care, around the clock. But she was a fighter. She was small. But she grew and flourished after a while.

Right from the start, she was so sweet and cute. She had lots of personality. With Her perfectly shaped, dark eyebrows and looong, silky, dark eyelashes framing dark brown, sparkling eyes, little turned-up nose, rosebud mouth and golden brown, silky hair, made her a most beautiful child. She had the most charming personality. All the family, including grandparents, aunts, uncles and cousins were charmed with her. At family gatherings, she was the center of attention. She liked to listen to our teen-age aunts tell about the handsome boys they knew.

One day one of them was telling about a certain boy that she especially liked, she said, "Oh, he's mine! Even if I never get him." Betty Jo was taking all this in. Dorothy was in first grade in school. There was a little boy she especially liked Doyle Dean Taylor. Every day she would tell us things Doyle Dean Taylor did or said. Betty wanted to go to school to see Doyle Dean Taylor. (Kids were allowed to take their little brothers or sisters to school with them sometimes for a visit.) So one day Mother let Betty Jo go to school with Dorothy.

In Dorothy's words, "At recess, the first thing Betty did was to ask me which one was Doyle Dean Taylah. I pointed him out. She ran up to him and grabbed his hand and looking deep into his eyes, said, "I luv you." she held onto his hand until he finally got away. Afterwards he told me, "Your sister is weird." Dorothy was so embarrassed. She never took Betty Jo to school again.

A few days later we were at Grandma's house for dinner. Betty Jo told them all about "Doyle Dean Taylah." Then she rolled her eyes, and sighed, "Oh, he's miiine, if I nevah get i'm."

After leaving Oklahoma, we traveled, picking cotton on the way; we spent some time in San Simon, Arizona. We went to school at San Simon from February until school was out in May. One day Pearl and I saw Betty Jo running and catching the little boys and kissing them.

We caught her and asked, "Why are you catching and kissing the boys?" She said, "Well, they kissed me first." The little boys were standing around, scratching their heads and wondering about this strange little girl.

Just before school was out, they put on a 3-act play. The principal had heard Betty Jo singing on the playground and asked her if she would sing some of her Shirley Temple songs on the stage between acts, while the scenery was being changed. Betty Jo answered, "Well, I get paid when I sing." (That is in another story I wrote about when we were traveling from Oklahoma.) The principal told her, "I'll give you a dollar, if you'll do it." Betty agreed to sing. The principal told Pearl and Dorothy and me about it and since the play was at night, we had to convince our parents to come to the play. Mother dressed Betty in a pretty little dress tied a bow in her hair. She was sooo pretty. She sang "On the Good Ship Lollypop" for the first intermission. Then for the next one, she sang "Animal Crackers in My Soup." She always put actions to her singing. On the way home, mother told her she could have anything she wanted to buy with her dollar. Betty Jo said, "All I want is a big can of tomatoes."

COLLEEN

R U B Y   G R E E N

Someone gave Mother a shower before Colleen was born. It was held at our house in Walters, Ok. All us kids went to Grandma's for the evening. One of the activities at the shower was to have Mother draw names out of a hat. She drew 2 girl's names and 2 boy's names. Depending on which sex the baby turned out to be these were the names she agreed to name the baby. I don't remember what the boy's names were, but the girl's names were Dolores and Colleen. They said if she had brown eyes like Mother, she would be called Dolores. If she was blue eyed like Daddy, she would be called Colleen.

I was so glad she turned out to have my coloring. Opal had blue eyes and blond hair, but all the rest except me had brown eyes and darker hair. Life was never dull around Colleen. She had a terrific imagination and was always making up stories. She may have had my coloring, but she was pretty, cute and funny like Pearl. Sometimes she had us going in circles, wondering if she was telling the truth, or if it was some figment of her imagination.

All the kids except Pearl, Dorothy and I had the measles when we lived near San Simon, AZ. One day a man from the Health Department came to post quarantine sign on the door. We were trying to keep Betty, Freddy, Colleen and Jerry in one bed and keep the room dark. Pearl, Dorothy and I were on the foot of the bed entertaining them. The man nailed the sign on the house, then just stood there looking in, in a very strange way. Then he turned and left. We, wondering what he had been looking at, looked around the room. There were three big King Snakes on the floor, and one was starting to crawl up the bedstead. Mother was in the kitchen. I was afraid to tell her there were snakes in the room. I just knew she would lose her head and run screaming from the house. We knew the snakes were not poisonous, but we didn't want them in the house, nor did we want them touching us! As we debated what to do, Mother heard us and came to see what the trouble was. That was one time she showed some bravery. She threw pans and spoons to us and got some for herself. We all banged on the pans and drove the snakes from the house. They went down threw a crack in the floor. By the way, Mother has always been terrified of snakes. The measles were hard on Colleen. They settled in her sinuses and were the source of much misery for her. If we could have afforded to take her to a Doctor, she would not have had to suffer for so many years.

Colleen had light blond hair. When she was about 3 years old, her hair started growing in, in a kind of ashy black. When it was about 1 ½ inches long, it came in blond again. When it was about 1 inch longer, it came in black again. Then when it was 1 inch longer, it came in blond and was blond from then on. She was a funny little striped headed girl for a year or two.

When I was 15, we moved to Safford. I had a boyfriend who would bring me a package of gum when he came to call. Colleen thought he was her boyfriend too and followed us around. Colleen liked the gum so much; he started bringing the gum for her. She was so cute; I think he came to see her more than me!

Colleen was only 2 when we left Oklahoma, so she doesn't have fond memories of Grandma and Grandpa and all the Aunts and Uncles and Cousins. Most of her memories must be of being hungry, and cotton fields, and traveling and very hard times. She was only 9 or 10 years old when Mother ran off with Spider. Some very cruel and sad years followed. Almost all of her early years were filled with misery. Threw it all she was cheerful for the most part. I am amazed at the way she has come through with flying colors. She must have absorbed her teaching in the Spirit world and her spirit has retained her brightness. I am sure our Heavenly Father is pleased with her. She is a brave and strong woman and I am so very happy she is my sister.

DON'T WORRY ABOUT IT

DOROTHY PATTON

My parents were worry mongers. They thrived on worry and my entire childhood was spent in terror of disasters that never happened. First there were the tornadoes in Oklahoma. I would often be dragged out of bed in the middle of the night during tornado season to go to the cellar. Our cellar wasn't under the house. We had to fight our way up a hill against the wind and the rain. The constant, furious lightening gave us more light than necessary to see the way, and along with the savage thunder, gave us the adrenaline rush we needed to get there.

The cellar was a hole dug in the ground with a mound of dirt on top like a giant grave. The door lay against this mound and had to be lifted up to open it. There was a strong latch on the inside because, although the door was heavy, sometimes the wind tried to suck it open. Steps led down to the small, musty smelling interior. It was lined with wood and canvas and there were several shelves along one wall for storage. Bunks were built along the opposite wall and there was a small table and two chairs in the center. A lantern hung on the wall near the door.

Once inside the cellar, Daddy would light the lantern and I would get cozy in a bunk. Then my parents would begin to talk. Some parents say things to calm their children's fears in times like this. Not my parents. They would recall every tornado they had ever heard about and all the disastrous results. Maybe they were trying to justify that trip to the cellar through the storm. After an especially loud clap of thunder Daddy would say, "Boy! that hit something." "Maybe our house," Mother would moan. "I wonder if everything we have is burning down right now." "Can't burn in this rain," Daddy would say soothingly. "More likely get washed away." "Oh, God, we could drown like rats in this cellar!" Mother could be very convincing. But Daddy's voice was always calm. "The cellar is on high ground and there's good drainage. 'Course if it's raining like this up river and all that water comes rushing down…well, the whole valley could be flooded."

I lay shivering under the covers and it was not from the cold. Once when we went in the cellar and Daddy lit the lantern, Mother screamed and pointed to the top shelf. We looked in time to see a snake slither behind some jars of canned food. There was instant panic but

Daddy barred the door so we couldn't get out and assured us that the snake was a harmless variety and that it was as afraid of us as we were of it and if we just left it alone it would leave us alone. When we were all calmed down and I was tucked in Mother said, "I wonder if that is the only snake in here." "Probably," Daddy said. "I don't believe what people say, that snakes go in pairs. I always see just one at a time. However, most anything could come in here to get out of this storm. Snakes, rats..." "Rats!" Mother shrieked. She must have climbed up on something at that point. I'm not sure because I was rolled up in a ball with my head covered and my eyes closed tight. But I heard Daddy say with a little chuckle in his voice, "Rats can climb, you know, almost as good as snakes."

We survived all that without getting blown away or washed away or snake bit. Then we moved to a little desert town in Arizona where there were no tornadoes. But there were other dangers for my parents to murmur about in dull moments. Every time we drove out of town Daddy would say, "Sure would hate to break down in this desert." The water and ice wouldn't last long in this heat," Mother would agree. "We would all be burned to a crisp, just like we were in an oven." I would spend the whole trip listening intently to the sound of the motor. But we never broke down in the desert so we survived the heat, too.

Then we moved to California. Before we even got there my parents began to talk about the earthquakes. "The earth opens up and swallows whole buildings," Mother said. "I don't think too many buildings actually get swallowed up," Daddy said. "The real danger is from fires set off by the earthquake. They can burn a whole city." When I asked why we would move to such a place they said with satisfaction that there was danger everywhere.

I've lived here in California for a lot of years now, survived the earthquakes and the big bomb scare with kids learning in the schools to "duck and cover" and people building fallout shelters in the back yard. "We're sitting ducks here on the coast," Daddy would say regularly. "Well, it doesn't matter," Mother would answer just as regularly. "Nobody anywhere can survive anyway."

Now we have entered the brave new world of computers. As the year two thousand approached, the great adversary was a computer bug that we couldn't even see. My parents were long gone but every time the year two thousand was mentioned I could hear their voices. They said that water and electricity would be shut off. Social security checks would stop. We couldn't even pump gas. Food and mail wouldn't be delivered. Couldn't withdraw money from the bank...etc...etc.

I don't know what the next threat will be but as a survivor of countless possible disasters, including being trapped in a cellar with snakes and rats and both parents, I can tell you, don't worry. Just have your emergency supplies ready, go to bed, pull the covers over your head, stuff your fingers in your ears, go to sleep and have faith that everything will be all right in the morning.

HAPPY CHILDHOOD

RUBY GREEN

I had a very happy childhood. Some of my earliest memories are of our little family at night. Daddy would make popcorn as he played his Jews harp and danced jigs. Pearl and I would try to jig like daddy, but we never mastered that skill. We would take a big bowl of popcorn and sit around as daddy read from a Zane Grey western. After the popcorn was all gone Daddy would put his book away and take one of us in his rocking chair, Mother would take the other one, in her rocking chair and they would sing songs and rock us to sleep. I remember Mother singing "The Little Brown Church in the Dale". Daddy would sing "Pretty Red Wing" and songs from the 1st world war, such as "its A Long Way to Tippirary", "Pack up your Troubles in Your Old Kit Bag and Smile, Smile, Smile" and "Oh, How I Hate to get up in the Morning". Mother and Daddy played with us a lot. They also told us stories about their parents and brothers and sisters. I would say we were a very happy family.

I remember Daddy making Dill pickles. He kept them in a barrel at the corner of the little house we lived in. We lived out in the country where there was lot of trees. Our salt box had a picture on it of a little girl sprinkling salt on a bird's tail. Pearl and I asked Daddy why she was doing that. He told us "That is the way to catch a bird." So one morning, Pearl and I found an empty Vick's salve jar and put some salt in it and started off to catch a bird. But the birds wouldn't stand still long enough for us to sprinkle salt on their tails. But we didn't give up. After a while, Pearl, being much younger than me- 17 months - wanted to quit and go back home. But I –being much older and wiser, and knowing that Daddy wouldn't tell us a lie, told Pearl, "Just a little while longer, I know we will catch one in a minute.

But when I looked around I realized we were lost. I told Pearl "We are lost just like the "Babes in the woods Mother is always singing about." That did it. Pearl began to cry. I was much too grown up to cry, but I was frightened. I could just see us lying down on the cold ground with birds covering us up with mulberry leaves. But I had to be brave. Soon I thought I heard Mother calling. I had to hold my hand over Pearl's mouth while I listened. (I think I almost suffocated Pearl) but I did hear mother calling. I told Pearl and we both began to holler as loud as we could. Mother's calls got closer and soon we were in her arms, safe and sound. That night, we were very mad at Daddy. We told him "THAT IS NOT THE WAY TO CATCH BIRDS."

Pearl says…. What she remembers about the bird adventure is after they were lost and frightened. Ruby picked up a little stick and said, "Don't worry Pearl if a big old bear comes after us I'll hit it with this." Pearl looked at the tiny stick. Realized how protected she was and really started bawling.

CADDELL IMMIGRATING FROM SCOTLAND

Hughes B. Caddell

(Mother's maiden name)

October 2nd, 1959. The story of the immigrant boy who founded the American family as related to me by my father, William Andrew Caddell, and my grandfather, Heazie Karr (Hezekiah) Caddell.

This young man lived in Edinburgh, Scotland, his father being one of the wealthiest men in Scotland. (Several years ago a friend was tracing his family tree and obtained some literature on the great clans of Scotland and the Caddell Clan was the in the pamphlet as the NUMBER THREE Clan of Scotland.)

The story goes that this young man was somewhat of a playboy, strutting around with a gold headed walking cane which denoted his father's rank of wealth, and one day when he returned home his father gave him a terrible beating for it. This unjust punishment made the boy so angry that he decided to run away from home and make his father sorry for mistreating him.

So he went to the shipyards at Edinburgh where the ships were being loaded for the American Colonies. While watching the activity on the docks he noticed his father coming at a distance, evidently looking for him, for he walked very slowly and making a careful search of everything as he walked along. The boy hid behind some bales of goods destined for America and watched his father as he slowly passed from view. This was the last time he saw his father.

By this time he was repentant of wanting to make his father sorry for mistreating him and wanted to return home and beg forgiveness, but since he had made a vow to run away and go to America, he did not know how to honorably break the vow. So he decided to leave it to fate and taking the walking cane he stood it straight up and said, "If it falls toward the sea I will go to America." It fell toward the sea, which was a terrible disappointment. Thinking that a small breeze may have caused it to fall this way he decided to repeat it and in order to cause it to fall toward the land, he leaned it in that direction and again it fell toward the sea.

This was heart breaking and he said, "I will try it the third time and whichever way it falls I will go." He wanted to return home so much that when he stood up the cane this third time he leaned it far over in order that it could fall no other but towards home, but fate caused it to fall toward the sea.

So he went on board a ship bound for the colonies and sold himself to the Captain for his passage, with the understanding that it would be for seven years as an indentured servant. Upon reaching Charleston, South Carolina, he was sold to a rich planter who took him to his plantation and giving him a hoe, put him to work in the fields. A short time later another plantation owner riding past the field noticed the boy crying, and stopping, he observed the boy's hands were raw and bleeding. Feeling sorry for the boy he took him to his master and offered to pay him what he had paid for the boy. Thus was he transferred from a harsh to a very kind master who took him to his home and gave him the light position as clerk over his plantation.

During this time he fell in love with the master's daughter and when the seven years of servitude were over, married her and they built their own plantation. From this marriage there were five boys. (Thomas, John Calvin, Andrew Henderson, William Riley, and Benjamin.) One of these five (Andrew Henderson) married and also had five boys. (Unknown, Andrew Henderson Jr., Thomas Webster, Lewis Green, and Maherschallal-hashbaz) and one of these married and moved westward to Indian Territory which later she was more talented than Shirley Temple, and cuter. They took her to town and got her on amateur night became Gadsden, Alabama, and also had five boys. (Hezekiah, Lewis Green, James Allen, Henderson, and Thomas Edward.)

One of these five (Andrew Henderson Caddell Jr.) married and moved westward to the headwaters of the Budahatchie River, which is in northern Alabama near the old settlement known as the old White House, a Baptist Church. This was Cherokee County between what is known today as the towns of Winfield and Haleyville, Alabama. This boy was born about 1814 and his grave is in the old White House Cemetery. From this marriage also were five boys, one of them being my grandfather (Heazie Karr or Hezekiah) born in 1842. He married after serving four years in the Confederate Cavalry as a scout under Nathan B. Forrest. He built his home and a cotton gin on the banks of the Budahatchie River and operated the Post Office in his home. These were wild days of terrorism and banditry.

From this marriage were five children, two boys and three girls. One of these boys was my father, born in 1872, who married Dollie Singleton in 1900 and from this marriage were five children, three boys and two girls. My father's brother was Frank Caddell, and my grandfather's brothers were Lewis, Tom, Henderson and James.

This text is taken from a copy that was given to me by Ernest Petrolia, Clay County. Texas. This is verbatim copy with the exception of additional information that I have inserted () in the interest of clarity. Ky W. White, great, great grandson of James Allen Caddell, 28 Dec. 1984

LEAVING OKLAHOMA IN 1936

RUBY GREEN

Dressed in blue and white bib overalls and a white blouse with big blue polka dots, I felt fresh and clean after my bath. I had worked hard all day. Aunt Bertha and Mother were selling produce from the farm in the shed, which Uncle Leonard had built out by the highway in front of the house. After preparing and feeding the little kids their lunch and cleaning the kitchen, I now had some time for myself.

I was fourteen and half years old. Glancing in the mirror while combing my blond curls, I thought I was beginning to look like a young lady. I slipped down to my favorite spot by the little creek near the bridge on the highway. Sitting on a low limb of a big tree, bare feet dangling, I could see and hear the little children playing in the yard. Pearl just turned 13 was playing with them.

Out on the highway was a steady stream of cars and trucks full of sad faced people. They were all going south. The cars all had rolled up mattresses tied on the fenders. Boxes, tubs, pots and pans were tucked in and tied on all over. The trucks had canvass stretched over bows and looked like covered wagons. They had barrels and tubs tied on the sides. An occasional car or truck would stop and buy melons and vegetables from Aunt Bertha and Mother. Caught up in this panorama of life going on around me, I recalled the pictures and stories in the newspapers of people starving to death and the top-soil being blown away and farmers having to just walk away from their farms which were worthless now. Cattle were starving too.

Uncle Leonard could still grow melons and vegetables on his farm, but it would not support two large families, so Daddy and Mother had decided to join the travelers on the highway in search for someplace where we could find work to sustain us. Daddy had bought a Model T Ford truck a few days ago and Uncle Leonard was helping him fit it with bows and canvas to look like a covered wagon. We were staying here on Uncle Leonard and Aunt Bertha's farm near Marlow Oklahoma, while Daddy fitted the truck for travel. Aunt Bertha and Uncle Leonard had left their farm at Walters and moved to this one, just before Grandma died. Thinking of her brought tears to my eyes. I missed her so much. She had been a stabilizing influence for our family. Now with the air always filled with dust and farmers leaving by the hundreds and no work to be found anywhere, I knew we had to leave too. My feelings were mixed. School would be starting in a week or two and I loved school. But there would be no school for me this year. Maybe never again. I was apprehensive, for I didn't know what would become of us. We were leaving Grandpa and all the dear relatives I loved so much. But I sensed a great adventure ahead and new places.

The next morning, we piled all our Earthly belongings into the truck. The mattress was put on the bed of the truck with the quilts spread on it. Boxes holding clothes and food were around the edges. Two tubs were tied onto the sides and a big canteen of water. Uncle Leonard put two big watermelons in the back end. All us kids except baby Jerry crawled into the back. Daddy cranked up the old Model T and we were on our way. We went by Walters to say goodbye to all the relatives there and visited Opal's and Grandma's graves. Then back on the highway to join all the other travelers.

We crossed the Red River and pulled into the campground with other travelers, near Wichita Falls, Texas. Our family consisted of Daddy and Mother, myself, Pearl, Dorothy 8, Betty Jo 5, Freddy Gene 4, Colleen 2 and baby Jerry, 5 months. We built a fire and cooked supper. Daddy talked to some of the other men. They said the cotton was just opening up around Waukcihatche, Texas. So we all headed that way the next morning.

While we were riding in the truck, we would sing. Betty and Freddy sang really cute together and Pearl and I taught them some cute songs. When we camped at night, Betty and Freddy would start to sing and soon a crowd would gather. Sometimes the other campers would give them money. Daddy protested at first, but people said it was the best show they had seen for a long time and was worth getting paid for. Sometimes they would be pressed to sing for an hour or more. Freddy got so he wouldn't sing unless he was going to get paid for it.

When we got close to Waukchiatche, there were lots and lots of big cotton fields. Cars and trucks would pull over to the side of the road while someone would go find the farmer. If they could use us, we would take our new cotton sacks out in the field and pick cotton. There were so many people; the field would be picked clean in no time. Then we would go on till we found another field we could pick. If a farmer had many cotton fields, he would provide a place for the pickers to live. Usually one room shacks with a dirt floor. There would be a water faucet or well nearby. We were glad to have it.

We were in such a place near Waukchiatche, Texas. One Saturday evening some girls our age asked Pearl and me if we could go into town with them and their brother (who could drive a car). Daddy gave Pearl and me 15 cents apiece. We planned to each buy a hamburger, a soda pop and an ice cream cone. That would be a splendid supper for us. But the kids went to an Ice Cream Parlor. They didn't sell hamburgers there. The other kids bought Banana Splits. They looked good and they cost 15 cents. So we both blew our whole 15 cents on a Banana Split. It was the most delicious stuff I had ever eaten. I thought I was in heaven. I enjoyed the memory of it for days. It was 15 cents well spent.

As the cotton fields were picked clean, we would move on in search of more white fields. We kept going South-West. When we were picking for a farmer near Roswell, New Mexico, Betty and Freddy drew the attention of the farmer and his wife. They thought Betty was the cutest little girl they ever saw. They said on the radio. She earned some money, I don't know how much. They wanted to adopt Betty. Of course that was out of the question. When the cotton was all picked, we moved into a campground near Roswell. Daddy went all over Roswell looking for work. There was none to be found. A week before Christmas, our money was all gone, we had only enough food for two more meals. There was no gas in the truck. It was rainy and cold. Mother and Daddy took to just sitting in the truck all day. I had my hands full to try to keep the little kids dry and warm and fed. Pearl and Dorothy kept busy gathering wood and keeping the fire going. At this very critical time, Pearl got a really good idea, one I never would have thought of. She washed Betty's and Freddy's faces and combed their hair and marched them off to town. She found a busy Street corner, stood them on it and told them to sing.

It was bitter cold, but Betty wouldn't sing with her coat on, for she put motions to her singing and the coat was big and cumbersome. Someone asked why they were here singing. Pearl told them "For money". People started throwing money at their feet. Pearl was afraid Betty would get sick from the cold, so when there was a lot of money on the ground, Pearl put Betty's coat back on her and they gathered up the money and headed back to the campground. They stopped at a store on the way and bought some bread and milk and a cake. When Mother and Daddy saw the food and the money, they revived a little bit and Daddy went and got more food and some gas for the truck and we got back on the highway. We stopped in every town in the back alleys while Daddy looked for work. Kids on their way to school would yell at us and call us poor white trash and other names. Pearl would yell back at them. Sometimes they would throw rocks at us. One hit Dorothy in the head and made it bleed.

Coming through the mountains, we ran out of gas. A new car with a young man and woman stopped to help us. The man siphoned gas out of his car and put it in the truck. He gave Daddy $1.00. They gave us a loaf of bread and some salami and some cheese. They were very nice to us. The young woman had tears in her eyes as she hugged Colleen and Jerry. We really enjoyed the food they gave us. We stayed that night in Las Cruses, New Mexico, in a motel for a dollar. The motel owner gave us a can of tomatoes and a loaf of bread. It was a good supper for us. There was hot running water and we all enjoyed a warm shower. The next morning, Daddy made some flapjacks for us to eat during the day. The man at the gas station told us to turn south, for the road was better. It seemed like the longest road. There was very little traffic on it. Late in the afternoon, the truck sputtered to a stop, out of gas.

Pearl and I built a fire and fed the little kids the last scraps of food we had, while Daddy walked up the road to see if he could find a house or something. He came back and said he thought he saw some smoke off to the east and pointed, but he wasn't sure, for the sky was filled with big black clouds. He just got into the truck and just sat there, it seemed ready for us all to die. Mother hadn't moved since we had stopped here. As I was checking on Jerry, between them, I could see Daddy and Mother both were burning up with fever. I wrapped Jerry and secured him on the seat between Mother and Daddy. I wrapped Betty and Freddy and Colleen in a quilt and told them not to move until Pearl and I got back, that we going to look for someone to help us. I told Dorothy she was in charge. Pearl and I put Daddy's old heavy overcoat on, her arm through one sleeve and mine through the other. We buttoned it up. Pearl suggested we pray for a miracle and stay here. Surely, someone would come along sooner or later. I reasoned it may be too late by the time someone came along. We hadn't seen another vehicle for hours. We said a prayer and checked the kids again. The three frightened faces stared at us from the quilt wrapped around them. Dorothy sat on a box in a heavy red sweater 3 sizes too big, looking out the back of the truck. Her white face and big brown eyes wore no expression, but tears were streaming down her face. It broke my heart and I knew I would remember this scene as long as I lived.

We started off in the direction Daddy said he had seen smoke. Darkness fell quickly. Then we could see a light in the distance. We kept going toward the light. We stumbled over rocks and cactus. Coyotes were howling and we were frightened, but we kept going. When we thought we were fairly close to the light, it went out. It started to snow. We hoped that we were still going in the right direction. After what seemed an eternity, we bumped into a house. We felt our way to a door and banged on it loudly. After a while, an old woman came to the door holding a candle. She looked like the Wicked Witch of the West. She was very surprised to see us, but she invited us in. We told her of our situation. She woke her husband up. He grumbled and said "You help out these poor white trash and they follow you around the rest of your life." Pearl and I begged with tears streaming down our faces. He grudgingly put on his boots and coat and took us in his truck to guide him back to our family. We had a hard time getting Daddy to respond or even speak to the man. Pearl told Daddy, "There's a lady up there, reminds me of grandma." I thought she must be out of her mind. The man fastened a chain from his truck to ours. When he thought Daddy was alert enough to steer, he pulled us down to his ranch. The next day, some friends of the rancher came by on horses. They said they had heard on the radio that a family of 8 had been found this morning a few miles ahead of where our truck

had run out of gas. Three of them were dead from exposure and 5 were in the hospital in Rodeo, New Mexico, which was the next town. I looked out on the snow-covered world and thought, we prayed for a miracle and we received one.

The rancher's friends told him that since he needed help badly, because his ranch in San Simone Arizona needed his attention too, why not let us stay and help. Daddy would be well in a few days and he could go on over to San Simon to his ranch there. He couldn't pay us, but we would have a place to stay and food. He needed us until about the last of March. I can't remember the Rancher's name, but that was the arrangement we made with them.

The rancher went on over to San Simon and we stayed there with his wife to help her. Pearl was a big help with the cows and horses. I nursed Mother and Daddy and cleaned and took care of the little kids. Daddy was well in a few days and was a help to the woman, taking her to Rodeo to shop, etc. When the rancher came back, Daddy was well enough to do hard work, so he took him to his ranch in San Simon with him. They took me with them to cook and clean for them. I wanted Dorothy to go with me to keep me company, so we left the rest of the family there, for Pearl was such a help for the woman.

When the rancher was through with Daddy, he got a job at a grocery store in San Simone for a dollar a day. We rented a house out in the country and moved the rest of the family over. At last we could start to school. I started in the 8th grade, having missed the year before. I really enjoyed living there and going to school. The kids were always talking about the Corn-fed Mormons who lived over in the Gila Valley. The way they talked about them, we thought they must be a breed of people like Indians or something. But we understood they were to be avoided. There was a rodeo ground between us and town. When they had Rodeos there, we would make fudge and take it and sell it to the people who came to the Rodeos. We made money doing that. The people liked the fudge and would look for us each time.

Even though we only went to school there for 4 months, I did some extra work and passed the 8th grade. That was the last of my formal schooling. When School was out we moved even father from town. In fact, it was out in the sticks. There was a well away from the house. One warm spring day I found some jeans that were tight on me; they were all torn in the legs, so I cut them off. I put on my blouse with blue polka-dots, tied it up, so my mid-drift was bare, the short cutoff jeans, combed my long blond hair. I thought I looked just like Daisy Mae in the funny paper. I took a bucket and pranced out to the well, really enjoying my beautiful self and drew a bucket of water, when Daddy happened to see me. He stormed over to me and bawled me out good and told me to go in the house and get some clothes on. I tried to explain that there was no one around to see me like this, but it didn't matter to him. "No daughter of mine is ever going to run around showing off her half dressed body". Needless to say, that was the last time I ever wore shorts or left my midriff bare.

When the time came to chop cotton, Daddy went over into the Gila Valley to chop cotton, for it would pay him more than a dollar a day. Mother and us kids stayed there for a while. We worried about Daddy being over in the Gila Valley among All those terrible Mormons. Daddy sent us some money to come join him. We had an old car; I don't remember where we got it. Mother loaded all of us and our belongings into the old car and we started for the Gila Valley. We had only gone a few miles, when (now, I'm not exaggerating one bit) the car literally fell apart right there on the road. The radiator fell down, the tires all went flat at once, and a fender fell off. It was like something you see in the funny papers or a funny movie. We sat there wondering what to do. We started laughing too, because it was such a funny thing to happen.

Soon a Baptist Preacher came along. He took us all in his car to the Gila Valley. It was a dark night when we were just entering the valley. We could see the lights of Safford. Then all at once I seemed to have a vision. I could see the whole valley at once. It was just beautiful, and I Knew this is where all the most important things in my life would happen and I felt that I had come home.

MIDNIGHT AND COTTON

COLLEEN CHAPMAN

I was somewhere between three and five years old. We lived in a little yellow house in Safford, Arizona. Although the house was not very big, a lot of people lived in it. I think it was Grandmas house to start with. We were the first to move in with her. "We" being Mother, Daddy, Dorothy, Betty, Fred, me, Jerry, and Donny. My two oldest sisters were married by then and my younger sister and two youngest brothers had not yet been born. Then Aunt Pearl left her husband. She and two of her kids, Verda Mae and Roy moved in. Next came Aunt Ada and two of her kids, Alice and Shirley. That made 15 people living in a two-bedroom house. I don't know how long we did it, much less <u>how</u> we did it. But do it we did and we all survived. No wonder Grandma Sullivan was so mean sometimes! Everyone use to say that Grandma Phillips was a saint and Grandma Sullivan was just the opposite. Never the less, the kids were left in her care quite often. Poor thing.

I often escaped to an irrigation ditch that was about ¼ mile from the house. Huge Cottonwood trees grew along the banks. It was my favorite place to play. I was not supposed to go there by myself, but that didn't stop me. Knowing I would be punished if I got caught, I went anyway. I got away with it most of the time so that made it worth risking the punishment. I felt safe and contented there. When I was in the ditch, I couldn't see over the side, so I knew I could not be seen from the house.

When the water had not been running for a day or so, as the mud dried it cracked and formed little patches about the size of a large cottonwood leaf. The edges curled up and got crunchy. One of my favorite childhood memories is walking along the bottom of the ditch and can almost feel the tickling crunch on my bare feet. How I loved that place! It was quiet and cool. At least it was the coolest place I could find in Arizona in the summertime. The other kids went there once in a while, but to me, it was <u>my</u> place. On the other side of the ditch a short distance away was a small settlement of colored people. Grandma told us kids to stay away from there but didn't tell us why. We were to have nothing to do with those people. We asked why but didn't get an answer. Just threats of punishment if we disobeyed.

One hot day I was in the ditch headed for my favorite shady spot. As I rounded a curve I saw a little girl in my place! Startled, I stopped and stared. Who was this stranger and how dare they not only be in my ditch, but in my very best spot? Suddenly I realized I had never seen a person like this before. Not up close anyway. She must be one of those people I was supposed to stay away from. She didn't look dangerous. She was about my age, maybe a little older and bigger. She sat there humming to herself as she dug down to get cool wet sand and put it on her feet. As if she felt my eyes staring at her, she turned and looked straight at me. She jumped up and started to climb out of the ditch. Changing her mind, she turned and stared back at me. She wiped her hands on her torn blue dress. After looking me up and down, she asked, "Are you one a them dam no count white trash? Cause if ya are, I ain't sapposta have nutten ta do with ya." "I don't know." I said, "Are you one a them dam black Nigers?" (Please excuse my use of that word, but I can't tell this story any other way.) She laughed and said, "Well I sho ain't Snow White." We both laughed and suddenly all the fear was gone. I said, "You must be a Pickin any. That's what my grandma calls Niger kids. I don't know what that means. Do you?" With furrowed brows she thought for a few seconds, then with a big smile she said, "Well, maybe out in the cotton fields, if the Boss man thinks we ain't workin fast enough, he yells at us 'Hey! Pickin any?'" She clapped her hands and said, "That was a good one." Her laughter made me think of tinkling bells. Never heard any like it before or since.

Her hair fascinated me. It was so black and curly! I wished mine was curly instead of straight as a board. It had been curled a few times but was straight again in no time. Daddy once said that not even an act of congress could do anything for my hair. What that meant, I hadn't a clue, but it sounded pretty hopeless. I wanted to touch her hair to see if it felt as good as it looked. She might not like that, but the urge grew stronger. Cautiously I put my hand on top of her head. O.K. so far. Scrunching a handful of hair, I asked, "How did your hair get so curly?" She smiled and tried to run her hand through my hair, but it was too tangled. "How did your hair get so strait? Did you iron it? My Aunt tried to iron hers once. You ever smelt burnt hair? Peeuuu!" she said pinching her nose. "And how did it get so white? Did ya bleach it? Cause it's as white as cotton, Hay! Can I call you Cotton? And you can call me Midnight cause mine is as dark as that."

Midnight and I became good friends. We met at the ditch almost every day. Using a stick and a scrap of cloth we found somewhere, we made a signal flag. The first one to the ditch would get the flag from its hiding place and put it in a certain spot where the other could see it. When water was in the ditch and was too deep to wade across, we crossed on a log that spanned the ditch. Grownups walked across but we crawled. There was a big Weeping Willow tree a few feet from the edge of the ditch near the place we had first met. Between the trunk and the branches that touched the ground, we found a space large enough to make a playhouse. A couple of wooden apple crates, two cushions from a discarded couch, some old dishes and various other things we thought might come in handy made it a cozie retreat.

I ain't sapposta have nutten ta do with no White Trash but I don't care. I got nobody ta play with. I got me two big brothers, but they can't be bothered with me. Her eyes looked as lonely as I felt. Yes, you can be lonely in a house full of people! "I ain't sapposta have nutten

168

ta do with no Dammed Nigers. Don't know why; just know I'll get a whippin if I do. That don't matter though, cause I'll get one anyway for bein here." We decided that if we were seen together we would pretend to argue. Maybe then we wouldn't be in quite as much trouble. We talked about how strange grown-ups are and wondered if we would be like them when we grew up. We figured the way it works is, the older you get, the stranger you get. So we had some time before we started getting strange.

The real world was shut out and we created one more to our liking. This little world of ours could be whatever we wanted it to be. Anything we had seen, or our older family members had seen and told us about, in the movies, or from a book, the radio, and our imaginations, could become an adventure.

One day it was our room in the tower of a castle. A terrible battle was being fought far below. Our Father, the King, and his men won of course. We had helped by pouring boiling oil onto the bad guys. The next day it could be a stagecoach and we were traveling to the gold mines of California. We had husbands waiting for us there. They had struck it rich and had sent for the children and us. We almost got run over by a heard of stampeding Buffalo. We managed to get behind some rocks just in time. We continued on our way and then a gang of outlaws were after us. We were worn out by the time that adventure ended. Where was the Cavalry when you needed them? On another adventure we had an airplane crash in the jungle and were saved by a monkey. It took us to Tarzan and Jane.

When we were in a fort in the desert and being attacked by Indians, we scared ourselves and almoscried at the thought of what would happen to us if the Indians got us. This time some cowboys on a cattle drive saved us. We argued about which one of us the handsome trail boss liked the best. We took care of that problem by giving him a twin brother.

We pretty well traveled the world by train, boat, plane, stagecoach, horseback, any and every other way to travel, we did it. A few times someone came looking for one or the other of us. We could hear them calling and see them coming in time to get on our own side of the ditch. Then we would yell at each other "You ole no count White Trash! You just ain't no good fer nuthin." "You ole Pickin any. Just ain't no count no how!" Then we did our secret signal that meant we didn't mean a word of it and I'll see ya later. It went like this: Put both hands on hips. Stomp both feet twice. Nod head three times while shaking a finger at the other. Turn back to back, bend over, stick out butts, and stick out tongues wiggle butts while making a fart noise. Don't ask me why we went through all this. I don't know!

About a week before school started, Midnight didn't come to the ditch any more. I went every day and put out our signal flag and waited. When school started I looked for her. By this time I was old enough to go to school at last! She had to be there someplace. I couldn't ask about her because I didn't know her real name. I got into trouble for going from room to room looking for her. She was not there! Where could she be? Was she sick? Had she been hurt? It was unbearable not knowing. After school was out the third day, I worked up my courage and sneaked up close to her Grandmother's house. She had pointed it out to me and said she was living there. Crawling under the house next to it, I hid and watched. I stayed for a long time in spite of the spiders and spider webs. There was a big rat in a pile of trash. It didn't run away like I thought it would when I tossed a piece of wood at it. I got as far away from it as I could. There wasn't as much space there so I had to lie on my tummy. A mangy old dog came and lay in front of me and kept licking my face and ears. I managed to push him to one side so I could see the house, but the darn thing kept licking my ears.

The people I saw coming and going at what had been her house was not her family. I wanted to ask about the girl that had lived there but didn't have enough courage to approach any of these strangers. I gave up and went home. When Grandma asked me why I had dirt and spider webs all over me, and where in the world did that mangy dog come from, I started crying. She whipped me for not telling, but it didn't hurt half as bad as loosing Midnight. Somehow, I knew I would never see her again. But I looked for her everywhere I went for a long time. I thought about her and missed her even longer. After all these years, I still miss her.

THE COTTON FIELDS

C OLLEEN C HAPMAN

When I was about 13, Mother left Spider. (The father of my half-brother, Skipper) Mother, Jerry, Donny, David, Linda, Skipper and I crowded into a car with Uncle Buddy and Aunt Doris. They took us to Coalinga or Huron, CA. to pick cotton. The poor old car had a hard time climbing up the mountain between highway 101 and Coalinga. It had been a long and tiring trip through the thick heavy fog.

We were in sunshine now and were glad when we found a place to get off the road and park. We got out to walk around and work the kinks out of our cramped bodies. We were high above the fog, and it was a beautiful sight. It looked like mounds of white and pink whipped cream as the rising sun sent rays skipping over them. Is life like that, I wondered, we have come through so much fog. Will we find our sunshine somewhere, somehow, sometime?

We went to a cotton camp. Uncle George, Aunt Ada, her daughters Shirley and Alice were there, and Aunt Doris's brother Joe. Alice, Shirley, Joe and I were close to the same age. I had not met Joe before, but I didn't like him and he didn't like me. When I stayed with Grandma, she talked about him a lot. Joe this and Joe that. He was such a good child. On and on. Not at all like me. She had done the same, I soon learned, when he stayed with her. Colleen this and Colleen that. We became friends in spite of it

I always wanted to pick cotton close to Uncle George. He would tell stories and sing while he worked. Late in the afternoon one hot day we were all quiet and trying to get the last sack full picked and go home. A song was running through my head, and I couldn't remember what came after....well what do you know its morning already, and over yonder....I stopped, stood straight and gazed off into space. Uncle George noticed. He straightened up, pulled off his hat, whipped the sweat from his forehead and looked in the direction I was looking, and looked back at me. I said, "Uncle George, what's over yonder?" He looked again. Everybody within earshot stood and looked. Soon everyone in the field was looking and asking each the whole valley and I knew as well as I ever knew anything, that all the most important things in my life, would happen to me here in this beautiful valley. It has proven to be true. We learned who the Mormons were, and even joined them two years later. When Mother wanted to go on to California, I told Daddy, "I know this is where I belong. I have work and can take care of myself." But Daddy wouldn't consent to go without me. They waited until I was married before the rest of the family went on to California.

UNCLE CARL

RUBY GREEN

Uncle Carl would play with all the little babies in the family. He would hold the very young ones - only a few weeks old - in his hand and raise them up high with them standing up in his hand. I used to hold my breath for fear he would drop them. I never figured out how he did that.

Also, he bought a new car each year. We would all admire the new car and he would take all the kids for a ride in it and buy us some candy. I really liked him. Pearl and I, Kenneth and Paul, used to play and run over the hills back of grandma's house. We would go down to the little creek near grandma's house and hide behind the trees and spy on Nettie and Ethel and their boy-friends. I have a lot of stories about our adventures with Kenneth and Paul.

WINGS IN THE NIGHT

RUBY GREEN

One day while I was at grandma's house, we were the only ones there. We were in her kitchen by the window shelling peas. We were talking about her and grandpa's three little babies who died. She told me this story. "One of my babies was very sick. We lived way out in the country. One night I was up with her and holding her in my arms in the rocking chair. She was asleep. I was very worried about her. As I was wondering what to do for her, I heard a sound like a big bird flying over the house, from east to west. It had to be bigger than any bird I had ever seen, by the sound of it. My baby died the next morning." When I went into labor with our third baby I was getting ready to go to the hospital. Carl was calling the neighbor lady to come stay with Catherine and Eddie. I went into the bathroom to get my tooth-brush, when I heard a sound like a big bird flying right over the house, from east to west. It had to be bigger than any bird I had ever seen, from the sound of it. I thought about what grandma had told me. But I quickly put it out of my mind. It was about 10 o'clock at night. Our baby boy was born that night. He only lived 17 hours.

My friend, Erdene Layton, (Pearl will remember Erdene Layton. She is Colleen Allen's sister-in-law.) told me this story several years ago. Erdene and three other girls who she grew up with, were very good friends. After they were all married and had children, they remained good and close friends. One of them lived in Duncan after she was married. They saw each other often. One day Erdine and two of the other women went there. It was a nice day and they had lunch on the patio. A white dove appeared and it flew around in circles above the head of the friend who lived there. It would fly away, then come back again in a little while and repeat flying around her head. They all wondered about it and even joked about it. She said it must have happened 5 or 6 times during the time they were out there.

Erdene and the two friends from Thatcher left and came home late in the afternoon. They had had a wonderful time together. They were all healthy and happy. Early the next morning, they got a phone call. Their friend in Duncan had died in her sleep in the night.

Shortly before Pearl and Louon,'s first baby was born they heard what sounded like a huge bird flying around the room. Louon lit a lamp, but they didn't see what was making the noise. They sat on the bed clinging to each other, scared half to death. The baby boy didn't survive and Pearl almost didn't. It was touch and go for several days.

BELIEVE

COLLEEN CHAPMAN

When we decided to move back into this house I came here by myself to get it ready. I didn't bring a radio or TV. I found some books that had been left here by the former tenants. In the evening after a hard day's work, I relaxed with one of them. It was a big disappointment, but I did get a laugh out of it. After a chapter or two I could tell when it was going to say....as the grey smoke curled up past his sky-blue eyes....I could not finish that book. The next day before starting work I went to get something better to read. There was a yard sale a few miles from the house and I bought a few books there instead of driving all the way into town.

That night I was sitting in the living room reading one of them. I don't remember the title of the book, but it presented some ideas, or beliefs that were new to me. I read this sentence… "I did not know if what I had just read was true or not. How am I to know, I thought. Perhaps if I am to believe, there will be a sign of some sort. Just then a bird hit my window. As it was rather dark in the room with only my reading lamp, and it was a moonless night, I took this as a message to believe." Just as I read the word believe, a bird hit my window! The circumstances were the same as in the book. The night was dark. The only light was my reading lamp. I was facing the window across the room as I read, and saw the bird hit the window and fall, as well as I would have if the porch light had been on. I went out to the porch after turning the light on. The bird was sitting on the porch. I had never seen one like it before and haven't since. As I reached for it, it flew away. To get to the window, that bird had to fly under the tree growing a few feet away and make its way through some branches hanging very close to the window. Was it a coincident? I think not!

LOVE AND BETRAYAL

Dorothy Patton

On the first day of first grade I fell in love with Doyle Dean Taylor, dark curly hair, sparkling brown eyes, mischievous smile. I was too shy to talk to him much but I managed to be near him most of the time at school no matter what we were doing. And I talked about him to my sister Betty. When a day came that younger siblings were allowed to visit school Betty wanted to visit my room first. I pointed Doyle Dean out to her and she walked right up to him and took his hand. "I love you." she said, gazing adoringly up at him. Embarrassed, outraged, betrayed, I stood there speechless. But I felt better when Doyle Dean leaned close to me and whispered, "Your sister's crazy." In days to come I felt betrayed by the whole family including aunts, uncles and cousins when they laughed and encouraged Betty to talk about how much she loved Doyle Dean Taylor. Nobody remembered or cared that I loved him too.

GENEY

Ruby Green

It never occurred to that all of our children didn't know all about what was wrong with Geney. That is, until Jeffery called last month to ask just what was wrong with Geney. He said he and Jody were asked to talk in Church on "Be of Good Cheer." H wanted to use Geney as an example of being cheerful. By the way Jeffery and Jody gave very good talks. When the Bishop announced them he said, "Since this St. Patrick's Day I thought it entirely appropriate to have brother & Sister Green talk.

At the time I found out I was going to have our 4th child, we were living in Superior, Arizona. Some of our friends there had gone to Mesa to a doctor there which they thought was very good. So we decided that I would go to the same doctor. I liked him. He was an osteopath. We had a lady who lived close by who would stay with the children when we needed her help. When the time came for Geney to be born, Carl took me to Mesa to the hospital. When she was born with a healthy cry, I asked the doctor, "Is it a boy or a girl?" He said "It is – a –girl. I asked, "Is she alright?" He said, "She – sure has a strong set of lungs". I didn't see her until much later. They were examining her. They didn't know at first what was wrong. But I didn't know anything was wrong with her. Carl hadn't told me anything before he left to go back home. The doctor had told him they thought she was a "hermaphrodite." (that is having both male and female organs.) I can just imagine how he must have agonized over that news until he came back in about 3 days to see us.

He sent for his mother to come and take care of the family. The first time they brought her to me to nurse her; I was examining her all over (as mothers do) when the nurse told me to be careful with her. Then she told me the baby had a deformity. She asked if I wanted to see in her diaper. I didn't feel strong enough to look at her until Carl could be there with me. When Carl came, the doctor came and told both of us that they had decided that her female organs were on the outside of her body. She didn't have a bladder. The kidney tubes were visible. She just hadn't come together in that area. She needed special care.

They made an appointment with a specialist in Las Angeles, to see what could be done for her. So 10 days after she was born, they let us take her home over night. We were to have her back in Mesa the next day. She was to be taken to a hospital in Los Angeles. I was going to take her there on an airplane. But the next morning I had a fever of 103. I was determined to go with my baby, but when we got to Mesa, the doctor determined I just could not go. The doctor would take her himself. I protested but I was too sick. I let the doctor take her. My heart was broken and I cried all the way home. I had to dry up my milk and it was very painful. But not as painful as having Geney so far away and not knowing how she was. It was good to have Grandma Green there to take care of everything.

They brought Geney back in about a week. Carl and I went to Mesa to bring her home. At the hospital in Los Angeles, they had put her female organs inside of her body where they belonged. Her kidney tubes were still exposed. She was constantly wet. We bought sterilized cotton in big boxes by the bulk. We had to use petroleum jelly to sooth on her, and then put the sterilized cotton between her legs then her diaper. She had to be changed quite often. She grew and flourished and was happy and delightful.

The doctor told us to take her to Mayo Clinic in Minnesota. I wrote to Mayo Clinic and told them about her and asked if they could do anything for her. A doctor wrote back – I can't remember his name – and said he could help her and asked if we could have her there by a certain date. I wrote back and assured him we could. He wrote back confirming the date. We made arrangements and borrowed $200.00 and got in the car and started out. (We had had Standard Oil corp. map out a rout for us. to travel.) It took 3 or 4 days to get there. Geney had gotten sick on the way with her first kidney infection.

She was very sick when we arrived at Mayo Clinic. The doctor we had an appointment with had gone on vacation. But they admitted Geney to the hospital. They wouldn't let us see her for about 3 days. Finally we told them we were going to see her anyway no matter what they said. We had contacted the missionaries and had them with us. They finally consented to let Carl and the missionaries go in and administer to her. Carl said she was lying there so pale and her tongue hanging out. She looked like she was dying. He and the missionaries administered to her. She improved quite a lot after Carl and the missionaries administered to her. They let us take her home in a day or two after that. The doctor who we had the appointment with never did see her at all. Someone at the Clinic gave me the name and address of Dr. Cummings who was a specialist in urology in Phoenix.

Making our way back home was hectic. We had thick fog and rain most of the way. Geney was so weak and it was hard to care for her properly. As soon as we arrived home, I made an appointment with Dr. Cummings. Geney had another urine infection before we saw Dr. Cummings. When he saw her, he gave instructions how to care for her. Also medicines and vitamins. He told me to bring her back in a year. (She was 7 months old when we took her to Mayo Clinic.) When I took her back after a year, she was so healthy and happy that Dr. Cummings could hardly believe she was the same baby. He said he thought she was going to die the first time he saw her. He didn't think he would ever see her again.

He praised me for taking such good care of her. He fell in love with her and promptly made an appointment to do surgery on her in a few days. She was 19 months old when she had her first surgery. Dr. Cummings transferred one kidney tube into the large bowel. Then when she was well and strong again – several months later, he transferred the other one. He saw her every few months. He called her his "Little Sweetheart." After a few months, he removed the remains of her bladder. While she was in the hospital, the nurses told me they could hear her singing in the middle of the night. They would peep around the door and she would be sitting up in her bed singing, "Down by the station uley in da monin, see da wittle puffa-bellies all in a woe, see da station mastah tun da wittle handle, Chug – Chug, toot – toot, way day go." The nurses loved her. She was always smiling and happy. She would talk to them.

After her surgeries, she grew and loved life. She was beautiful. She did very well in school. But she would get urine infections frequently and had to have kidney stones removed twice. Also she had to be constantly alert to keep from leaking from her bowel. The urine made her bowels loose all the time. When she went to sleep she would relax and she had to wear padded plastic panties, which I designed and made. The house would smell bad sometimes because of her inability to control it. She must have been in pain almost all the time all her life. But she didn't know the difference, so she made the best of what she had. She was a twirler in high school, As Catherine had been. In her first year at E.A. she met a handsome young man and they planned to get married. I took her to see Dr. Cummings. He examined her and determined she didn't have a vagina. She had had normal periods of ministration, but there wasn't a real vagina there. So she underwent a surgery to make her one. She told her fiancé about her kidney problems. He decided not to marry her. It broke her heart. But she got over it.

After more kidney infections, Dr. Cummings proposed taking her kidney tubes out of her bowel and giving her a colostomy, (a bag on her side to drain her kidneys into,) which had been perfected recently. We agreed and she went to the hospital for the surgery. (Each time she had surgery in the hospital in Phoenix. I would take her over there and stay with Carl's aunt Dessie while Geney was in the hospital.) I spent each day with her in the hospital. She got along very well after that. When she went to Mesa to go to A.S.U., she did real well. She lived with other girls and worked and went to school. She met Michael Luster, a return missionary. About a year after she was there they fell in love. Geney told Mike about her problems before he asked her to marry him. He wanted to marry her anyway. She was so happy. They were married in the Temple and were happy together. Geney graduated and taught school for two years, while Mike finished school. But she continued to have kidney infections and spent a lot of time in the hospital. When she got to having kidney infections more often, she had to resign from teaching school and began to taking in sewing. She even made Mike a suit. She was very good at sewing. Her Bishop asked her to be the Relief Society President, but Mike told him about her problems and that she wouldn't be able to do all the work which would be required. It was very disappointing for Geney. But she realized she wouldn't be able to do it.

She got a severe liver abscess which had to be lanced. The doctor did it in his office and let her go home. He told Mike how to take care of it. It had to be cleaned and dressed and medicated every day. Mike was so good in taking care of her. She was on dialysis twice a week 6 months before she died. She wanted more than anything to have babies and raise a family. But that wasn't to be. Her body wasn't strong enough to allow her even to get pregnant. But she had a cheerful attitude in spite of the disappointment. She taught the Mia Maid class in

Primary. Her Mia Maid class sang "I am A Child of God, at her funeral. She made her family happy. She loved her husband and made him happy. She was a joy to me and her Dad all her life. Her dad called her his "Little Chickadee, "I still miss her, but hopefully, we will be together in Eternity.

Portrait of Geney by Ruby Green

PAPER DOLLS AND UNRULY HANDS

Dorothy Patton

I loved to play with paper dolls when I was a kid. If I didn't have the store bought kind I would cut them out of old catalogs. And I made paper furniture for them. I could make tables, chairs, beds and even a car so that they could all take a ride. I would spend hours at this.

My little brother and sister, Freddy and Betty were just toddlers. There was over a year's difference between them, but Betty, who was the oldest, was small for her age, and that made them about the same size. They looked like twins and were always together. One day when I was playing with the paper dolls they wanted to play with me and I wouldn't let them. Paper dolls are fragile and I was sure their awkward little hands would ruin everything. I told them they were not old enough to play with paper dolls and to go play with their own toys. They went away and soon I heard a fuss in the kitchen. Mother was scolding and the kids were crying. I went in the kitchen to see what was going on. Oh! What a mess. The lids had gotten into the flour bin and they were covered from head to toe with flour, and it was all over the floor. Mother had brushed the kids off but not too gently. She told me to clean the floor and I hurried to get the broom and dust pan.

Mother asked the kids why they had gotten into the flour. They said they didn't know. "Well, I guess your hands just got out of control." She said. They nodded in agreement. "Okay, I'll just have to tie them up." She grabbed an old flour sack that we had been using for a dish towel and started viciously it into strips. She tied their hands behind them, sat them each in a kitchen chair, and tied them to the chairs. By this time I had finished cleaning the floor and watched in disbelief. She told me to get out. I did. "Now you will sit there until your hands learn not to get into mischief." She said to them.

I went back to my paper dolls but couldn't keep my mind on what I was doing. It was my fault the kids were tied up, I thought. I should have let them play with me. I wondered how long it would be before my two older sisters came home from school. Maybe they could think of a way to rescue the kids and maybe they couldn't. And it would be even longer before Daddy came home from work. What if the kids had to go to the bathroom? Well, she would surely untie them for that, I thought. I peeked in Mother's bedroom and she was lying on the bed nursing the baby and reading a magazine. I sneaked into the kitchen and looked at the wide-eyed tear stained faces. I went over to them and whispered to them "Call Mother and tell her you have to go to the bathroom." They started calling right away and I ran on tip toe back to my paper dolls.

The kids called and called, their sobbing voices getting more and more pitiful. Finely I heard Mother's angry voice in the kitchen telling them she would untie their hands this time. "But if you feel like they are going to get out of control again, let me know and I will tie them up again and leave them that way so they won't get you into any more trouble." Soon the kids came back in where I was playing, and this time I let them play with me. I even tried to show them how to make the furniture.

EARLY SUNDAY MORNINGS LONG AGO

RUBY GREEN

I have been thinking of those early Sunday mornings when Daddy didn't have to go to work, kids didn't have to go to school and there was about an hour before we had to get ready for Sunday school. I would change and feed the baby. Then we would take it in our bed and play with him-or-her. Soon one little brother or sister would come in and jump up onto the bed to join in the fun. Then another would come, soon the whole family would be on our bed playing with the baby. The baby would squeal with delight at the funny things little boys and girls do to make the baby laugh out loud. Amid gales of laughter and hugs and kisses and love pats, we would spend several minutes like this. It was such a happy, delightful time. I treasure the memory of those early Sunday mornings in my heart.

THE OLD HOUSE

R U B Y   G R E E N

The old house stands--- full of memories. Memories of the love and laughter, the heart aches and tears. The struggles and sorrows, the joys and the triumphs of raising a family. The memories of children growing up, going away and starting families of their own. But together still, one happy family, forever growing. The old house waits, with always welcoming doors, for brief visits, from members of the happy family.

REMINISCENCE

Ruby Green

On the way to the temple today, as we drove through the desert, I am caught up in the beauty of the flowers making a colorful carpet for the cactus and other desert plants. It is spring of 1991. We are approaching our golden wedding anniversary. In my mind's eye I go back in time and see myself knee at the altar in the temple with a handsome young man. All dressed in white, we are being sealed together for time and all eternity. It is a beautiful ceremony and wonderful promises are made to us.

I remember such sweet little spirits coming to bless our home. As I held my first soft cuddly little baby in my arms, I thought… no joy could be greater than this. My heart nearly burst with love for this little one. As each sweet baby came to us, I felt the same way as I cradled the little one in my arms. I see again the irresistible little toddlers filling us with joy and laughter. How we thrilled with each new word and each faltering step. It was amazing how fast our kisses healed their little bumps and bruises.

Our home quickly filled with bouncy bubbly little girls with sparkling eyes and shinny hair. Rough and tumble little boys with freckles sprinkled across their noses, which we called angle kisses. They grew in knowledge and experience. We thrilled with each new accomplishment. They were very lively and filled our hearts with love and joy. We thought… nothing could be better than this.

I saw boys grow into serious young men and go off on their missions. The bittersweet partings. The inspirational and spiritual letters. The joyful reunions after their missions had been honorably fulfilled. I see again the lovely young ladies the girls grew into. They each went off to college and on week-ends they occasionally brought home boys for the family's appraisal. How joyful to see each of our children choose the very best companion for themselves and what a spiritual feast to go with them to the House of the Lord to be sealed to their eternal companion for eternity. Our hearts were so full we thought they would surly burst.

About this time there started coming into our family the most wondrous little creatures, wrapping themselves around our hearts and loving us unconditionally. They are called grandchildren. What a special blessing they are. Somehow our hearts grew to include them. We thought… nothing could be better than this. Then other little beings started coming. They are called great-grandchildren. They are just as wonderful as the rest. Our hearts are full to overflowing.

I see myself and my companion kneeling at the altar so long ago and am so thankful we made that choice. Carl takes my hand, bringing me back to the present. Our eyes meet and we smile. I think… the best is yet to come.

STINKY

RUBY GREEN

When Colleen was about two years old she had really bad sinus trouble. She stunk so bad it was hard to pick her up and cuddle her, which we wanted to do since she was so sweet. We lived out in the desert near San Simone, Arizona We had no neighbors and we didn't know a doctor. We couldn't have gone to one anyway, for we had no money. She never cried or acted like she hurt. I know she must have been miserable, for she could hardly breathe. She tried to be her bright and funny self. We loved her, but it was hard to cuddle her, for the awful smell. I can't get over the fact that she never cried. I prayed for her but I don't think any of the family but me thought prayer would do any good. I was the one who tended her most. I think if we could have afforded a doctor, she wouldn't have such a hard time with her sinuses now.

This is a cute story about her. When she was about three years old, her hair was blond. Then it started coming in black. It was kind of a Smokey black. After it was about one inch longer, it started coming in blond again. After it was about an inch longer, it came in black again. After several months of this, she looked like a little stripped skunk. Mother cut her hair very short and it came in all blond again the rest of her life.

MY BROTHER'S DRESS

DOROTHY PATTON

There were four girls in our family before my little brother Fred was born. I remember the celebration. "We finally got a boy!" my Dad kept saying. We were all so proud. But when my brother was about three years old he decided that he should wear a dress like the rest of us kids. That was back when girls always wore dresses. My little sister was a year and a half older than my brother and he would take one of her dresses and put it on over his other cloths. But my sister was tiny while my brother was robust, and with the boy cloths underneath, the dresses was too tight. Finally my Mother took one of my outgrown dresses and gave it to him. "This can be tour little dress," she said. He was delighted, and when my little sister played with her doll, he insisted on playing with mine. Of course I protested, but Mother said, "You must share your toys." It was absolutely scandalous, my brother sitting in one of our little rocking chairs wearing a dress and rocking a doll! I appealed to my Dad. He would put an end to this nonsense I thought. But he only laughed about it. "He's just trying to fit in." he said.

I was ashamed when any of our friends or neighbors saw my brother in a dress. One day when we were going out to play I convinced him that he should leave the dress inside so it wouldn't get dirty. He finally agreed. A friend of mine came over to play and I was so proud that my little brother looked like a boy. We were playing very nicely when he looked at my friend and said, "I have a little dress." "No you don't." I said, "That is my dress." He called through the screen door, "Mom, don't I have a little dress?" And the answer came back. "Yes Honey, you have a little dress." I was so humiliated! Fred grew up a little and learned to act like a boy...too much like a boy. And through the years, when I thought he was being too macho, I taunted him with the fact that he once insisted on wearing a dress.

From the writings of Chief Tecumseh, Shawnee Nation

So live your life that the fear of death can never enter your heart. Trouble no one about their religion; respect others in their view, and demand that they respect yours. Love your life, perfect your life, and beautify all things in your life. Seek to make your life long and its purpose in the service of your people. Prepare a noble death song for the day when you go over the great divide. Always give a word or a sign of salute when meeting or passing a friend, even a stranger, when in a lonely place. Show respect to all people and grovel to none. When you arise in the morning give thanks for the food and for the joy of living. If you see no reason for giving thanks, the fault lies only in yourself. Abuse no one and no thing, for abuse turns the wise ones to fools and robs the spirit of its vision. When it comes your time to die, be not like those whose hearts are filled with the fear of death, so that when their time comes they weep and pray for a little more time to live their lives over again in a different way. Sing your death song and die like a hero going home."

PHILLIPS NAME

COLLEEN CHAPMAN

Copied from the genealogy of Andrew Phillips Sr.

An early morning, in ancient Wales, the night spirits swiftly fled the land as a layered fog was snatched skyward by the warmth of a rising sun. Cadivor Vawr, the Prince of Pembroke and one of the fifteen peers of Wales, stood and watched the action as the earth turned friendly with light, never thinking of the stir he was going to cause in the future. Today, Cadivor's bones lie peacefully in the priory at Carmarthen, Wales, placed there in 1037, but his genes are singing, sighing, laughing, crying, dancing and prancing at a great rate with a family and its branches names Phillips.

Without a family name, which was not uncommon in eleventh century Wales, recordsof family lineage soon ended mysteriously with Ted, brother of Alex, father Joe, an adverse situation at best. Then, early in the 12th century, a man d Ff ylib ap Jevan, claimed to be descendant of Cadivor Vawr. By the end of the century, due to the individuals' choices in spelling, Ffylib had become Phillips. The Phillips family is well traced to the 12th century in Wales. The family is indebted to ffylib ap Jevan for letting them know they are descendants of Cadivor Vawr of Pembroke.

Aaron, a great grandson of Cadivor, was given a family coat of arms by King Richard 1 (1189-1199) Aaron received the crest as a token of his services during the third crusade to the Holy Land.

The name Phillips, spelledin many ways, goes back to a more ancient time than Ffylib ap Jevan's day. It was present when the town of Phillipi was founded by Philip of Macedon, 359-336 B.C. A multitude of Phillips's have walked the earth from that time to this. Six Kings of France and five Kings of Spain were named Philip. There are three Saints named Philip. Phillips families were at Warwick, Stafford, Liecester, Devon, Suffolk, and Stratford upon Avon. A bust of John Phillips, a poet, is in Westminster Abby's Poet's Corner. (He keeps company with Shakespeare and Chaucer) The Phillips name is of Greek origin and is as old as recorded history.

DOROTHY'S FIRST DAY AT SCHOOL

RUBY GREEN

It isn't quite daylight yet. I woke up a while ago, freezing. I had been dreaming about the time Pearl, Dorothy and I were walking to school in Oklahoma. I thought the story was worth telling, so I got up, put on my warmest robe and turned the Furness on, and sat down to the computer. I am still shaking, for the Furness hasn't had time to warm the house yet.

We were living in a one room shack on a hill out in the country, in Oklahoma where Daddy had landed a job with a farmer, share cropping, we went to school at Little Beaver, a mile and a half from where we lived. There was a general store and a post office and a "filling station" across the road from the school house. The depression was getting really bad. We were lucky to be where we were, for the farmer had cows, which Daddy milked so we had milk.

We got potatoes and apples that were stored in Grandma's basement in Walters, and we got jars of canned vegetables and fruit from the basement too. We were living high on the hog. It was Dorothy's 6th birthday. So, she insisted that she was going to start school today, for she was 6years old. We tried to talk her out of it, but those of you who know her, know how stubborn she is. Well we bundled her up as well as we could and started out. The sky was blue, but there was a stiff wind.

It was the 1st of February and the world was covered with snow. It had frozen over and we lived about 6 hills from school. The only way we could get up the hills, was to go over to the side of the road to the barbed wire fence which ran along the side and pull ourselves up. When we got to the top of the hill, we could slide down the other side. I can still remember how we strained and ached, trying to get to school that day. Pearl and I took turns carrying Dorothy on our backs and trying to keep her warm. It was an experience I would never want to repeat.

We had peanut butter and crackers in our lunches and our homework books to carry too. We finally made it to school. There were other kids at school too, the ones who only lived a skip-a-n-a-hop- n-a- jump from the school. The two teachers in that little country school, were furious at our mother for sending little Dorothy out on such a day as that. Dorothy was almost frozen stiff. Her little lips were blue, and she was shakings furiously. But she was brave and didn't cry. The teachers put a blanket around her and held her near the big black woodstove, until she was alright again. I don't remember how we got home that day.

Ohooo, I ache all over, just remembering that experience!!! The house is warming up and the sun is shining, so I guess I will get dressed and fix myself some breakfast.

I got to thinking about Grandma's and Grandpa's garden and how much we depended on the canned vegetables from it during the start of the Great Depression. Grandma died while we were living out at Little Beaver. Grandma and Grandpa always had a really big garden. They worked in it every day when grandpa got home from work at Sullivan's Park in Walters. Pearl and I would help them pull the weeds. The big potato patch work was relegated to Pearl and me to pick the potato bugs off the vines and drop them into cans which grandma poured coal oil in and burned them in the middle of the yard. We also helped dig the potatoes when grandma said they were ready. When we pealed the potatoes for cooking, we would cut out the (eyes)–buds–and save them to plant in the spring. The garden was beautiful. There would b 2 to 5 rows of one vegetable, then 2 rows of Zinnias, more rows of another vegetable, and then two more rows of zinnias. Grandma taught me to snap the string green beans and pull off the strings to prepare them for cooking or canning. I helped her shell the peas. I helped her slip the skins off the beets. She made the best pickled beets I ever tasted. In the fall, she would buy a truck load of apples from a peddler. We helped grandma take the potatoes and apples and pile them ––Potatoes in one corner in her basement and apples in another corner. They would last us until time to put fresh ones in. She would buy concord grapes from a peddler and make delicious grape jelly. She also canned peaches and apricots and made applesauce. When Daddy got bumped off the railroad, and he couldn't find work during the first part of the depression, we would have starved if it hadn't been for the food grandma had stored. I am so thankful. She really was an angel.

CHANGING OF THE SEASON

COLLEEN CHAPMAN

My brother David worked for the B.L.M. At one time He, his wife and daughter lived on the side of San Benito Mountain overlooking New Idria Mines. David was the care taker and the town was population three. His daughter, Ara was a little girl at the time. Every summer and winter solstice she and David would get out his gun, which was a .357 magnum. They would make a special bullet together by selecting the right primer and he would weigh out a young girls' portion of black powder. When they were done they would go out in the yard and they would together both fire the bullet straight at the Sun. He told her it was to scare the sun back to the other side of the sky so the season would change. They did this for years when Ara was very little. It was like Santa to her. She was always excited and honored to make the seasons change for everyone.

GOOD-BY MR. PRESIDENT

DOROTHY PATTON

I met Ronald Reagan in person when he was running for president the first time. Nancy's parents, Edith and Dr. Loyal Davis, had retired to Phoenix and Edith had some health problems. I was working for a nursing agency in Phoenix as a home health aide and was sent to her home to take care of her. She was a lively and interesting person and loved to sing the praises of "Ronnie" She told me that when he and Nancy became engaged they were both actors in Hollywood and he insisted on flying to Chicago, where she and Dr. Davis lived at the time, to ask for Nancy's hand in marriage. He had old fashion ideas and values, she said

When I met him he had brought his campaign to Phoenix for the Easter weekend. When I arrived for work on Friday I found Nancy sitting at the table sipping tea. She had come ahead the night before and said Ronnie would arrive later that day. I asked if she would like breakfast. "I guess I should have something," she said, laying her hand on her stomach and looking at me questioningly. She was so thin and I remembered Mrs. Davis saying that Nancy watched their diet closely. I suggested a pouched egg and toast. She smiled. "Dry toast," she said. My hands were almost shaking when I started the egg and I scolded myself for even offering to make her breakfast. But it turned out perfectly, she was very appreciative and then I was proud of myself.

The day before an advance crew had come and spent hours setting up a communication center in the garage. Two men came in and checked out every inch of the house. One of them asked me a series of questions about where Mr. Reagan would sit to eat, to watch TV and where he would sleep. His eyes were sharp and penetrating. He seemed to be watching me suspiciously and it made me feel guilty even though I had never had a subversive thought in my life. Finally the motorcade arrived. The string of cars almost filled the circular driveway. People piled out and walked toward the house in a large group. I was at the kitchen window trying to pick Mr. Reagan out from among them. I expected that he would be surrounded by security personal but as they got closer I realized that he was the one out in front. He was striding youthfully along, swinging a briefcase, his jacket unbuttoned and flapping in the breeze. The others seemed to be having trouble keeping up.

The house was full of dignitaries there to meet him but soon Mrs. Davis brought him over and introduced him to me. He shook hands and thanked me for taking care of Edith. I felt at ease even though the security man from the day before was glaring at me over his shoulder. On Saturday there was a fundraising dinner and speeches at the coliseum in Phoenix. I didn't work on weekends but Mrs. Davis made sure I had tickets for myself and a couple of friends who were anxious to meet him.

governor than you were an actor." He looked shocked, Kathy stomped her foot and said "Oh shit, Colleen!" Regan laughed very hard and long and gave me a big hug. The other people laughed except for Kathy and the secret service men whose expressions never changed.

A LETTER FROM UNCLE ODIS

Hi Colleen,

I am Odis Caddel, I guess that would make me your uncle, or that would be 1/2 uncle since my mother is not your bio. grandma. I don't know how you and Bob got together, but I'm glad you did. Bob is amazing on this family tree business, apparently, he has spent a tremendous amount of time checking all this stuff out. (He is also pretty sharp.) It gives me a head ache just thinking what all is involved. As Beverly has already told you, we met your mother several years ago. I had never met her until then, Beverly and I met her at the same time about a year after I retired, about 1985. She was visiting Jody (Buddy) and Doris in Weatherford, Texas and we were there at the KOA Campground on our way to Houston, and we got to meet Buddy's family, and Ada and George (Ada's husband) who was a genuine real cowboy. We really enjoyed listening to some of his ranching stories. Of course, you know that I am the half-brother of your mother, but for simplicity sake I will refer to all of them as sisters and brothers. You may not know that I am the youngest of Joseph Wilborn's kids. My only full brother is Wilburn H.

Caddel, who was living in Billings, Montana the last we heard from him. We tried a few times to call Buddy, but always got an answering machine with a voice we didn't recognize. I met Clark for the first time in 1956. I had just got a job with Southwestern Public service Company in Artesia, NM, and he was visiting some friends next door to us, and they told him our name was the same as his. So he strolled over nonchalant like, and asked me what my name was. I told him, and he said what was your dad's first name, I told him, then he stuck out his hand and said "Hi, I'm your brother Clark." You could have knocked me over with a feather. So, we had a good visit and I didn't know if I would ever see him again. Then about 30 years later, we were at a campground in Colorado, and I kept seeing this guy that looked very familiar, and I heard someone call him Clark. I found out that he was the teacher in a square dance program that they were having there. So, we invited him to sit with us in the restaurant, I ask him his name, and when he told me it was Clark Caddel, I said "Hi, I'm your brother Odis Caddel." It really did my heart good to get even with him. They moved to Ariz. and lived there a few more years and they both died in a few more years. Glenn and Elsie are living north of Fredericksburg, TX. Address is 12482 N. ST. Hwy. 16, Fredericksburg, TX.,

78624-6822---ph 216-685-3600. We only saw them once. We stopped there on one of our trips in the 1980's. We heard from them last Christmas, and Elsie said Glenn wasn't doing very good. By the way, your mother told us while we were at Buddy's that Willis left home at a very young age and joined a circus. I forgot which one, but I think it was Barnum and Baily or however you spell it. I don't think anyone has heard from him in years. Let us hear-Odis

PS Bob says hi to the kids and Pearl. And let us know if the horses or the cowboys or the cowgirls are in charge.

TECUMSEH

JOSEPH TOMPKINS - SON OF TECUMSEH

Samuel Phillips' wife, Elizabeth Tompkins was the daughter of Joseph and Mary Jenkins Tompkins. A "cousin" reports that their story goes that he was the son of Tecumseh the great Indian Warrior (my apologies to our Native American Cousins). In my own family the story was more like this....

The Tompkins family founded the town of Tompkinsville, KY and settled in the area at the same time of war between the natives and the white settlers. As was custom by the "Indians" in that time, they would "adopt" the son of an enemy to replace a son lost in battle. One of the Tompkins' sons (unnamed in the story) and his sister had been kidnapped and raised in such a manner. He grew into a strong, brave and wise man that was called Tecumseh, because the name Tomkins was difficult in the Shawnee tongue. Tompkins, tompkinseh, tekinseh, Tecumseh.....The story says that as a dark haired white man, this Tompkins fit into both societies and could "blend in" and that was why he was able to bring the Cherokee nations together and could still "rub elbows" with the white governors. The proof of the story, so it is said, is to look at the etchings of Tecumseh... He doesn't appear to have the characteristics of a Native American. I'll leave that decision up to you. What I find interesting about this story is that two branches of the family separated by four generations and hundreds of miles and years have stories based on the same person. And that Tecumseh was, in fact, adopted by his Indian father, along with his sister.

INDIAN FAIR

RUBY GREEN

Several years ago, Carl and I took 3 of our granddaughters out to Oklahoma for a reunion at the Rhoads' (Aunt Bertha's family). They had invited all the Phillips cousins. Before we came home, Uncle Walter took us to Marlow, to see Mary Lois. Her father, Jesse Stultz was living with her and her husband. While Mary Lois was showing me her files and we were talking Genealogy, The girls went upstairs and explored. When we joined the men - Carl, Uncle Walter and Jesse, Jesse told this story.

It seems - in the early days of Oklahoma, Jesse's father or grandfather, I don't remember which -- took his family to an Indian fair, or Pow-wow. The family had a real pretty little girl with blond curly hair. An Indian Chief was watching her and seemed to be fascinated with her. After a while, he came over to her father and pointing to the little girl, asked "How much?" Her dad said, "Oh, about two ponies".

The Indian Chief left and after a time returned with two ponies and picked up the little girl and started off. He said they did some tall talking and explaining. They were frightened and worried and thought for a while they would lose their child. But the Indian Chief finally gave the child back and took back his ponies. They were thankful to get away from there and had learned to take any trade with an Indian seriously.

When we were on our way home in our car, the girls told us of the upstairs in Mary Lois's home. They were real impressed. They said it was like something out of "House Beautiful" magazine. I wished I had gone for a tour as they did. The ground floor was beautiful too, as was the outside, and yard.

A GOOD NIGHT SLEEP

COLLEEN CHAPMAN

Dorothy was on her way from Arizona to Salinas. She stopped at our place on the Tule River. She was looking forward to a swim in the river, and a few days of some much needed rest and relaxation. More than anything, she needed some sleep. Debra took her sleeping bag and settled down on the couch, giving Dorothy the use of her bedroom. About midnight a bushy haired man at the window awakened her. As sternly as she could, she ordered him to leave. He told her it was Steven. She informed him he could not fool her, she knew that none of Colleen's sons had long hair. (Steve's hair was very curly. He wanted straight hair. When it got a little bit long it was straight next to his scalp. He decided to let it get long, and when it was long enough to be the length he wanted it, he would get a haircut, and would have straight hair. Or so he thought!) He was in his twenties and living in Van Nuys. He had not told us he was coming. Not wanting to wake everyone, he had gone to Debra's window to wake her to let him in.

Ken came to pick Debra up as usual. I told him that she wasn't up yet and to get her up. He sat on the edge of the bed and rubbed Dorothy's back and told her to get up and came back into the kitchen. I had forgotten to tell him Debra was on the couch.

The next night she and Debra changed places. Dorothy said she sometimes had to get up and walk some to relieve leg cramps. This way she would not disturb anyone. And she needed to sleep on the floor. Her back needed the firmness. Early the next morning she was awakened by a shake and was told to get up and get ready for school. Ken came to take Debra to school as usual. He knew she had slept in the living room the night before, and of course didn't know about the change. He almost gave Dorothy a kiss before discovering it was not Debra. Dorothy might not have minded a kiss on the forehead but didn't like the shake and being told to get ready for school *twice!*

About 2 o'clock the next night, we were awakened by thunder and lightning. (When my kids were little and were scared by thunder and lightning, I convinced them that God was putting on a show for us. I explained what caused them, and they learned to love the nighttime storms. We turned off the lights, and when we tired of watching, we made popcorn and hot cocoa, and told ghost stories.) There was no rain, and it was a warm night, so we went outside to watch. We could see the lightening going from the mountaintop to the sky. We saw this often during hot weather, when there was no storm. The kids thought it had something to do with UFO's. I was not about to spoil their fun and explain that lightening usually goes from the earth to the sky. When it does go from sky to earth, it is caused by reverse polarity. When they observed lightening going from cloud to cloud, (heat lightening) they just KNEW there were UFO's hiding in the clouds. Dorothy's sleep was interrupted once again. She might not have minded a kiss on the forehead and hot cocoa, but the other things! The bushy haired man at her window, the shaking and being ordered to school, thunder, lightning, talk about UFO's, she could do without! All she wanted was a good night's sleep!

MY YOUNGER YEARS

COLLEEN CHAPMAN

Perhaps this should be sub-titled…..OK kids; this is why your Mom turned out to be a tough old biddy.

Mother left home when I was nine or ten. I knew she was going to a few months before she did, but I won't go into that. Dorothy had a toddler, but she came to stay with me, Jerry and Donny. Betty was a teen-ager, and I think she got married shortly after Mother left. Mother had taken the two youngest, David and Linda with her. Fred, who was in a cast from the waist down, from him being hit by a train, was taken to stay with Pearl and Louon. I don't remember all the things that happened during the next few years. It gets all mixed up. I don't know how long after Mother left Daddy too me, Jerry and Donny and went looking for her and David and Linda.

We went to Safford, Arizona where Grandma Sullivan lived. While going over the mountains somewhere between Phoenix and Safford, the boys and I were sleeping on the back seat. I was suddenly wide awake. I looked around; trying to figure out what woke me up. It was very dark and quiet. I noticed the headlights of our car shinning on an aluminum house trailer in front of us. It was so bright it hurt my eyes. I wandered how Daddy could see how to drive. I stood up behind him so I could see him in the rear-view mirror. He was staring, unblinking at the trailer and getting closer and closer, until our car was less than two feet or so behind it.

The car ahead speeded up, but so did Daddy. I told him several times that he was too close. Then I was really scared because he didn't seem to hear me. I screamed at him to slow down. He didn't. Not knowing what else to do, standing behind him I slapped him with both hands, on his cheeks. He jerked his head, batted his eyes and slowed down. As soon as he could find a safe place to pull over and stop, he got out and walked around. I turned on the dome light to see if Jerry and Donny were OK. They were both very pale. We sat in silence, watching Daddy as he walked back and forth. Then Donny shook his head and said, "Dang! Did you see that? Colleen slapped the holy hell out of Daddy!" Jerry said nothing, he just looked straight ahead.

Linda and David were at Grandma's, but Mother was not. Daddy took Linda to stay with Uncle Buddy and Aunt Doris. David went with us to Ruby's in Superior, Az. I was left with her. I don't know where Daddy and the boys went. For the next few years I was with Ruby and Carl twice, Grandma twice, Uncle Buddy and Aunt Doris once, and with Mother and the other kids at Spider's twice. Spider was the father of my youngest brother, and the reason she left home.

I left Ruby's the second time when I was 12. I got a letter from Jerry and Donny telling me that they were at Spiders. Spider was mean to them and hit Mother a lot and they were hungry all the time. Something was wrong with Linda. She wouldn't talk, didn't cry, and as they put it, looked blank. She was three years old. I didn't tell Ruby why but told her I was going back to Salinas even if I had to walk. She reluctantly let me go. Years later she said she had always felt guilty for sending me back. She shouldn't. One way or the other, I was going. There is nothing she could have done to stop me.

I had to change buses in Los Angeles. There was a two hour wait for the bus I had to take. I walked around and saw a snack bar. I went to get something to eat and discovered my wallet was gone. No money, no ticket. While sitting and trying to think what I should do, a man sat beside me. He said I looked like I was lost and asked if he could help me. I didn't trust him and said I was waiting for my Dad who had gone to the restroom nearby. He said he knew better, he had been watching me since I got off of the bus. I got up and started to walk away. He grabbed my arm. I kicked his shin, scratched his face with my free hand and shouted at him to let go. Someone said something to him and he told them I was his unruly daughter. I bit his hand, he let go, and I ran. I hid in the restroom for about half an hour.

When I came out I didn't know where I was going or what I was going to do. I started walking. I thought to myself, "God, I know you're busy with problems bigger than mine, but if there's such thing as Guardian Angles, I sure do need one now!" I turned a corner and I saw a big sign that said TRAVELER'S AID. I have believed in Guardian Angles ever since. I went there and told them my situation. Mother didn't have a phone, so they called the Salinas Police. I didn't know the address, but I could tell them exactly where she lived. She sent money for a ticket on to Salinas. The bus arrived in Salinas about 2 am. No one was there to meet me. The only way I knew to get to Spider's place was to walk several blocks down Main Street, then down East Market Street, past some seedy bars that were just closing. Good thing I could run fast.

Spider claimed to have been a prize fighter, and Spider was his fighting name. He worked the night shift at Spreckels sugar plant and he went to bed about four in the afternoon. So everyone else had to. He went to work at midnight, I think. Jerry, Donny, David and Linda all slept on an army cot in the kitchen. They were supposed to get in bed and be quiet. I was expected to sleep there, too, but took Linda and got on the couch after Mother and Spider went to bed.

There wasn't much food in the house. Mother was not working and was in bed most of the time. Skipper was just a few months old, and I guess she had not quite recovered. I guess she didn't have the money to do better. I saw that I had to take charge of the kids. I informed Mother and Spider that two of us would sleep on the couch. There would be no more taking turns staying up at night to keep the buggy rolling to keep Skipper from crying. He belonged to her and Spider and the buggy would be put in the bedroom with them. Spider had a fit! "No smarty pants kid was going to tell him what to do. He used to be a prize fighter" he said "and he could knock out all my teeth with one punch." "That's right!" I said, sticking out my chin, "That's all you are! An old has been. Go ahead and hit me. I would love to have something to show the cops!" He didn't hit me. He sure did want to though.

School was out a few days after I got there. I took Jerry with me and we worked in the carrots and garlic. A bus was provided for the workers. It picked us up at 6 am and we got home about 3 pm. Donny, about nine years old was in charge of David and Linda. In the evening after feeding the kids, I walked several miles to a babysitting job. I had to be there by 7pm. The woman didn't have a car. She rode to and from work with a co-worker. She got home a little after 2 AM. I walked home. To get there I had to walk down Main Street and Market Street again, in the bad part of town as the drunken creeps were leaving the bars. It's a good thing I could out run them. I had no idea what they wanted me for. I thought they were after whatever money I might have. One night I decided I was not going to run from them anymore. I had learned about the horoscope and that I am a Leo. When the creep who had chased me every night started following me, instead of running, I turned and faced him. With all my might I summoned up my "inner Lion," and stared at him trying to look like a ferocious Lion. I also had asked my Guardian Angles to be with me in case it didn't work. It did.

I knew I had to make Spider afraid of me. With a hammer I found somewhere I put a stop to the abuse and the attempted sexual abuse. I didn't know anything about sex, but knew he shouldn't try to remove my cloths at night when I was asleep. I started sleeping in my Levis with the hammer in my hand. One Sunday I had fixed dinner (with the money Jerry and I made, we had better food now) and had just poured the gravy from the skillet into a bowl. Mother's friend Lola and her two boys were there. Everyone was seated at the table. Instead of putting the bowl on the table, I put it upside down on Spiders head. He yelled and went to the sink. Mother helped him, both of them yelling at me. The kids didn't move or make a sound. Lola giggled.

I wanted to run, but knew I had to act like I wasn't scared half to death. I don't think I could have made my feet move anyway. I think I could feel my knees knocking. After everything settled down Mother asked me why I did such a terrible thing. I said as calmly as I could, "He knows." I said. Looking at him I said, "Keep it up and see what you get." I had forgotten all about that event until Jerry mentioned it several years ago. We wandered what else I might have forgotten. I didn't want to know. I still don't. What I do know is I became a stronger and hopefully better person by overcoming difficult situations in my life. There have been many, but I know I didn't overcome them alone. There was always help and guidance available. I just had to ask, open my mind and heart and listen and do my best to make things better.

When I was 14 I became pregnant. When Mother told me I was pregnant, I thought she was lying. Why would God want me to have a baby when I already had my hands full? She told me the baby was Buds.(the nephew of a friend of Mother's.) He had been hanging around a lot. His Aunt and Uncle lived next door. What did she mean the baby was Bud's? Now I knew she had lost her mind! If I had a baby in my body, how could it be his? It was in my body, not his. And men didn't have babies!

No, I did not know how one gets pregnant. I thought that when God wanted a woman to have a baby, he blessed her with one. I had heard that many times. I didn't know men had anything to do with it. I learned later how I became pregnant. Mother had to make a choice between me and Spider. She had tried to send me away again, but I refused to go. Bud had told her that he loved me and wanted to marry me. He had told me that and I had told him I was not old enough, and anyway I hardly knew him.

So he and Mother decided that she and Spider would take the kids for an outing and tell me I couldn't go because there was not enough room in the car. Bud would take me to a movie. After the others were gone, Bud said it was too early to leave for the movies, so we would have some coke that he had brought. I woke up lying on the army cot. Bud was gone. I was bleeding a little bit and hurting. I thought I had started my period.

In the following two or three months, several times I would wake up and not remember going to sleep. I learned later that I had been drugged by Bud, and he had sex with me, intending to get me pregnant. His and Mother's plan worked. I went to the library and learned about sex. Mother told me if I didn't get married Ithe baby would be taken away from me. Bud and I were married in June, I was 15 in August. Bud wasn't a "bad guy" on purpose. Trouble just seemed to find him. He was very charming, and everyone thought he was wonderful. When I saw that he would never be the kind of father my kids deserved I wanted a divorce. I had no money and no car. I went to see an attorney, and he told me I couldn't get a divorce if we lived in the same house. I was stuck. I was not yet of legal age and Bud was my guardian, or so I was told. I had no say so about anything. My body was not my own. He did as he pleased with it. I am not sorry I have all my kids. I love them whole heartedly. What I do regret is that my first seven were not conceived with love. Bud never left any bruises on me. Not ones that could be seen.

One day I had been hanging cloths on the line and walked into the house just as Bud backhanded Vincent and knocked him off of the kitchen chair he was standing on. I didn't say anything to him, I took care of Vincent. Bud was drunk again. I waited until he passed out on the couch. The kids were all in bed sleeping. I rolled Bud onto the floor, took some cloths line rope and hog tied him. Then I stuffed hid mouth full of his dirty socks, and then gagged him with a baby diaper. The diapers back then were big square cloths. Taking one of his leather belts, I whipped him from his shoulders to his knees, as hard as I could. That woke him up. I whipped some more, while telling him if he ever dared to hurt my kids I would use a knife next time instead of a belt. I called the Sheriffs Dept. and told them what I had done and wanted them to be there before he managed to get loose. Four officers arrived. They made him promise he would not hurt me before they untied him. And said if he didn't behave, they would arrest him. He behaved very well after that. If he started anything, I would remind him he had to sleep sometime. Four months after that he was in jail again for writing bad checks and theft.

In 1958 I was pregnant with my seventh child and with the help of the Legal Aid Society, managed to at last end a very bad marriage. They had just opened an office in Salinas. Louon took me there. After hearing my story, Mr. Stewart, the lawyer, informed us that their job was to defend people who have been charged with a crime and can't afford an attorney. I got up and started for the door. Louon asked where I was going. I told him I was going to go kill my husband so my kids could have a chance for a better life. I had tried every way I could to get away from him and nothing worked. Then I asked Mr. Stewart if he would defend me if I did that. He told me to sit down. He went to consult with the other lawyers. When he came back he said they would do it, and all it would cost me was court costs.

When I met Howard the kids and I were living on Strawberry Canyon Road in Prundale. Debra was just a few months old. My oldest was ten. My whole life was dedicated to taking care of my kids and building a life for us. The night I met Howard, he and his nephew Jim, who was in the army, had met a waitress, who was a tenant of a cousin of my ex. Bonny and I were friends. I stopped by to see her occasionally when I had to go to Salinas. She was always telling me I had to have some recreation. So when her tenant called her from work and asked if she, Jim and Howard could come over to her place after she got off work, Bonny said yes. Howard and Jim went there, but the waitress had not arrived. I didn't have a phone, and she, Howard and Jim came to ask me to come to her place. I was not about to get in a car with two guys I didn't know but told them if I could get a baby sitter, I would drive myself there. A teenage boy reluctantly agreed to baby sit for a couple of hours. The kids were asleep in bed. I went to Bonny's, but the waitress never showed up. Jim turned on the radio and asked me to dance with him. He was getting a little too friendly. He was a child of 19, and I was a mature woman of 24. I was rather nervous about the whole situation. I went into the kitchen to get a drink of water and to get away from him. I felt a kiss on the back of my neck. Thinking it was Jim, I said sternly, "Alright now!" Howard said, "Right now?" Up to then he had been sitting quietly, not saying a word. When I whirled around, I must have looked funny because he snorted and some snot escaped from his nose. There he stood, wiping his nose, wearing a faded flannel shirt and jeans. He looked like he had not had a haircut for a long time. His curly hair reminded me of Bamba the Jungle Boy.

He then went into the living room and with a leap, grabbed hold of the beam going across the middle of the room, where a wall had been removed. He hung by his knees and did a very good imitation of a monkey, scratching, blinking his eyes and making monkey noises. Well, with that I decided it was time for me to go home! Somewhere along the way, the brother of the waitress arrived. His name was Jimmy and he was also 19. He asked if he could go home with me. I told him no. He begged. I told him I didn't have any place for him to sleep. I had seven kids, and I slept on a couch. No, it never occurred to me he wanted to do more than sleep.

I went out to the car, but discovered my keys were missing. I went back in the house. Howard and Jim took Jimmy outside and returned with my keys. Howard followed me out to the car and asked if he could come to see me. I said if he was interested in coffee and conversation, OK. But if he was interested in anything else, go someplace else, and drove off. He had heard me say I had seven kids, so I figured I didn't have to worry about him showing up.

A few days later he came to call. At first, I didn't recognize him. He'd gotten a haircut and was nicely dressed. While we were talking threw the screen door, I latched it. As he was telling me he lived just over the hill in the next little canyon, he took out his pocket knife and slipped it in the crack and flipped the latch, opened the screen door and walked in. He said, "You offered me some coffee." I had a fresh pot which I had made for Daddy, who had come to visit, and left a few minutes before. In my nervousness, I poured three cups. He asked who the third cup was for. Thinking fast, I said it was for the flies. My landlord had pigs, they attracted flies and with the kids coming in and out all day, I was always fighting the flies. When we finished our coffee, there was three flies in the third cup, and none in ours. He came over almost every day for a couple of weeks in the daytime, because I told him he couldn't come after dark. It was summertime, and the kids were always at home. Then he started coming at night, after the kids were in bed. I often went to sleep when he was there. Taking care of seven kids, two of them not very healthy, was exhausting. He would put a blanket over me; turn off the light and TV and leave. After about six months I decided this couldn't go on. He was 29 and had never been married. I asked him to stay away, but he didn't. So I found another place to rent in Salinas, packed up and moved without telling him my plans. About a month later he opened the door and walked in, pulled his shoes off, picked up a newspaper, and asked for a cup of coffee. He said I couldn't get rid of him that easy, so I might as well marry him. We were living just down the street from Betty and her family. The word spread about Howard. Louon came to talk to me about it. I asked him if he would buy a pair of shoes without trying them on, or if he would buy a car without taking it for a test drive. He would not. Well, marriage was a lot more important than those things, and I was taking it for a test drive. He said OK, you know what you are doing so I will shut up and go home.

He has been in our lives ever since. We agreed we would try it out, living as man and wife for two years. At the end of that time, if either of us wanted to end it, we could. Or if it was working out, we would get married. I had been stuck for ten years in a bad marriage and was not going to take a chance on repeating that mistake. It hasn't been perfect, but we are still together. Howard always treated my kids as well as he did the two we had together.

This was written several years ago. The following is an update.

Howard was diagnosed with Lymphoma in 2002. He had surgery and Chemotherapy. It didn't make him as sick as the horror stories we had heard about it. He didn't lose all his hair, but his beautiful curly hair got brittle and a lot of it broke off. There's several kinds of Lymphoma, and he didn't have the deadly ones. He seemed to recover, but never really regained his strength. A year or two later, he was getting weaker by the day. I never left the house more than a few minutes at a time unless I could get someone to stay with him. After a while I never left the room he was in for more than a few minutes. At first, he refused to see a Doctor. His feet and legs were turning black. Then the time came when I could not get him into bed. I helped him to the bed and helped him sit on it. We managed to get him turned straight, but his legs, from the knees on down were hanging off the bed. Our cedar chest is at the foot of the bed and I put pillows and blankets on it and managed to make him as comfortable as possible. The next day he let me take him to my Doctor. Loren and Jay helped get him in the car. I had to get the Fire Department to help get him into the office. The DR. said he had never seen such dead looking legs on a live person. He said they might have to be amputated. The next several days are a blur but he was admitted to the Hospital. He was there for one week, and then I was told there was nothing more they could do for him and he should be placed in a nursing home. No way! I arranged for a hospital bed to be set up in our living room facing the big windows so he could look out and see the birds he loved so much. Loren helped me take care of him. It was painful for him when he had to be touched. Repositioning him was torture for him and for us. But we did manage to keep him and his bedding dry. When he couldn't eat I fed him broth and water with a big syringe. He died in a week. He was cremated and his ashes are scattered in my garden. I saved some for Loren. He wants to scatter them in some of their special places.

It was heart wrenching to watch a man who had been so very strong and very smart waste away for all those years. I held myself together and didn't cry except at night while in bed with my face buried in a pillow. Until one day about a month later, I went to Costco to do the regular shopping. I put some things I always got for Howard in the cart and then I dropped to the floor and let it all out. Let it hell. I could not have stopped it. I alarmed a lot of people with loud sobbing. Someone called the Paramedics. They took me out to the ambulance and gave me oxygen. I had more or less gotten control of myself and explained what had happened. I did not need to go to the hospital. They stayed there until I was ready to go back to finish my shopping. One of them went with me. Since I was the widow of a retired fireman, there was no charge for the help.

This November 2018 will be three years since he died. I think of him every day and miss him so very much. We had been married for 53 years and together 55 years.

My oldest daughter, Diane was hit by a Sheriff's car answering a fake call. He was not using a siren or flashing lights. It was New Year's Eve 1985. She was only 26 years old. She and the son of a friend were crossing a street, in a crosswalk. Diane saw the car speeding towards them. She shoved the boy out of the way, and she was hit. When you lose a loved one, especially a child, it is like a piece has been torn from a blanket. You may learn to live with it, but that blanket will never be whole again. I still miss her and always will.

I am the seventh of twelve offspring. There's only three of us left. I'm afraid my blanket is very tattered. But it my blanket.

HERE COMES THE BRIDE

ALMOST DONE IN

COLLEEN CHAPMAN

Susan was getting married and there was no way I could make her dress. She lived in Ventura, Ca. and we lived at the river (by the Tule River, between Porterville and Springville, Ca.) We met at the house in Van Nuys. I think Vince, Teri and the kids lived there then. Anyway it was still in the family, so we could stay overnight there, and go shopping the next day. The first thing we did was to get her a long line bra with good, firm support. She is a big girl and has a very large breast. (size double Dang) She wore it to try on dresses, and when we got back to the house, she still had it on. We were pleased that we had found everything she needed for her wedding, and I could go home the next day.

As Sue was leaving, we stood in the doorway saying good-by. Just as she put her arm around my neck and pulled me close to her, someone said something to her. As she stood there talking with them, she didn't notice that her firm, well supported right breast was firmly pressed against my throat and face. I couldn't move. Couldn't breathe. My nose and mouth were muffled by her breast. My left arm was pinned between us, and my right arm was in a sling because I had a badly sprained wrist. The only thing I could do was try to pull away, but Sue just held me tighter. At last someone noticed I was in trouble and told Sue to let me go. She got teased a lot about her lethal weapons. Loren had a lot of fun telling everyone how Mom almost got done in by Sue's boobs.

CULTURE SHOCK

SANDRA JOHNSON

In 1962, I, a Californian, went to the Arkansas delta country to meet my husband's family. I was sixteen years old at the time. The experience was my first time out of central California. His family was a God fearing matriarchal family. It didn't take me long to figure out I wasn't in California any more. His people spent most of their time cooking, eating and praying. The main activity was church three times a week. The underground philosophy was the men tried to get away with all they could. Smoking, drinking and women. The women were in charge of the souls of the family. It all seemed a little childish to me. I was soon taken in hand by the young women of the clan and instructed on proper behavior.

GoGee, the matron of the clan was not to know I smoked. We all took a walk after meals and had a cigarette. On the way back, we would get weeds growing next to the road, crush them and rub them on ourselves to deaden the smell. Then took mints for our breaths. We then smelled like herbs, mints and cigarettes. Paw, the old man of the family, would sneak out of the house for his cigarette. They had indoor plumbing for years, but he went out every morning for his smoke. I asked if they thought all this fooled GoGee. It was generally accepted that she knew.

Men had fun and women didn't, was the basic message. The guys were playing basketball and I tried to join in. I was told to go in the kitchen and have coffee with the women. At an uncle's house, the men were shooting pool. I asked when my turn was. I was again told to go have coffee with the women. Coffee with the women was basically telling me how to be a good wife. I was to be my husband's Mama. Since he had a strong southern Mama, I figured I was off the hook.

One day I needed to wash cloths. My sister-in –law, who I still think is one of the neatest people I know, took me to town. I really needed to get away from *the family.* She did too. Our excuse was she needed a new red coat. There was a lot of joking about white people not wearing red in Arkansas. Anyway I thought it was a joke.

In this little delta town there were three stores. On one side of Main Street was the white store, and on the other side was the black store. Between the two was a groceries store run by a Chinese family and was referred to as the Chink store. We went to all three. The white store was a genealogy information place. "Where yawl from? Who are you related to? Tell Abbey Hi and I'll see yawl in church Sunday. Ain't got no red coat. Try that Nigger store across the street."

That store had the coat my sister-in –law wanted. We were invisible. There was no eye contact.

We did not belong and it was made very clear. That was OK. We had wasted a lot of time at the other store answering questions. I had to get detergent and stuff to do my laundry, so we went to the Chinese owned store. By the time we got through shopping our cart was full. We went up to pay and a black girl about my age stepped out of line for me to go before her. She only had a few things in her hand so I said, "Go ahead. I'm in no hurry." Again, no eye contact. She just stood there with her head down. I thought maybe she didn't hear me so again I said, "You go ahead. You have only a few things and I have all this. You go ahead." Things started feeling tense. My sister-in-law told me to go ahead. The girl didn't move. She just stood there looking at her shoes. So unwillingly I went before the girl. My sister-in-law laughed and told the clerk I was from California. All laugh, we go through who we are related to and do a genealogy rundown again. We'll see her in church too.

It was time to do the laundry. I go into the Laundromat and over the washers and dryers are signs. **Color, White.** No explanation as to why. I felt very fortunate to have a color machine and a white machine together. I always prided myself on having a logical mind. The best logic I could come up with was maybe they did a lot of dying of cloths and to put white cloths in a machine that had been used for dying would be a bad thing. I was putting my cloths in the colored machine, trying to think what that has to do with colored dryers, when a black gentleman came up to me and told me I couldn't do that. I pointed out that my clothes were colored and I was putting them in the colored machine. From the stopping of all the action in laundry, I got the impression my logic was wrong. My sister-in-law came over and explained I was from California. Then she explained to me the white and black referred to race, not fabric. My culture shock was constant the two weeks we were there. The family tried to educate me about the concept of race segregation, and I was a constant source of embarrassment and entertainment for them

GETTING MARRIED

C OLLEEN C HAPMAN

When Pearl got married it made quite an impression on me. I didn't know what married was, really. All I knew was she didn't live at home any more, and she and Louon seemed to have an awful lot of fun. One day I had a really good idea. Louon's family, the Fishers, lived next door to us. His brother Randall was about my age. I convinced him we didn't have to mind our parents any more if we were married and lived in the chicken coop. The coop hadn't been used in a long time, so we got busy. We got a rake somewhere and an old broom. After raking and sweeping, we squirted it out with a hose. We got as wet as the coop did. Daddy came to see what we were up to. All we told him was that we wanted to make a playhouse in the coop. He helped us get it washed down and told us to stay out of it until it got dry. Then he sent us in the house to get washed up and changed.

We scoured the neighborhood looking for things to use. By the next day the coop was dry and we put furniture inside. We had apple boxes, old dishes and a few bent up tin pans and an old baby bed mattress. We took some cloths and a blanket for each of us and put them in the boxes. The mattress wasn't big enough for both of us. It took some doing, but Randall agreed that since I could beat him at wrestling, I could have it. He would get another blanket to sleep on.

We didn't know where to go to get married, but we knew Pearl and Louon had gone someplace important to do it, because they had gotten all dressed up. We decided they must have gotten married at the Post Office. That's where everyone went for important papers. We knew they had a paper that said they were married. We cleaned ourselves up, and away we went. We lived in Safford, which was a small town. I was pretty sure I knew the way to the Post Office. We didn't realize that Daddy and Mr. Fisher were following us. Just as we started up the steps to the Post Office, they picked us up and asked what we were doing. When we told them, they sat on a bench and laughed.

"Where will you live if you get married? With us or with the Fishers?" Daddy asked. "We would live by ourselves in the chicken coop." said I, standing in front of him with my hands on my hips. "Yeah. The chicken coop." Randall said.Mr. Fisher said, "can you cook, do house work, the washing, all that kind of stuff?" "We don't have to! I have that all figerd out. Duz will do it!" I said, feeling smug. "Who?" said Daddy and Mr. Fisher at the same time. I took a deep breath and rolled my eyes. They were so dumb! "You know, that lady on the pancake box. Her name is Duz. And the radio is always telling us that Duz does everything. So we are going to get Duz to come live with us. After we get married we're gonna go to the radio station to get her." I explained patiently. "Yeah, Radio Station." Randall said. Daddy and Mr. Fisher asked more questions for which we had no answers. We began to realize we didn't have things worked out as well as we thought we did.

They picked us up and carried us home, laughing most of the way. Randall and I decided we would live in the chicken coop anyway, and go home only to eat. I sneaked out of the house that night and waited for Randall. Soon he came out dragging a blanket. Wrapped in our blankets and lying on our stomaches, we had just gotten as comfortable as possible, when we noticed it was VERY dark! Then we heard a noise nearby. All we could see was a pair of eyes glowing in the dark. Coming closer! Maybe this was not such a good idea after all! We sat up, huddled together on our knees and pulled the blankets over our heads, peering out into the darkness.

"What's that?" Randall whispered in a trembling voice. "I don't know!" "Is it a lion?" "I don't know!"

"Is it going to eat us?" "I don't know. I think we better go home!" "I know!"

Terrified, we broke a speed record getting back in our houses. No more talk about leaving home!

An explanation for the young ones. I was obviously mixed up. I thought the picture of Aunt Jemima on the pancake box was a woman named Duz. Duz was the name of a detergent. The radio commercials said Duz does everything. Yeah, I know. Pretty dumb, huh. But after all, we were just four or five years old.

UNCLE WALTER AND AUNT JESSIE

RUBY GREEN

Uncle Walter was my favorite before he met Aunt Jessie. He used to joust me on his knee and he called me cotton top. He called Pearl Fatty Arbuckle. He played with us a lot. Mother told me he worked under cover for a while for the police. I am guessing it was for a local police station.

It seems there was a gang of young men doing a lot of mischief, really doing a lot of bad damage and causing the Police a lot of trouble. They needed someone to spy on them, so they could put a stop to it. Uncle Walter joined the gang and spied on them, under cover. It was a dangerous thing to do, but he was able to get the information the Police needed without getting hurt.

I remember the first time he brought Jessie Osbourn home to meet the folks. She was a big girl. She was strong. Her dad had a farm and she was used to doing work on the farm. I thought it was so funny when to show how strong she was, she picked Uncle Walter up and carried him around the house. She laughed and talked a lot.

I was a little jealous when they got married. But she was so friendly and was always happy and cheerful. She paid a lot of attention to all us kids. She quickly became a favorite aunt. I never saw her angry or unhappy. Uncle Walter loved her very much. The both of them just adopted all the nieces and nephews and loved us and we loved them. We were always glad when they came to visit. They were not blessed with children of their own. They would have been good parents. They loved kids so much. We all loved them dearly. I have fond memories of them.

Sandra...I am a great grandniece of Walter and Jessie. Jessie is the first person I ever met who was a hugger. I loved to see them come for a visit but I would try to hide from the first greetings. It never worked. Jessie was loud and when she got hold of us kids she would hug and kiss us until we thought we would be suffocated by her love. She had big breasts and it was a little scary to be caught up in there. I loved her and always knew she was extra special. She was such a happy person and a joy to be around. I never heard anything but good things about Walter and Jessie. I can't think about them without smiling. They were a gift to our family.

DEBRA'S WEDDING

COLLEEN CHAPMAN

The day Debra and Ken got married was cold, windy and raining. Howard had to work the day before. His shift ended at six or seven AM, but the firefighter who replaced him was late. Howard had to drive from LA to Porterville, bad weather all the way. The road over the mountain was bad enough in good weather. It is called the Grapevine. He got there, very tired, just in time to get ready to go to the church. He had forgotten his dark blue suit which was in his locker at the station. He had worn it to a firemen's retirement dinner the week before. The only suit he had at home was a light tan suit meant for summer. He did not like wearing a suit and tie.

The best man, Winston, was standing by a back door, letting people in from the parking lot. When the wind shifted and blew rain onto him, he stepped just inside the door, leaving it open a crack, so he could see people when they approached. There was a very loud clap of thunder just as he closed the door all the way. He looked at his grandmother who was frowning at him. He pointed to himself and shook his head, then pointed up and nodded.

I was talking to someone when the organist began playing "Here comes the bride", and we just kept talking. When she started over, and I realized it was otherwise quiet, it got my attention. I stood up and turned to look at a giggling Debra on Howard's arm, waiting. Susan, the maid of honor, came first. She was slightly limping. Oh no. Another sprained ankle? Then Debra and Howard started down the aisle.

Her veil was crooked and sliding slowly. She managed to tilt her head a little to the left to keep it from slipping more. They made it through the ceremony with the Preacher pausing during the many claps of rumbling thunder. After the ceremony, I went to the rest room and when I came back there was no one in the church. I knew there was to be a reception, but I didn't know where the room was, where it was to be held. Then I heard noise coming from below, found the stairs, and the room.

Several things had gone wrong. The bridesmaid's dresses had not been delivered to the church, so they had to wear what they had on. Fortunately, they all looked nice. Sue had to walk down the aisle with the heel broken off of her left shoe. She managed to do it gracefully by walking on her tiptoes of her left foot. I wandered if the storm and all that had gone wrong was an indication of what might lay ahead for Debra and Ken. But after we left the church and reached the highway, the rain stopped, the sun came out and there ahead of us were three …yes, three rainbows! We could see them from end to end very clear and bright, going from one side of the road to the other. I had left my camera with Debra, so didn't get a picture, but that sight still lives in my memory.

HOLIDAYS

A SPECIAL EASTER

C O L L E E N   C H A P M A N

When my children began families of their own, I decided I would not cause a conflict about where they would spend the holidays. They could do whatever they wanted, and it was OK with me. Except for Easter. That was mine. Everyone who could came home for Easter. Even some of my kid's friends and their kids wanted to come to our place for Easter. It was not unusual to have 30 or 40 people there for the whole week-end. Everyone did their share of work and bringing supplies, and everything went smoothly.

One Easter was more special than usual because it was the first Easter, since the kids had started leaving home, that we would all be together. My niece and nephew, Michael and Angie were with us too. I was troubled by the fact that those two had no idea what Easter was really all about. And although some of my grandkids had been taught about it, it was not done in a way that they could really understand. Besides that, I didn't like the way some of my sons had let their hair grow long and had beards. Yeah, I know, they are adults and have a right...... But I still didn't like it and had a right to let my feelings be known. This Leo learned a long time ago that roar, and you just might get roared back at. I do not roar. Well, not very often. When I do, it seems to scare everyone half to death. Or tickle them half to death in some cases. Anyway, I hit upon a way to take care of both problems at the same time. I went to a turkey ranch and bought some eggs. Most of the eggs I cleaned, boiled, and decorated them extra nice. I left 4 of them just as they came. Really yucky!

On Easter Sunday after telling the little kids the Easter story; I showed them a raw egg. I broke it into a bowl. Then I cracked a hardboiled egg. They could understand that they were both eggs, and how one egg had been changed, but was still an egg. That helped them to understand the change in the body of Jesus when he was raised from the dead. I also worked in some other things they needed to know or understand, then (of course the older kids were listening) we talked about what is on the inside is more important than what is on the outside. Then I put the yucky eggs (that no one had seen yet) next to the pretty clean and decorated eggs, and asked which they would choose, if they didn't know what was on the inside. If all they had to go by was what they could see. The point being, a first impression is formed by what is seen. Not many people would want to get to know a yucky looking person but would be attracted by a nice looking clean one. The kids said they understood. I hoped my older sons got the point also. I was very pleased with my success when my sons showed up a weekend later, with haircuts and clean shaven. AFTER THE JACKASS MAIL RUN WHICH IS A BIG DEAL IN SPRINGVILLE. WHICH IS WHAT THEY GREW THE BEARD AND HAIR FOR AND DIDN'T TELL ME AND NO DOUBT HAD A BALL WATCHING ME STEW ABOUT IT!

I think that was the Easter I rented a rabbit costume. Howard had brought home some motorcycle helmets which had no padding. With a bail of hay I made a big nest. Then turned some of the helmets upside down and snuggled into the hay. Robert was the first one to get into the bunny suit and sat on the nest. I told the kids the eggs were hidden on a level clearing below the house. I led them down the hill and around a bend in the trail. There they saw the giant rabbit and giant eggs. They all stopped and stared. Brian recovered first and shouted, "holey shit!" They tried to figure out who was in the suit while hunting eggs. I managed to get them around the bend so Rob Had a chance to get out of the suit and Vince got in.

They had decided it had to be Rob because they had not seen him with the rest of us. Just then Rob came trotting down the hill and said he was sorry he was late. The kids ran to see if the bunny was still there. The kids looked around to see who was missing. Someone said it must be Vince. But no, he had gone to the house to get some sodas. Well, they would go to the house to see if Vince was there. I slowed them down by telling them that eggs were hidden along the trail too. Rob and Vince did the quick change again. Vince came down the trail with the sodas. One of the kids said they didn't know how Vince and Rob did it, but they wanted to see them at the same time.

It was a drizzly day and Debra said some of the kids in Springville didn't get to have an Easter Egg Hunt. Sooo, we put a box in the bed of Debra and Ken's pick-up. All the kids sat on blankets on the bed of the pick-up. They took all the candy we had and went to Springville. (about three miles up the road.) When they saw kids they tossed candy to them and Rob occasionally got out and talked to them. Pearl and I were following them in my car. As Debra was stopped for traffic before pulling back onto the highway a little boy was standing in his yard. Rob waved at him and the kids tossed the last of the candy. While Pearl and I were waiting our turn to get on the highway, the boy went to the door and yelled, "MOM! I SAW A GIANT EASTER BUNNY!" The mother said, "What did I tell you about saying things that are not true? Now get in here and go to your room!"

When we got home I told what we had heard. Deb and Rob looked at each other, Rob zipped up the suit and they went to the pick-up. When they got back they said Rob knocked on the door. The mother opened the door, screamed and slammed it.

CHRISTMAS SPIRIT

COLLEEN CHAPMAN

December of 1958 I was 24 years old, pregnant with my seventh child, and had just sued for divorce. We were living in Chular CA., a very small town. When we had to move because I didn't have money to pay the rent, Louon, Pearl's husband, arranged for us to move into a storage room attached to an empty building that had once been a grocery store. It was only $25.00 a month rent.

The furniture consisted of an old table with a two burner camp stove, and a set of bunk beds for the four boys. There was not room for the girl beds, so Diane, Susan and I shared a full size bed. We had no radio or TV. We had a few children's books, and a few little toys. That and our few boxes of clothing, our bedding and dishes were all we had.

A week or so before school was out for Christmas, the kids and I all had chest colds. To make matters worse, it rained and rained and rained. The roof leaked, and the only way I could keep all of us dry was to put all of us on the full size bed. Thankfully, the roof didn't leak over that bed!I found a sheet of plastic and draped it over the bunk bed to keep it dry.

Two days before school was out for Christmas, Diane was well enough to go to school. When she came home, her eyes were all aglow, and with a radiant smile she described the Christmas tree at school, and sang some of the songs they had sung that day. Then she asked, "Mom, what can I take to school tomorrow? We are all going to bring something to school to give to the poor people." The poor people? What does she think *we* are! "Who are these poor people?" I asked. "You know, people who don't have any body that cares about them". She said.

We managed to find a dry spot for the stove. Using the last of our sugar and butter, we began to make a batch of fudge for the poor people. The roof began to leak on the stove. Dave remembered seeing a piece of plastic in the old store. He got it, and the four bigger kids stood on boxes and chairs and held the plastic over the stove. Laughing at the ridiculous situation, a big batch of fudge was finished. We each had a piece and then took a piece of cloth left over from a dress I had made for one of the girls, and a hair ribbon, we made a pretty bundle for Diane to take to school.

I learned a valuable lesson from my innocent little girl that day. You can be without material things, have no money, and still be rich.

DON'T OPEN THE DOOR

DOROTHY PATTON

I got Halloween flashlights for Jared and Leif the weekend before Halloween, and after dark on Sunday night they wanted to try them out. They also wanted to make a fort. So we set chairs around the room and spread a sheet over them, turned off the lights and lay down under the sheet with the flashlights and made shadow figures on the sheet.

Both the boys can make really good alligators with their mouths opening and closing. And with the sheet so close they were very big and scary. Then I made a giant hand with bony fingers reaching down, all the while moaning and groaning. Finally, Jared said, "Granma, stop making that noise. It's too scary." "Let's turn on the lights." Leif said.

Just then a knock came on the back door. "If it's your parents they'll come on in," I said. We waited and the knock came again, louder this time. I started to crawl out from under the sheet but both boys held me back. "Don't open the door!" they said. "It's probably Betty," (my neighbor) I said. Finally they let me go and I turned on the light and opened the door and it was Geoff come to pick them up. I didn't remember locking the door. "Oh, Daddy, I'm glad it's you." Jared said. "I thought it was a ghost!"

DON'T TELL ME I CAN'T

COLLEEN CHAPMAN

As Howard was getting ready to leave for work one Halloween he asked what my plans were. I answered, "Oh, I don't know. I'll take the little kids around the neighborhood, I guess, the others are going to parties, and then I guess I'll go TP the fire station." I really didn't mean that, but when he said, "Hah! Don't even try. You won't be able to do it." Well, he shouldn't have said I couldn't!

The younger kids were in bed, worn out from the excitement of trick or treating. Our neighbors, Diana and Skipper were spending the night, and their mother, Kathy had agreed to babysit for a couple of hours. Diane and her friend Vicki were getting ready to go to a party. Diane asked why I was dressed in black and putting six rolls of toilet paper in a bag. I explained what I was up to. She and Vicki asked if they could go with me. And if TP'ing one station was good, wouldn't every station Howard had ever been stationed at be better? I put more TP in the bag.

We went to Howard's station first. We couldn't get to the parking lot without driving alongside the building, so we parked next to the brick wall that separated the station and a grocery store parking lot. We climbed on top of the car, got on top of the fence, and jumped to the ground. We TP'd all the cars in the lot, then the fire engines, being careful not to do anything to interfere with driving if they had to go on a run.

For a finishing touch I made a big bow with TP, and crawled, holding the bow with my teeth, toward the screen door separating the garage from the kitchen. The door opened. I froze, about 10 feet from the door. Herb stopped, looking back and talking to someone. What am I going to do if he sees me? Say trick or treat, or meow, I thought as I waited. He closed the door and went back to finish the conversation. That was close. I tied the bow to the door and made my escape.

To get back over the wall, Vicki and I raised Diane enough for her to get on top of the wall. She got on the car and leaned over the wall. She pulled and I pushed Vicki up. Then they leaned over the wall and pulled me up.

Next, we went to two stations Howard had been assigned to in the past, then to the one closest to home. The gate to the parking lot was locked. We entered and left the same way we had at the first station. I almost got caught again. I was between two engines that were parked one behind the other in the garage. I keep calling it garage. It is called the apparatus floor by the firemen.

A fireman came out of the office, looking at a paper. I froze. He walked right by me on his way to the kitchen. I didn't finish that engine, thinking it best to leave. As we were leaving we didn't see the police car parked just down the alley. A policeman appeared out of the dark and asked what we were up to. After we explained, he took a look at the TP'd cars and said he wouldn't "run us in" if we would TP the police cars in the police parking garage. He said it is guarded, so be careful. We had Vicki act as our decoy, and flirt with the guard while Diane and I TP'd the cars. So there! Don't tell ME I can't!

EASTER APPARRAL

RUBY GREEN

When Pearl and I were little girls, we had some neighbors, the Gentry's. Dorothy Gentry was my age. She was a really good friend. I loved her voice. I can still hear her saying, "my name is Dorothy Fay Gentry. I was born on the 28th-a-June in 1922" She, Pearl and I had lots of fun playing together. Her mother (Ruby Gentry) worked cleaning house for a rich woman. Every year at Easter time, Ruby Gentry would buy pretty fabric for Easter dresses. She would buy enough for Dorothy and Pearl and me and have our mother make them. We would be so pretty in our new Easter dresses.

One year she also bought some anklets (socks) and some pretty silky rayon panties for all of us. It was the first store bought panties we ever had. They felt sooo silky and luxurious. They were so pretty. When we went to church, Pearl just couldn't stand to have such pretty panties on and no one knowing it. So while sitting in the Church bench, she would pull up her dress very primly, at the side of her thigh and little bottom, so everyone could see that she had on pretty silky panties.

I was so embarrassed and would reach over and pull her dress down to cover her panties. But when she thought I was not paying any more attention to her, she would pull up her dress again. I would repeat pulling her dress down. That went on all through the service. Walking home from church, She would jump and hop and accidentally get her dress caught in her hand, so her pretty pink panties would show. When we got home, I told Mother what had happened and Pearl said "what good does it do to wear pretty silky panties if no knows it?" Mother seemed to agree, so I just had to live with my embarrassment.

LIVERTY

COLLEEN CHAPMAN

Debra was in the first grade and very proud that she had learned The Pledge of Allegiance, God Bless America and other old, patriotic songs we all learned in school. As we sat around the table for our Thanksgiving dinner, we did the usual thing, each one telling what they are thankful for. Debra said she was glad and thankful that our country, Tizovthee, is a land of liverty. She innocently munched on a piece of turkey, not noticing everyone else had stopped eating and sat looking at her. "Why did you say our land is named Tizovthee?" I asked. "A song says so. It says. 'My country, Tizovthee, sweet land of Liverty'. See?" "And what is liverty?" "That means there is plenty of liver to eat so we can be healthy and strong." Some explanations were needed. And maybe a word or two to her school teacher

Debra was anemic and I had brain washed her into liking liver when she was old enough to eat solid food. She knew liver had a lot to do with her growing healthy and strong. I agree. God bless liver!

THERE'S NO SUCH THING

COLLEEN CHAPMAN

Christmas was coming soon. Our little neighbor Diana was very excited about Santa coming and talked about it a lot. One day she was sitting on our front steps waiting for Loren. Rusty came out of the back yard and sat on the steps to tie his shoelaces. Diana started talking about Santa again. In exasperation Rusty said, "Oh Diana! There's no such thing as Santa Clause!" Diana looked shocked and exclaimed, "Yes there is!" Rusty, being a very practical nine-year-old, said, "Think about it. In the first place, if there was a Santa, he could live anyplace he wanted to, so why would he live in a miserable, cold place like the North Pole? That's dumb. Where would he get the supplies to make all the stuff? And how could one sleigh be big enough to carry stuff for everyone? Besides, reindeer can't fly. Even if they could the sleigh would hang down and all the stuff would fall out. How could he go all around the whole world in one night? And he's supposed to come down the chimneys? Did you ever see a picture of Santa with soot and ashes on his cloths? What if there's a fire in the fireplace? What about houses that don't have fire places? Is he supposed to go through the gas pipes and into the furnaces and heaters? So you can see it's just a dumb fairy tale. It seems to me they could have thought up something that makes a little bit of sense."

Diana sat staring into space. She didn't make a sound as big tears ran down her face. Rusty looked at her and obviously wished he hadn't said all those things. After all, she was only four years old. He hung his head and started to walk away. He looked at her again and sat back down. He put his hand on her shoulder and said, "Don't cry Diana. I wasn't through yet. You see, what he really is, is a rich old man with a go-cart. He lives in New York and he hires a lot of other old men all over the world to help him. They use go-carts and trailers because go-carts are low to the ground and can get around without us seeing them if we look out the window. They made quiet motors for them. They made up the other story so we would be watching the sky if we are awake and looking for him and wouldn't see them delivering stuff." Diana thought this over. Smiling as she wiped away the tears she asked, "Then there really is a Santa Clause?" "Yes Diana." Rusty said with a sigh.

WHO IS SCARING WHOM?

COLLEEN CHAPMAN

In the "olden days" when I was about nine years old, Betty and her friend Laura, who were about 13, were babysitting one night for Pearl and Louon. It was the night before Halloween, and I thought it would be fun to sneak up and scare them. I waited until about 9 o'clock and tried to get Fred to go with me. He wouldn't, so I asked Jerry. He said no, he was not getting out of bed. I took off by myself.

It was a very dark and cold night. The two-mile walk seemed to take much longer than it ever had before. I heard strange animal sounds but couldn't see anything. I stood still and looked around, nothing on the right, nothing on the left, but when I turned to look behind me, I saw two glowing eyes! It was too dark to run, I might stumble on something, but I ran anyway. Sure enough, I tripped on something and fell.

Before I could get up, the glowing eyes came closer! I lay on my stomach and buried my face in my arms, waiting to be eaten by some horrible animal. It came closer. I couldn't see it but could hear it breathing. Then I felt its breath on my neck. It sniffed, and then licked my neck. Oh God, I begged, don't let it like the taste! Then it licked and whined, and nudged me, and whined again. Peeking out of my arms, I saw it! It was a dog that followed us kids around all the time. For once I didn't tell him to go home. I hugged him.

When we got to Pearl's house the dog ran off to play with another dog. I could see Betty and Laura in the living room, dancing to music playing softly from the radio. Taking the string from my pocket, I attached it to a nail, and then attached it to a window screen. Holding the other end of the string, I stood in the dark past the light that came from the big window. I took the piece of rosin from my pocket and rubbed it slowly up and down on the string. It made a creepy sound. Betty and Laura stopped dancing and stood very still. Then Betty turned the radio off. I made the noise again. They hugged each other and stared at the window, their eyes big with fright. I did the string thing again. They both ran and crouched down behind the rocking chair, holding on to the slats, and looking through them, at the window. After making the noise a few more times, I let the string go, and went a distance from the house so they wouldn't hear me laugh. Then I started home.

By this time there was a small sliver of moon giving a little light. Deciding to take a shortcut through a pasture, I climbed over the fence. There were a lot of cows in the pasture, but I had done this before, and knew they wouldn't bother me. But some of the cows seemed to be a little upset about something. Then I heard a noise off to one side that didn't sound like a cow. I didn't want to look! But how could I not? Turning slowly toward the low, moaning sound, I saw a slight movement of something white. These cows didn't have any white on them. I wanted to run, but my feet wouldn't cooperate. The moaning came nearer, but I couldn't see the white thing. It wasn't where I saw it before. Then the moaning stopped. Everything was very still and quiet. Even the cows were quiet and still. I began to relax a little bit and turned to continue on my way. Then the white thing was in the air and coming toward me! Screaming, I turned to run, and ran into a cow, and fell on my back. The white thing landed on top of me...and I could hear Jerry laughing. The white thing was a sheet. He had it over him, and after letting me get a glimpse of him, he hid behind a cow. Then He slid up on the cows back while I was not looking in that direction, and crouched there, holding the sheet, and waiting for me to look in that direction. When I did, he jumped into the air, holding the sheet high over his head, and then threw it over me as I lay on the ground. After I recovered from the awful scare he had given me, we started home. We kept telling each other that the noises we heard were the same ones we hear in the daytime, nothing to be afraid of. Now all we had to do was sneak back in the house and get to bed without waking anyone. Especially Mother!

There was a big tree in the yard, and it cast some scary shadows between the house and us. There was some light coming from some windows, so we had to walk under the tree to stay out of the light. Just as we approached the tree, a shining skeleton, with a rope around its neck, dropped from the tree right in front of us. We both screamed and fell backwards. Fred and two of his friends, Sonny and Hootie, jumped down and rolled on the ground with laughter. The skeleton was Sonny's Halloween costume, filled with crumpled up newspaper. Then we saw the light come on in Mother and Daddy's bedroom. Sonny and Hootie took off for home.

We rushed to climb in a window and got into bed with our clothes on and pulled the covers up to our necks. We could hear Mother and Daddy talking. Daddy had gone outside but didn't see anyone. Mother checked us kids. Mother knew darn well she had heard a scream, and hysterical crying. She wandered if they should call the police. Daddy said if they heard any more noise, he would call. I was tempted to stick my head out of the window and scream but decided there had been enough excitement for one night.

A SCARY HALLOWEEN

DOROTHY PATTON

I experienced the most terrifying Halloweens of my life when I was about fourteen years old. Kids didn't go trick or treating then in our part of the country, but some kids did play pranks. They would soap windows, turn over outhouses, make scary noises and whatever ornery thing they could think of. But I never took part in anything like that. I was babysitting that night with two little boys. It was getting pretty late, the boys had been asleep a long time, and I was in the living room reading by lamplight and trying to stay awake. Suddenly I heard a loud thump and the sound of breaking glass. The sound came from a room at the back of the house. I ran into the room where the boys were sleeping and locked the door. I thought it might be a Halloween prank, but couldn't believe that anyone would actually break a window as a prank. The only other explanation I thought was that a burglar had broken in. There was no telephone to call for help, but I knew there was a baseball bat in the corner of the bedroom. I felt around in the dark until I found it. For what seemed like forever, I stood behind the door with the bat ready for attack and said my prayers.

Finally, I heard a car in the driveway and knew the parents had come home. I told them what I had heard and they took the lamp and went to the back room but the window was not broken. We checked every window in the house, but none of them were broken. Then the man lit a lantern and went out and looked all around the house and yard but found no broken glass. By this time, they were giving me funny looks and I went home thinking they were sure I was losing my mind and would not let me babysit again. I depended on that money for movies and such. I was pretty mystified but knew that I had heard breaking glass. When I told my younger brother and sister about it the next morning we reached the conclusion that it had to have been a Halloween ghost. Because what else could have made the sound of breaking glass without actually breaking glass?

But later that day the lady I had been babysitting for came over to tell me that the mystery had been solved. There was a double chest of drawers in the back bedroom. A large, heavy mirror had been hanging on the wall above it. The mirror come loose from the wall and fell down behind the chest and broke. I was glad the people no longer thought that I was crazy and would let me babysit for them. But my sister and brother and I were disappointed that we had to give up the ghost story.

SHE MELTED!

COLLEEN CHAPMAN

This was not a prank, but it happened on April 1st many years ago. I don't remember if it involved Pearl, Sandra and Larry or Dorothy, Richard and Jackie. Whichever it was came to visit on a very cold day. She parked her car at the foot of the driveway because she didn't like to back down our rather long driveway. Although there was room to turn around in front of the house, she wouldn't, afraid she would run over or into something. I was fixing lunch when Pearl...or was it Dorothy....from now on I will refer to whoever it was as she......said she had brought some cookies she had made, but forgot to bring them in. She was about halfway down the driveway when a very cold, strong wind and a very heavy rain began. By the time she got back to the house she was soaked. As she went through the living room and kitchen, and into the playroom where the wood burning heater had a nice fire going, dripping water all the way, she said, "Brrrrrrr! I feel like a popsicle!"

The kids were sitting at the table in the kitchen. I told her to stay by the fire and thaw out and went to get some of my clothes for her to wear. I handed her the cloths and went back to finish getting lunch on the table. When finished, I put some lunch on a tray and..... Sandra, if "she" was Pearl, or Richard if "she" was Dorothy, went to take it to her. They came back into the kitchen looking upset. "I think Mom melted!" On a chair by the stove was a shirt draped over the back, a pair of jeans on the seat with the legs hanging down the front, and a pair of shoes on the floor next to the pants legs. She had spread them out to dry. There was water on the floor. The child was very relieved to learn she had decided to warm up in a bathtub full of hot water. Maybe she was Dorothy. She loved our big old fashion tub. I once accused her of not coming to see me, but to soak in my tub.

Yes, it was Dorothy. I remember teasing Richard about thinking his mom had melted. For years if he asked anyone where his mom was, the answer would be "look for a puddle" or "I don't know. She probably melted."

One day we were picnicking by the river and Richard was very mad a t Larry and Jacky. He said he wished he would hurry up and get as big as they are. Dorothy, Pearl and I buried him up to his chest in a hole we dug in the sand. While we did it we told him it would make him grow as fast as a weed. We would come and water him and feed him every day. He thought it was funny and didn't resist. Then we started gathering up our stuff, getting ready to go. The other kids were getting in the car and he began to look a little worried. He tried to get out of the sand but couldn't. We kissed him on the forehead and told him we would be back in the morning. He told us he really didn't want to grow all that fast. We let him convince us and dug him out.

AN ANGLE IN THE SKY

TAKEN FROM THE FAMILY SITE

Sue…..Our weather across the nation has seen its extremes in the past month or so. The weather brought us an extreme angel in the sky on Christmas Eve. As we were returning from visiting Aunt Pearl in Soledad, Mom and Aunt Dorothy looked up into the sky and saw the most awesomely perfect angel with beautiful wings and a flowing gown. At first, she looked like she was holding a book, and then it looked like she was blowing on a horn or bugle. It was inspiring

Dorothy…The cloud kept changing a little till it was out of sight but it always looked like an angel.

Ruby…I am reminded of the time--about two years before we left Oklahoma. It was in the summer. The clouds were stormy. Pearl and Dorothy Gentry were playing between our houses with the Gentry dogs. It was late afternoon or early evening. Daddy and Mr. Gentry were on our front porch talking. I was listening to their conversation. They were afraid Germany was going to have a war soon. Pearl and Dorothy came running up to the porch telling of a man's head in the clouds and had been there for a long time. They tried to get daddy and Mr. Gentry to come see. I wanted to see but the head had disappeared before I went to see. Daddy and Mr. Gentry just went on with their talking. A few weeks later, Dorothy Gentry came running over to our house to show us a man's picture in the paper. When Pearl saw it, she exclaimed "Oh, that's the man we saw in the sky!!!" Dorothy cried, "That's why I brought it for you to see". Then we started to read the paper. The man's name was Adolph Hitler. When daddy and Mr. Gentry saw it that night, they were really afraid a war was coming.

An angel appeared to the Sheppard the night Jesus was born. Do you think this angel you saw holding a book or a horn or bugle was trying to tell you something?

Colleen…I didn't think it was trying to tell us something. I did think it was more than a coincidence it appeared on Christmas Eve. I took a picture of it but had forgotten to put the scan disc back in after taking it out the night before to look at some pictures. Several years ago on Easter Day, I was on my way home after taking some Easter baskets to some kids. As I went up the hill on San Miguel Canyon Road, just before reaching my turn off, in the sky directly ahead was a perfect cross formed by a cloud. There were very few clouds, so this really stood out. I pulled over and got out of the car and stared. Four or five other cars pulled over too. No one had a camera. The cross cloud and the Angle cloud both warmed my heart, made me feel love flowing between me and my maker.

CUTE THINGS KID SAY AND DO

R U B Y   G R E E N

Darvel was cutting Loren's hair. Loren, Darvel's son, was about 4 years old. Darvel asked, "How do you want your hair cut?" Loren replied, "Like Grandpa's." Darvel finished the haircut and held him up to the mirror and asked, "How's that?" Loren started to cry and said, "No! I wanted it like Grandpa's with a hole on top!"

One morning after family prayer, Kellie, age three, asked, "Daddy, where does Heavenly father live?" Pointing upward, Joe replied, "Up there." That night when they were ready for bed and they knelt in prayer, it was Kellie's turn to say the prayer. She began the prayer with, "Heavenly Father, who lives in the ceiling..."

One afternoon at Grandma's house, the teenagers allowed Jill and Elysa, 11 years old, to play Taboo with them. When the word to guess was positive, they were having a lot of trouble with it. They were giving clues like upbeat, cheerful, etc. Finally Jill said HIV. Right away Elysa replied positive!

Jedediah was 7 years old. The whole family was caught up in the preparations of Carla's family moving to Louisiana. Jedediah asked, "Grandma, where is Louisiana anyway?" I pointed eastward and said, "It is way, way, way, and far away that way." To which he quickly replied, "Oh no, that can't be, for just a little way passed Safford that way, it's a dead end!"

Tyson, the city cousin, came to stay with Grandma and Grandpa and spend time with his country cousins. They were all having fun riding Grandpa's horses-Star and her colt Frisky, Darvel's mare Babe, and Jeffery's mare Cutie. There were lots of cousins to play with. Tyson, (Carla's son), Jeremy, (Darvel's son) and Janna (Jeffery's daughter) were all 11 years old. One morning as Grandpa and Tyson were feeding the horses, Tyson asked, "Grandpa, when you want your horse to have a baby, why do you feed her bread?" Grandpa asked, "Where did you get that idea?" Tyson replied, "Well, Janna said her dad is going to take Cutie down to Keith Smith's pasture with his big pinto and get them bread so Cutie will have a colt that looks just like Keith Smith's pinto. Grandpa allowed he would have to tell Tyson about the birds and the bees.

We went to visit Danny's Family in Taylor. Garret, Danny's oldest son, said, "Grandma, my 4th birthday already passed and you didn't even send me a tard." Shrugging his shoulders, he told me "All I needed was a tard." I told him I was sorry, I just forgot. He said, "I tell you what you tould do. You tould dit a talender and write everybody's name on it. Then you tould dit a box of tards and put it by the talender. Then when you look at the talender, you tould see it is time to send a tard." I always remember birthdays now. All they need is a tard.

Jeremy was 5 years old and his big brothers were getting him ready for Sunday school. When they started to comb his hair, he said, "Comb it like Uncle Danny's. You know, with a real big forehead. (Uncle Danny had a receding hairline-losing his hair-like in going bald.)

I took two-and-a-half-year-old Eddie to the doctor with a fever and a sore throat. After examining him, the doctor gave him a shot of penicillin. Eddie didn't cry, but he was really mad. He told the Dr., "If Ida known yous a-gona-do dat, I wouldna tum!"

In the movie, the posse was hot on the trail of the outlaws who had just robbed a bank. The outlaws came to a fork in the road. Without hesitation, they spurred their horses on. The posse came to the same fork and stopped to try to decide which way the outlaws went. 2-½ year old Eddie yelled excitedly. "Dey went dat-a-way"!

One morning I told Carl I needed the car that morning. I was going to get sister Pomroy to spend the day with me. Carl said, "Oh, you're going to have a hen party." About mid-morning we were enjoying our visit as I ironed. We heard a terrific noise, the door burst open, and there stood Catherine, Brusie (a neighbor boy) and Eddie. They were all dusty and disheveled. Eddie was holding a big red hen by the legs. It was almost as big as he was. She was trying her best to get away. But Eddie hung on. There was no way he was going to let go. He proudly announced, "Mommy, heah's da hen foah youah hen poughty!"

Pearl loved Grandmas beans. When we had a baby who was nursing, and we were eating at Grandma's house, Mother would say, "I would really like some beans, but I'm afraid they would give the baby colic." One day when we were eating at Grandma's, someone noticed Pearl didn't have any beans and offered her some. Pearl sighed and said, "Oh I would love some but I'm afraid they will give the baby colic."

When Pearl was about three years old, Daddy was in the habit of taking her outside at night before putting her to bed and showing her the moon and stars. One night the rain was coming down in sheets. There was a lot of thunder and lightning. Pearl was crying non-stop. Daddy was trying to get her quieted down. In exasperation he said, "Pearl, what can I do to get you to hush?" Pearl wailed, "Well, take me outside and show me the moon and stars and maybe I'll hush."

When Uncle Walter was about 4 years old, the family lived on a farm. One day Harvey (Daddy), Uncle Joe and Uncle Martin climbed up a tree near the front gate. Uncle Walter was too little to get up into the tree, so he sat on the gate and began to cry. A man rode up on a horse. He couldn't see the boys in the tree. This conversation took place:

Man on horse- "Hello, young man. What is your name?"

Walter, sobbing- "Walter."

Man on horse- "Walter who?"

Walter-still sobbing- "Just Walter."

Man on horse- "Who lives here?"

Walter- "We do."

Man on horse - "What is your Pa's name?"

Walter- "Pa."

Man on horse- "Pa who"

Walter- "Just Pa."

Man on horse- "What is your ma's name?"

Walter - "Just Ma."

Man on horse "Does Emit Phillips lives here?"

Walter– "Nope. Just Ma an Pa an us kids."

Grandma looked out the window and came to see what was going on. The man on the horse was a long-lost friend of Grandpa's.

Eddie used to deliver newspapers in Central, 3 miles west of Thatcher. One Saturday I took all the kids for Eddie to collect from his customers. Some of the houses had out houses. Joe (about 3 years old) asked what those little houses were. I told him they were their bathrooms. He said, "Evewybody has a baff woom outside. I want a baff woom outside."

KIDS

COLLEEN CHAPMAN

Three-year-old Vincent came into the house fighting back tears. He said, "I dropped me and bumpered my head!"

Grand daughter Jennifer came running up the driveway. She stubbed her toe and fell in the dirt. She got up; brushed the dirt from her dress, then examined her shiny black shoes. She frowned at the dust on them. Taking a Kleenex from her pocket, she cleaned them and brushed some dirt from her stockings and straightened them and arranged the little ruffles just so. When she was satisfied that she had restored herself to the neat little lady she had been before her fall, she stood erect, pushed back her long blond hair and patted it into place. She looked up at me with an embarrassed grin, then wiped her nose with the back of her arm and said breathlessly, "I falled me down."

Debra-Fighting back tears, "I fell down and tore my pants and peeled my knee!"

Diane-very sleepy 5 years old "My eyes are broken. I can't keep them open."

Steven sat on the floor near the ironing board. He had been still and quiet for a long time. Much too long for a 6-year-old boy! I kept an eye on him as I ironed. He was deep in thought. He would ask his question sooner or later if he didn't get it figured out for himself. Finally, he asked, "Mom, why did God move and change his name?" "What makes you think he did?"

"That prayer everyone says a lot."

"Which one?"

"The one that goes 'Our Father which aren't in heaven, Hollow Ed be thy name..."

As I turned the car onto the road we live on, grandson Howard, about 6 years old, looked at the sign by the side of the road. "That sign says 'not a through road', right?" "Yes" "That sign was there the last time I was here. How long has it been there?" "Oh, I don't know. It was there the first time I was ever on this road in 1960." "Wow! That's a long time. Grandma, just what is it that it's doing that it's not through with after all this time?"

Loren saw Debra and Ken kissing after Ken brought her home from church one Sunday. He came running in to tell me, "Mom, you better get out there fast! Debra and Ken are out there (he slapped the palms of his hands together) mouth to mouth!"

James and Jennifer had asked about their ancestors, wanting to know what nationalities they are. Judy told them they are a mixture of a lot of things. They have a little Irish, a little French, etc. James, upon hearing that one of his ancestors was an Indian Chief, which made his daughter, which would be the great, great grandmother of Jennifer and James, an Indian princess, he popped his hands to his face and said, "Oh no! I've got a little Indian Princess in me!"

Shortly after Robert started school, we went to visit Pearl. As we were leaving, Pearl said, "Oh, Mickey (that is what we use to call him) you're going to school now aren't you!" He said, "No, silly, we are going home now. It's almost bedtime. I go to school in the afternoons!"

Robert got sick while at school, and I had to go get him. As we were leaving the school, his teacher asked Robert, you have your new book, right?" "No Ma'am." He answered. "You didn't get a new book when they were passed out?" she asked. "Yes Ma'am, I did." "Then you have your new book." "No ma'am, I don't." Robert and his teacher stood looking at each other, both confused. I said, "Were new books issued today, and you want to know if Robert received his before he went to the nurses' office?" "Yes." she said. "Robert, did you receive a new book but you don't have it with you right now?" "Yes! It's in my desk! Can we go now?" he said, sounding exasperated. With a sigh his teacher said, "One of these days I will learn how to talk to that boy!"

Loren arrived home from school with a stuffy nose and a cough. My home remedy for colds is a hot shower, bundle up and get in bed. Then a hot toddy consisting of hot tea, lemon juice, honey, and brandy. In Loren's toddy, I put about a teaspoon of brandy. When I went back into his bedroom to see about him, He was still propped up, holding the big empty mug. He said, "Boy am I shinnin'!" What he meant was, he thought he was drunk. He had heard someone say they had a glow on, meaning they had too much to drink.

The first time I saw Jennifer after moving from the river to Prundale, she hid her face on Loren's shoulder. She wouldn't talk to me or look at me. After several minutes she looked at me and shaking her finger at me said, "I'm mad to you!"

AUNT MYRTLE

Ruby Green

Grandma and Myrtle went outside to call the kids. Grandma called, "Harvey, Joe, Annie," and then listened for their answer. There was a mocking bird high in a tree nearby. It was singing and making an awful racket. If the kids had answered, Grandma would not have been able to hear them. Grandma called again. Still no answer was heard from the kids. Three-year-old Myrtle could stand it no longer. She looked up at the bird and yelled, "Won't you hush up? Can't you hear Ma calling them kids?"

THE TWINS

DOROTHY PATTON

Jared and Leif are three years old and they seem to believe in reincarnation because they are always talking about something that happened when they were big. And now it seems that they also believe in transmigration or whatever it is called when life forms are changed. We were watching wild horses on television and I asked them if they rode wild horses when they were big. "No," Jared said, "But when I was a horse I could run like that." "Me too," said Leif. "I could run like that horse."

One weekend when they stayed over, they decided that there were bears in a small wooded area nearby and wanted to go bear hunting. I took them bear hunting, hoping they wouldn't be too disappointed when we didn't find any bears. But I needn't have worried. After following invisible bear tracks for a while, they picked up a small limb that had fallen from a tree. It was large enough that it took both of them to pick it up.

At first, I thought they were having a tug of war over it but then saw that they seemed to be working together. After waving it around awhile, they threw it down and Jared said "Gramma, we killed a bear." "A big, big bear." Leif said. So a successful bear hunt doesn't depend on real live bears. But what I thought was most remarkable was that neither of them said anything when they picked up the limb and started to do battle. But they both knew that they were killing a bear.

While playing with the twins one day, I said to Leif, "You're my sweetie pie."

"You're my sweetie pie, too." He said.

Then I said to Jared, "You're my honey bun."

In his sweetest voice he replied, "You're my sandwich."

They seem to think it is their duty to keep me informed about all the bad words they have learned that they are not supposed to say. The last time they came, they had learned that it is bad to call someone stupid and that you never; never say shut your mouth to your mom.

The boys and I were relaxing in lounge chairs on my deck. Jared said "when I grow up and get married, I think I'll have sex. Leif said in a scolding voice, "Jared!" Jared said, "it was just a thought. It probably would never happen."

On my birthday card the boys wrote…. Happy Birthday Grandma. We hope you have a pleasant aging process.

One nice sunny day when the boys were about 10, we were relaxing in lawn chairs on my little deck. We had all been quiet for awhile and I was half asleep. Jared said, "Ya know, when I get married I think I'll probably have sex." Leif said, "Jared!" in a scolding voice. Jared said, oh it was just a thought. It'll probably never happen. Just a thought."

MALISSA

SANDRA JOHNSON

When my Granddaughter Malissa was about 5 years old she was exposed to the God and Goddess mythologies. One day she was in the bath tub while I was putting on my make-up and getting ready for work.

She say's "Grandma, the Mother makes things." Referring to Mother earth and Mother Nature, etc.

I respond "That's right dear"

"And God gives it energy." She says.

"Yes he does." I state.

She starts making waves in the bath tub and her toys dance in the water. "Look Grandma, I'm God."

"You got it kid." I agree.

We believe that God cannot be male or female because that would be an incomplete energy. So God must be both. We also believe that every person has God within to be loved and honored.

LEAVING HOME

COLLEEN CHAPMAN

The conversation went something like this with 7-year-old Rusty:

"Mom, I won't be here for dinner. I'm leaving."

"You are? Where are you going and how long will you be gone?"

"I'm just leaving. I'm not coming back."

"Going out on your own, huh, you are kind of young for that, don't you think?"

"I don't care. I'm going. I'm leaving on my bike."

"Well, it sounds like you have made up your mind. I sure do hate to see you go. We'll all miss you a lot. There are some things you should know and some things you'll need; so hang around for a while. I'll make some sandwiches for you. Better put in some fruit and cookies. Have you thought about where you'll sleep tonight?" I packed the food in his school lunch box. I rolled up an old blanket and tied it to his bike and put the lunch box on top and tied it in place; all the while giving him all kinds of advice.

Do not talk to strangers. Look out for cars. Get a job as soon as possible. Always find a place to sleep before it gets dark. Check it out for snakes, bugs, and other things that like to crawl all over people. While I was doing this, Rusty was becoming less certain he wanted to go. And why was I being so helpful instead of stopping him? After getting all of this done, I handed him $ 3.00, said I wished I had more than that to give him, kissed him good-by, and walked to the front door, opened it and looked back. Rusty was standing beside his bike looking miserable and confused. Over my shoulder I said "Oh yeah. Remember you are not allowed to go any farther than the corner, and you are not allowed to cross the street." "Then how can I run away from home?" "You'll have to figure that out for yourself. I have helped you all I can."

After a few minutes he went to the back yard. He was there for dinner.

IT JUST ISN'T WORTH IT

C OLLEEN C HAPMAN

My sister-in-law, Sierra, her daughter Lynn, and grandson Jimmy were spending a week with us. Jimmy and Loren were about three years old, Jimmy being the oldest by nineteen days. Jimmy was trying to get Lynn's attention. She and Sierra were talking, and she ignored him. Frustrated, he climbed up on her lap saying, "Mamma, Mamma, Mamma." Didn't do any good. Jimmy became more insistent. Taking her face in his hands, he turned her face toward his, saying, "MAMMA, MAMMA, MAMMA!" Still she paid no attention. He started patting her face with one hand, the other hand still trying to keep her face turned to him, **"MAMMA! MAMMA! MAMMA!"** I don't know how she did it, but she still ignored him. He patted her cheek harder and harder. He finally hauled off and slapped her hard. That got her attention "WHAT, JIMMY!" she said. Loren watched all this with interest. His eyes popped wide open in surprise when Jimmy slapped Lynn. I knew what I could expect sooner or later. It came much sooner than I thought it would.

Our normal routine was; Loren would have his "kid coffee" otherwise known as Ovaltine while Howard had his breakfast. He had his juice while the school kids had their breakfast, then the rest of his breakfast with me. This morning Howard had left for work, the kids were off to school, and I had breakfast on the table for Sierra, Lynn, Loren, Jimmy and myself. I put Loren in his place at the table and sat down to wait for the others. Loren immediately appeared at my side. He informed me he wanted to go outside. I informed him he could go outside after he had his breakfast and got dressed and put him back where he belonged. Again, he was by my side as soon as I sat down.

"I want to go outside *now!*" he said.

"*You* can go outside *after you eat!*" I put him back.

"I DON'T WANT TO EAT NOW! I WANT TO GO OUTSIDE NOW!" he said from beside my chair.

"*No." YES!" "NO!"* "I want to *hit* you!" he said. "Oh you do? Are you sure about that?"

He thought for a few seconds. "Yes I am." "Do you know what will happen to you if you do?"

"Yes." "If you are really sure you want to and if you think it will be worth it, go ahead." He did. He hit me *hard.* I put him over my knees and gave him his first spanking. It couldn't have hurt much, those three swats, over his thick Dr. Denton pajamas. I don't know if he thought that is what would happen. I put him in his room and told him he could come out when he was ready to have his breakfast. He was back in about five minutes. After sitting on my lap for ten minutes or so, he was ready for breakfast. For years after that when he was mad at me he would say, "I want to hit you *but it just isn't worth it!*"

I CAN DO ANYTHING YOU CAN DO!

COLLEEN CHAPMAN

Rusty had Loren "suckered" in again. He was doing things and Loren copied him. "I can jump from here to here." "So can I." "I can jump over that." "So can I." I noticed Rusty was being careful not to do anything he knew Loren could not do. Rusty went up on the porch, took hold of the trunks of two banana trees, pulled them apart, and stuck his head between them. He let go and held his arms out and waved them up and down. He then freed himself and stepped aside. Loren stepped up to the trees. He got a firm grasp on the trees and pulled. Rusty was standing behind him. Loren did not realize Rusty helped him pull the trees apart. Loren had to stand on tiptoe to reach the gap between the trunks. He stuck his head in and did as Rusty had done. Rusty gently let go of the trunks. Loren's look of smug satisfaction turned to embarrassed anger as he discovered he was stuck. There he was, on tiptoe with his head stuck between the banana trees, yelling at Rusty "Dang you Rusty! I am going to kill you, you jackass, you ole poop head! When I get out of here you're gonna be really sorry."

HOT PEACH PIE

COLLEEN CHAPMAN

There was a fast food place in Van Nuys that had hot peach pie. Grandson Howard loved it. One day when he was about 4 years old, he asked me to take him there. I told him I didn't know where it was. He said he could tell me how to get there. "It's easy Grandma, you just mosey on out to the car, go to the corner of Oxnard, and that will be easy cause the car is already pointed that way, toward Oxnard. When you get to the corner of Oxnard, hang a right. Then you go bookin' straight on down to Van Nuys Vulabard, hang a left, and boogie on down to Sherman Way, flip a U turn, and come back a little ways, and you can't help but miss it." I followed his instructions and found it. We drove up to the order window. He told me he always ordered for himself. He got on my lap on his knees, stuck his head out the window, ready to order. The young woman at the window smiled when she saw him. "Hello Mr. Listner, what will you have today?" she said. "I'll have a small cheese bugger, a small coke an a hot bitch pie, please." "Coming right up." Smiling at me she said, "I look forward to him coming in about once a month. I just love taking his order for a cheese bugger and hot bitch pie."

HOOF AND MOUTH DISEAS

Colleen Chapman

When Loren was about ten years old he developed the habit of biting his toe nails. Yes, toe nails. I kept telling him if he didn't stop he might get hoof and mouth disease. Of course he didn't believe me, and would say Ha Ha, and went right ahead and bit his toe nails. About a month after he had started that habit he got a sore on his mouth. It didn't look like anything I had seen before so I took him to our Doctor. He took one look and said it was Hoof and Mouth disease. From the look Loren shot at me I could tell what he was thinking.... that I had told the Dr. to say that...then confusion, because he had been in the room when I had made the appointment that morning and all I had said was that I was concerned about the sore and felt it should be looked at as soon as possible... Dang! Maybe humans really could get it! The Dr. was confused by my laughter and Loren's scowl. I explained and the Dr. had a good laugh, then explained the sore was caused by the same germ (or whatever) that caused hoof and mouth disease. I don't remember if Loren got a shot or what, but the sore was gone in a matter of days. He didn't bite his toe nails anymore.

JERRY

COLLEEN CHAPMAN

The car was packed and we were ready to go. Mother and Daddy were going over the check list. Did you get this, did you do that? When they were satisfied all was ok, Daddy started the car. They were taking Jerry to Phoenix to see a specialist. He was three years old and had not begun to talk. As the car rolled slowly toward the street, Jerry said, "Did you get the tea kettle on the stove?" Daddy stopped the car. We were all shocked. Daddy said, "You can talk!" Jerry nodded his head. "Well why in the dickens haven't you talked before now?" Daddy demanded. Jerry said, "I, I, I didn't need to."

MARCI

Colleen Chapman

Marci was a cute little four-year-old blue-eyed blond. She was the daughter of the girlfriend of a fireman Howard worked with. Herb asked me if I would take care of her. She had some emotional problems that seemed to be getting worse. We had Marci every day from 6:00 AM to 6:30 PM, except Sunday. If we went out of town that summer, we took her with us.

I don't know the details, but Marci had seen a lot of blood from an injured person and knew that person had died. She went into hysterics at the sight of blood. It was time for her to have a check-up. Her mother, Myra, agreed to let me take her to our Dr. I talked to Dr. Chung ahead of time and explained her fear of blood. He agreed to do things my way. I had an appointment the same morning for my regular physical. He would see me first. When he was ready to take blood from Marci, he would show her a vial of my blood, and tell her she needed some new blood, and he was going to put some in her. That way, when he drew her blood, she would think he was giving her some instead, and she would be spared the trauma of losing her blood. I would tell her it wouldn't hurt as much if she didn't watch. It worked. One of the rules I try to live by is you do not lie to a child. However, there are exceptions to every rule!

The Sunday before New Year's Eve was stormy with lots of thunder and lightning. Marci called me. She said she was home alone and was scared. I told her that her mom had probably stepped outside for something and would be right back. She called back a little later and said her mom had been gone for a long time. Her mouth was bleeding. I could tell she was on the verge of hysteria. I told her I would be there as fast as I could.

She had lost her first tooth, and the bleeding had stopped by the time I got there. I was writing a note to tell Myra I had taken Marci home with me when she and a new boyfriend came home. Myra had left her little daughter home alone, during a severe storm, to go shopping for a dress to wear on New Year's Eve. I lost it, and read Myra the riot act, and then was afraid she wouldn't let me have Marci anymore, but she did.

Marci got over her fear of blood. Being around so many rough and tumble kids, she saw them bleed and also saw that they didn't die. My kids and all the neighborhood kids were very good with and for her. I swear some of the kids made themselves bleed to show her it wasn't anything to be afraid of.

GAMES

Remember kick the can, red rover, and all those other games? I taught them to my kids, and we played them sometimes. Some of the neighbors thought we were nuts, and others joined in. I kept my kids at home so I knew where they were and what they were doing. Most of the kids in the neighborhood were in our back yard, and it was always a mess. They built things–skate boards, stilts, there was always a pile of wood and hammers and other tools for their use. Howard brought home a truck tire. Two kids could fit inside, and it took two kids to roll it down the sidewalk. I got an old bed spring and mattress from the Salvation Army for them to jump on. We brought home refrigerator packing crates and the kids built a fort. There was a very small German car with no engine. Loren and his friend Greg would pile their camping stuff in the car and go camping. Then they would make a tent with an old army blanket. One day a neighbor looked over the tall fence into our back yard. He was appalled at the mess and said he was going to report us. His two kids who were in the middle of a project started crying. They wouldn't have any place to play, they said. He didn't report us. We had a rule that anyone who spent time in our back yard had to help put tools away and clean up before they went home in the evening.

MATTHEW

C O L L E E N C H A P M A N

I was on the way to the store and stopped by Vince and Teri's to see if Matt wanted to go with me. Teri didn't think he would go, since he had never been any place without her or Vincent. She was sure he would be crying before we were a block from the house. I told her I would circle the block and if he cried, I would stop. If not, I would keep going.

Teri and Vince stood on the sidewalk waving good bye as we drove off. He stood up on the front seat (we didn't have seat belts then.) waving to them. He turned and looked out the rear window until we turned the corner, and he could no longer see them. He then faced forward, looked out the side and front windows, jabbering about the things he saw. He turned and looked out the rear window several times. I wondered if he was feeling insecure and was looking for his Mom and Dad, although he didn't act the least bit insecure. He had just turned to face forward again when I turned the last corner, and there was Vince and Teri waiting on the sidewalk.

Matt looked surprised and then mad. He crossed his arms and plopped down on the seat beside me and said, "Dam it to heyow!" I asked him if he wanted to stop at his house. He shook his head and said, **"NO! Go wit you!"** "OK, we won't stop." He stood up and smiled and waved as we passed. I told him I would go faster now, so he needed to sit down. He happily sat beside me and talked about what he wanted to get at the store. So much for him feeling insecure!

ROBBY

COLLEEN CHAPMAN

Robby is a little boy I took care of for a couple of years when we lived in Van Nuys. He was a cute little guy, eight years old, with curly red hair and blue eyes. It took some getting used to, being around a large family. My kids were very good with him, as they were with all the kids we took in over the years. He soon learned the rules and tried hard to obey them. When he got excited about something, the rules were forgotten. Like when I took them to Sea World. I was always taking the kids, mine and usually several others, on outings. It was not unusual for me to be the only adult with 11 or 12 kids ranging in age from infant to young teenager. Therefore, there had to be rules and the rules had to be obeyed. I had to mean what I said and say what I meant. The kids knew exactly where they stood. They knew what was expected of them and knew what unacceptable behavior was. I very seldom had a problem with any of them. We always received compliments on their behavior and manners. When we arrived at Sea World, before we got out of the car, I asked, "O.K. guys, what are the rules?" They answered in unison, "No running. Stay together. If we do get separated, stand still. You will find us. Don't go with a stranger no matter who they are or what they say." We had not been there more than a few minutes, when Robby got excited about something and ran ahead of us. I called to him, but he kept running. We were passing by some benches just then, and I told the kids to sit down. I stood on one end of a bench so I could see over the crowd and keep an eye on Robby. Fortunately, it was not very crowded. Robby did as I thought he would. He soon realized what he had done, and that we were not with him. He came running back and, in his panic, did not see us as he ran back and forth. As he passed us the third or fourth time, I stepped in front of him. He came screeching to a halt. I led him to the bench and sat down.

He sat beside me choking back sobs. I asked him "Now do you know why it is important not to run, to stay with the group, and stand still if you do get lost?" He nodded his head and said, "Oh yes! Yes I do! I sure do!" I had told the kids if they disobeyed, or broke any rules, they would be taken to the childcare center where they would stay until the rest of us were ready to leave. Everyone agreed that he had learned his lesson and should be allowed to stay with us. He stayed really close.

On another trip, we went to Crystal Cave in the Sequoia National Forest. As we stood in line waiting for it to open, Robby noticed the ornate gate that spanned the opening to the cave. It was made of metal grillwork in the shape of a giant spider web. Off to one side on the web was a big metal spider. Robby said in a rather loud voice, "Oh look! That looks like a Whore House!" Everyone turned to look at us. I said, "Yes, Robby, it looks like a House of Horror." He said, "Yeah, that's what I said. A Whore House."

We took him to the river with us. We had a cabin on the Tule River, a few miles below Springville. Using some rope, empty plastic jugs and rocks, we made buoys and roped off an area on the beach and in the water for the little kids. They were not to leave that area unless they had permission to do so, or were with an adult or one of the older kids. They were told they would be safe there, and it would be easier for me to keep an eye on them. The water outside that area was over their heads, and they might drown before anybody knew what was happening. And a very important rule was, no screaming, unless you got into trouble. If they did get into trouble, then they were to scream for help as loud and as long as they could, or until they get help. By this time Robby had learned to pay special attention if I said something was very important. Robby was having a great time. He had learned to swim, but as yet could not swim very well or very far, but he could swim! One afternoon he suddenly realized he was outside of the markers and started screaming and thrashing around. He was not in danger because we had left plenty of space outside the markers, which was shallow enough to be safe. We all started laughing. I called out to him but he wasn't listening. When he saw us laughing, he was so stunned he quit screaming. I said, "Robby, listen to me." He said "I'm gonna drown!" Again I said, "Robby, listen!" He said "O.K. but I'm gonna drown!" "No you are not! Stand up!" "What?" "Stand up." He stopped splashing and stood up. The water was just a bit higher than his waist. He was embarrassed, but relieved. "Man! I thought I was a goner! I guess I shoulda known if I was gonna drown you guys wouldn't be laughing. But you said…" He stopped to catch his breath. I explained to him that it would be stupid to put the markers right at the edge of the deep water. One of the teenagers waded from the shallow water to the deep water to show him it did indeed get deep. He grinned and said, "So this time you meant what you said, but not exactly. Because I got out of the area, and I wasn't in over my head. But I would have been if I went a little farther. So you were right, but not exactly." To which I replied, "And aren't you glad?" "I am. Yes I am. I sure am!" he said with a sigh.

RUN HOME SUZI

COLLEEN CHAPMAN

When Suzi was just a little squirt she decided she wanted to play baseball with the bigger kids. Of course they were not seeing things her way. I finally intervened on her behalf and told them if they would let her play for a little while she would soon tire of it and leave them alone. And anyway, how did they think she was supposed to learn how to play? They agreed but were not happy about it. I went on about my business.

A few minutes later Suzi was in the house. She sat on the floor, crossed her legs, and had a slight frown on her face. I thought, "She sure didn't play long. Now what is she thinking so hard about?" She sat like that for 5 or 6 minutes then said "Mom, how do you catch flies?"

"That isn't very easy to do. Why do you want to catch flies?"

"I need three of them. Do you think we could catch them and put them in a jar and put a lid on it?"

"I suppose so, but why do you want three flies?"

"Will you help me? Please?"

"Yes, if you need three flies I will help you but WHY DO YOU NEED THREE FLIES?!!"

"Cause the kids said I could play baseball, but I have to catch three flies before I can try to hit the ball. I DON'T KNOW WHY I HAVE TO HAVE THREE FLIES!!"

Back outside we went to get this straightened out. The kids decided to let her go up to bat with Dave's help, without catching three flies first. Everything should be o.k. now. So I went back into the house. In no time at all, Suzi came running into the house crying.

"Now what's wrong?"

"I don't know! I hit the ball and everyone started yelling at me to run home!"

SHE'S TOUGH BUT CUTE

COLLEEN CHAPMAN

Some boys were teasing our neighbor girl and Debra as they walked home from school. She and Laura tried to ignore them. They went too far when they grabbed Laura's book and ran. She had a crippled leg, and Debra was protective of her. Now she was angry. Those boys didn't know they had taken on more than they could handle. Debra handed her books to Laura and took off after the boys. She caught up with the first boy, got a handful of hair and threw him to the ground without slowing down. She easily caught up with the second boy and threw him to the ground, rolled him onto his back, put the heel of her shoe on his throat and said, "If you bother us again, I'll…I'll…I'll…**bit your nose off!**"

GAMES

C OLLEEN C HAPMAN

One winter I taught the kids some of the games we use to play. Hide and seek was first. Diane was about four years old the first time we played it. I was it and she told me, "I'm gonna hide under my bed." I explained that I wasn't supposed to know where she was. I was supposed to hunt for her. The kids just stood and stared at me. Dave, about five, asked when I changed the rule about me knowing where they were at all times. To get around that one, I told them that as long as they didn't leave the house, they could hide from me, but only if we were playing a game.

Kick the can...Steven, about three years old, after having Dave or Diane run and kick the can while he was looking for them, decided to take the can with him.

One rainy day the kids, my nine and I don't remember how many others, were in the house. They had to think of things to do without making much noise, and without moving around very much. A real challenge. Howard had been at a brushfire for twenty hours and was trying to get some sleep. The kids did things like make shadows on the wall with their hands, finger dexterity exercises, see how many coins they could get spinning at one time, string and finger stuff, etc. They were running out of things to do, so I suggested they play Simon Says.

The person who was being Simon would stand next to the door, facing the group. One of the kids, whose turn it was to be Simon, said to cross your eyes. Then try to touch your nose with your tongues. While this was going on, there was a knock on the door. I opened the door, and there was the Fuller Brush man. I loved some of the products, but this salesman was very strange. If he was told no thank you, I don't need anything today; he would stand there and go through his whole routine anyway, even if the door was closed. The poor man saw wall to wall cross-eyed kids with tongue's sticking out. He left and never came back.

SPAGHETTI

COLLEEN CHAPMAN

When Rusty was seven years old, he asked questions about childbirth. I got my big Medical book, and sat beside him on the couch. This book has a picture of the bone structure and successive pages with the different parts of the body on transparent pages. I do not know if I am making this clear. The first page to cover the skeleton has muscles on it. You can see through the page and see the bones. This continues up to the skin and hair. It also has a pregnant woman, and the pictures show the baby growing in the womb, month by month, up to and including the birth.

A few days later, we had spaghetti for dinner. Rusty said, "I know how come Diane can eat so much spaghetti. It goes down in her legs and in her arms." When asked where he got that idea, he said, "I saw it in the Medical book. Remember Mom? It showed that woman's arms and legs full of spaghetti." No, Rusty, those were tendons.

WHAT AM I SUPPOSTA DO?

COLLEEN CHAPMAN

Loren was really mad one day. He went to his room and slammed the door so hard the whole house shook. I had been allowing him to slam the door, but this was the first time he had done it when Howard was home. Howard was almost asleep in his chair when the door slammed. He was on his feet immediately. He went to Loren's door and ordered him into the living room. Before Howard could say a word, Loren said, "O.K.! I know I'm in trouble. I can tell. But what am I supposta do to work off my frustrations? I'm not allowed to cuss. I'm not allowed to throw things. I'm not allowed to hit anybody. They're all bigger than me anyway. And the last time I kicked the kicking tire I almost broke my toe. So what am I supposed to do? *Huh? What!*"

He was trying hard not to cry. After all he had told Dave just this morning not to call him a baby anymore because he was almost old enough to start Kindergarten. Loren stood there with his hands on his hips, chin stuck out, and head back staring up as Howard loomed over him, hands on hips, staring down and looking less stern all the time.

Howard said, "You can go back to your room and you will be allowed to slam the door. Just don't slam it so hard." Howard said to me, "We will have to make that exception to the rule for him. Just get him to not slam it so hard." I didn't tell him I had made that exception a long time ago.

TIE IT TO THE DOOR

COLLEEN CHAPMAN

Suzi's loose tooth was dangling. It moved with each breath she took. It moved with each step she took. We all watched in fascination. Her mouth was open all the time. It was fun to watch as she tried to eat and to talk without putting any pressure on her tooth. The kids were betting on how long it would be before the tooth would fall off. She wouldn't let anyone touch it. I told her to let me tie a string to it, and tie the other end of the string to the doorknob. Then for her to sit on a chair in front of the door, and the next time the door was opened, the tooth would be jerked out so fast she wouldn't feel a thing and it would be all over with. She thought that was a good idea. It shouldn't take long, either. Our front door opened and closed so often we joked about needing a revolving door.

I tied the string to her tooth, Sue put a chair in front of the door, tied the string to the doorknob, and sat on the chair *inside the house!* Rusty came in the back door and saw Sue. He asked her what she was doing. He controlled himself very well. He went back out, using the back door. He told the kids what she was doing and they all decided not to use the front door. They quietly came in the back door. They went into the hallway and peeked through the door into the living room, the small kids on their knees, then the next size kid, until there were five heads next to the door jam. Others peeked at her from the kitchen, trying not to laugh. After half an hour without the door opening, the suspense was too much for her and she was about to give up. Then the door opened! *Inward.* Sue looked at the sagging string, looked at Vincent standing in the doorway staring at her sitting on a chair with a string coming out of her mouth. Sue jumped up, yelled, "Shut up!" and started to cry. Vince looked bewildered, and said, "I haven't said anything! I just got home and…. what are you doing, anyway!"

All the kids were laughing and teasing Suzi. She ran from one to another, the string trailing along, telling them to shut up, and trying to hit them. Then someone noticed the tooth was no longer dangling. The string lay on the floor, but we never did find that tooth!

WATCHING TV

COLLEEN CHAPMAN

We got our first T.V. in 1959 or 60. Vincent and Robert were five and six years old. They didn't just watch the program, they lived it. When a western was on, and the characters rode horses, so did they. During a fistfight, they went through the motions. We stayed out of their way. If the Three Stooges ran back and forth, so did they, never taking their eyes off of the screen. A scary movie? They started out sitting on the floor, and as the movie got scarier, side by side they scooted backward to the couch, slid up onto the couch, then onto the back of the couch, stood on it with their backs pressed against the wall. I'd get them down and turn to another channel. They would beg me to turn it back. I did. They would get behind my rocking chair and peer out between the slats while thoroughly enjoying being scared.

WAYNE'S KISS

COLLEEN CHAPMAN

One day Diane came barging into the house very angry and pushing three-year-old Wayne in front of her. Crying, he ran to me and crawled up on my lap. "What's wrong?" I asked. Diane replied, "I washed his pants." Wayne, speaking at the same time said "Mom washed my pants!" Diane explained "He came in when I was putting pants in the washer. The pair he had on was dirty so I pulled them off and put them in the washer. He started bawling and hasn't shut up since. He just kept saying take me to Grandma." Wayne, between sobs, also tried to explain. "Gramma, your kiss was in my pocket and she didn't gived me time ta get it out!" Diane looked puzzled and said: "What?" "Gramma's kiss was in my pocket. You put it in the washer, and it's all ruined." "What is he talking about? How can a kiss be in a pocket?"

At first, I was as puzzled as she was. Then I remembered. I was getting ready to go on a trip and would be gone about a week. Wayne said I couldn't go because he had to have a goodnight kiss from me before he went to bed. They lived a 'stone's throw' from us, and we saw each other several times a day. He and his brother Howard always came to get a good night kiss before going to bed.

I kissed the palm of Wayne's hand and told him that was a special good night kiss. He was to put it in his pocket, and when it was time to go to bed, he should put his hand in his pocket, and the kiss would hop on. Then he was to kiss his hand where I had kissed it, and he would have his good night kiss. Then I had him to kiss my hand, so I would have one of his to take with me.

Diane was not amused. "Is that why you had hysterics when I tried to put those pants without pockets on you?" "Yes! I toldded you I had ta have pockets. I knowd Gramma would give me another kiss if she didn't left yet. An I needs a pocket ta put it in." Diane grabbed Wayne and stormed out muttering something about dammed foolish nonsense. That's OK; Wayne had another kiss in his closed hand.

DON'T LET ME SEE YOU

COLLEEN CHAPMAN

Matt was playing with a Frisbee. It went over the fence into the yard next door. The fence was made of wood and was about 6 feet high. It was not easy for a 6-year-old to climb over, but he managed, more than once. I could see him from where I sat. He obviously had done this many time. I think he liked to do it, and once in a while deliberately threw the Frisbee over the fence. Teri looked out to check on him just as he was jumping off of the over into the neighbor's yard. She gasped and waited while he got the frisby then came running back. Said, "Matt, do not let me see you do that again! It scares me half to death!" Matt replied, "O.K. Mom, sorry."

A few minutes later, the Frisbee went over the fence again. Matt looked at the door, moved further up the driveway, and looked at the door again. He moved the box further down the driveway. Thinking he was out of sight, he proceeded to stand on the box, grab the top of the fence, and pull himself up and over the fence.

He again tossed his Frisbee over the fence. I laughed, and Teri looked to see what was happening. There was Matt, on top of the fence, ready to drop on the other side "Get in here right now, young man!" He jumped down and came in wondering what he had done now. Teri said, "I told you not to climb that fence again. Now go to your room!"

Matt, looking innocent, said, "No you didn't."

Teri, "YES I DID!!"

Matt "No you DIDN'T"

Teri "Matthew!!!!"

Matt, "She didn't, did she Grandma!"

Me, "No you didn't, Teri, you told him not to let you SEE him do it."

Matt, "Yeah, Mom, so I moved up the driveway. You wouldn't have seen me if you hadn't looked out the door! Now don't look out the door cause I need to go get my Frisbee! I'll tell you when I get back."

HELP ME DOWN!

JERRY PHILLIPS

I climbed up the tree to see the baby birds Colleen told me about. I couldn't get high enough to see them. Then to my dismay, discovered I was stuck. I could go neither up nor down. As I pondered what to do, Colleen came around the house into sight. When she got close enough I called to her, "Hey, Colleen!" She paused and looked around. Not seeing anyone, she started on to where ever she was going. I called out again, "Colleen! Up here in the tree!" She looked up and saw me. "What are you doing?" she asked. "I wanted to see the baby birds. I can't get down." She said, "I guess I'd better help you. If Mother sees you we'll both get it." She climbed up to where I was but couldn't get me started down. She climbed down and told me we would have to find another way. She stood thinking for a while, then said she would be right back, and took off. She came back with a rope. She told me to catch and tossed one end of the rope. I didn't catch it. We tried again….and again. Either the rope wasn't thrown high enough, or I just couldn't grab it. Then she got another idea and took off. She came back with a piece of wood about eight inches long and a couple or so wide. She tied it to the rope. The wood gave it enough weight to be thrown high enough to hit my head. Three times! After three tries, she threw it just right and I caught it. "Now sit on that limb, hold on tight to the rope and shut your eyes." she said. I did like she said and the next thing I knew I was laying on the ground. She had jerked me out of the tree! She had tried to catch me and since I was almost as big as she was, we both were a little worse the wear. I was probably only a few feet up the tree, but to a four-year-old, it looked pretty high.

I SURE AM SORRY

COLLEEN CHAPMAN

About six months after Jerry was born Fred and I were sitting under a tree talking. Fred was quiet for a while and looked sad. Then he shook his head slowly, looking down. I asked what was wrong, but he said he probably shouldn't tell me. After some urging, he told me. "I sure hate what's gonna happen to you. I don't know when, but it will happen." "What's gonna happen?" "I don't know exactly, but….well, member when Mr. (I don't remember the name) got some new baby chickens?" "Yes." "Ya member what he did with the older ones? The ones that were babies not too long ago?" "Yeah, they killed em and ate em." "They sure did, sold some too. And member when they got another calf? They butchered the one that was a calf last year. And the pigs, when they ain't baby no more. They kill um or sell um. Member when he got a new horse? He got rid of the other one, I hate ta tell ya this, but you ain't the baby here now. I don't know if you'll be killed or sold or just got rid of because that's what happens when ya ain't the baby no more. And just when you was gitten old enough ta play with."

He got up and walked away, shaking his head. I sat stunned, heart pounding. I visualized my neck being wrung like a chicken or hung by my feet with my stomach cut open like I had seen pigs. I remembered a stranger leading the neighbor's horse away. Should I hide? But where? I was in quite a tizzy until I knew what I had to do. I had to get rid of Jerry. (I am 18 months older than Jerry.so I must have 24 months. Not old enough to reason that if what Fred said was true I wouldn't have older siblings. Fred is about two and a half years older than me.)

I went in the house through the back door. Jerry was sleeping on Mother and Daddy's bed. I pulled slowly on his baby blanket until he was at the edge of the bed. I put a pillow on the floor, and pulled Jerry, still on his blanket, off of the bed and onto the pillow. I got under the bed and pulled the blanket and pillow until he was close to some boxes and then pulled him behind them. He was still asleep. I lay beside him, thinking I could rest for a while. The terror and crying had worn me out. While we slept, someone noticed Jerry was gone. Sometime later during the search, someone noticed I was missing too. The whole neighborhood was in an uproar, but it was the sound of Mother's hysterics that woke me up. It woke Jerry and he began to cry. I joined in, knowing I was a goner. Somebody moved the boxes and found us.

While I was being pulled out from under the bed I was screaming. Daddy tried to calm me down. Finally, between sobs, I asked if he was going to kill me. He looked shocked and said no. I asked if he was going to sell me or just get rid of me. It took some doing to get me calmed down and assure me that nothing was going to happen to me and learn why I thought it would.

Mother told me that Jerry was actually my baby, and since I was not old enough to take care of him she had to. Like I said, I was very young and bought the story. For quite some time I nearly drove her nuts, telling her…go see if my baby is wet –my baby is hungry– my baby needs his face washed–my baby…

HELP ME UP

COLLEEN CHAPMAN

Louon was lying on the floor. Loren, very proud of his new cowboy boots, sat next to Louon and pulled of his boots so Louon could see how wonderful they were. Louon admired them and then asked Loren to help him up. He said he had to go pee and couldn't get up by himself. Loren stood and taking one of Louon's big hands in his two little ones, pulled and pulled with all his might. He then got behind Louon and pushed. He gave up and told Louon he was sorry, but he was just too big. Louon told him to go in the back yard and look in the trash and get a can and bring it to him. He would just have to pee in the can. Loren said he hoped he could find a big one. Drawing by Sandra Johnson

While Loren was gone, Louon dribbled a little water out of his glass into one of the boots. When Loren came back with a can, Louon said he was sorry, but he just couldn't wait, and had to use one of the boots. With a look of alarm, Loren picked up the boot next to Louon, put his nose inside and sniffed, Looked at Louon, and then sniffed again. He then put his hand into the boot, pulled it out and licked his fingers. "You did not!" he said in relief. Louon laughed so hard he had a hard time getting up and to the bathroom in time.

WILD FLOWERS

COLLEEN CHAPMAN

Every spring we take a wildflower excursion. The wildflowers were extra prolific the spring Nicholas was four or five. We slowly drove our favorite route at the foot of the mountains. "What are those flowers?" Nick asked as we passed a sea of yellow swaying in the light breeze. "That is wild mustard. The mustard that we eat is made from flowers like those." When we passed a meadow billowing with white flowers Nick said, "I surmise mayonnaise is made from those?" "No, mayonnaise is made with eggs, oil and milk, mainly." Surmise? Where did he get that and know how to use it correctl

POEMS AND THINGS

CATHERINE

R UBY G REEN

Her warm eyes charm you, while
She caresses you with her smile.
And you hear angels sing.
She ennobles you with her words.
She encourages you with her works.
And you hear angels sing.
We thank God for her each day.
Because of her, along life's way,
We hear angels sing.

CARLA

R U B Y M A E G R E E N

Where did my little tomboy go?
The one with the bright blue, long lashed eyes.
Well, she grew up a little while ago.
She's baking bread and making pies...

Once a lively, mischievous little tomboy
with golden curls flying, running to and fro,
then a giggly teenager, bubbling with joy
with a string of adoring boys in tow.

Now she's just as happy as she can be.
She's a patient loving mother and wife.
She's a very special spirit you see.
Happy and cheerful all her life.

She's grown into a lovely lady.
Her busy schedule would make your mind whirl.
But I remember my beautiful baby –
My precious little tomboy girl

GENNY

RUBY GREEN

She was a beautiful baby
More than physical beauty
It was her happy spirit,
As a little girl, she just bubbled over
with the joy of just being alive.
As she entered her teenage years,
Overnight, she turned into a prim
And proper young lady, still bubbling
over with the joy of living.
She had her dark days, pain and
Sickness, heartaches and tears were
a part of her life. But mostly, she was happy.

I made her a yellow chiffon dress.
Standing in it on high school graduation day
With her golden hair and radiant face,
It seemed as if the sun was shinning
from within her. A joy to behold.

When she was married, she bubbled
over into the song of
full flowering womanhood.
Now, she has passed over into the
Spirit world. The pain and sickness
which for so long had been

her constant companions have
been taken from her.
Sometimes, I think I hear faint strains of the
song of her bubbling joy of life.

RICHARD LEEMAN

Ruby Green

I loved him while his body was growing inside me.
Oh, how my arms ached to hold him.
But it wasn't to be. His body lies beneath the
ground in his tiny casket.
But his spirit is alive and I carry him in my heart.

COLLEEN

RUBY GREEN

She has long flowing blond hair
Blown like a vapor on the soft summer air.
You can tell what she is thinking when you look in her eyes
Which borrowed their color from the bright blue skies
She is mischievous, happy and gay.
We wouldn't have her any other way.
Sometimes she is sober, thoughtful and deep.
But her pains and sorrows to herself she will keep.
She's a fun person to be around.
To her family she is tightly bound.
She is a wonderful creation,
My sister Colleen.

MY HUSBAND'S HANDS

RUBY GREEN

When first he took my hand in his
I felt truth and glimpsed eternity.
Kneeling at the alter in the Temple,
I placed my heart, my future life
And my trusting hands in his firm
His firm strong hands.
And I knew it was right.

In pain and fear during childbirth,
He would hold my hand in his and I
Would feel strength and peace.
When weary from childcaring, work
Ravaged day, I would slip my tired hand
Into his strong one and feel
Courage and tranquility.

In sorrow, his loving hands lent me
Hope and comfort.
Now his loving hands are workworn and
Rough from caring for his family.
I take his hand in mine and feel
Gratitude and love eternal.

INVISABLE WALLS

Dorothy Patton

The strongest walls are those we can't see. Walls of brick come down eventually.
Like the one that devastated Germany for so long.
But what about the devastation caused by the wall around the
heart of that S.O.B. that cannot understand that you are only trying
to make your relationship what you know it should be.
And the walls around your own heart, your intellect, your tongue,
that keeps you blundering and blathering when you have only the most noble of intentions.
How about the wall between the conscious and unconscious mind?
That wall is a teaser, allowing just enough of a glimpse now and then to let you know
There is a world of stuff in there. Stuff that you want desperately to know.
But maybe stuff that you don't really want to know.
The wall between those in the body and those in spirit may be the same wall
Because it is also a teaser, hinting at the most fabulous possibilities.
But perhaps the greatest tease of all is the wall between myself and my computer!

THE TREE IS DEAD

DOROTHY PATTON

No foliage conceals the magnificent ivory limbs
Lifting countless bare erratic branches
Creating delicate patterns against the sky
The tree is dead
But it doesn't seem to know
Unmindful of its nakedness among lush companions
It stands proudly pointing upward
The tree is dead
The skeleton dry and brittle
But dutifully holding the pose of life
Offering this last bit of beauty to the world

LITA

DOROTHY PATTON

If I do or if I don't'
If I will or if I won't,
It's okay with you.
If I'm happy or if I'm sad,
If I'm good or if I'm bad,
It's okay with you.
If I'm as dense as I can be,
If there are things I just don't see,
That's okay with you.
Grateful to the end,
I'll forever call you friend.
If it's okay with you.

A SISTER?

DOROTHY PATTON

At first, I wondered if she was really a girl.
She seemed so determined to outdo her
Older brother in getting into mischief.
Not at all dainty and manageable like my
Other little sister.

Now I know I have a sister.
When I need a place to stay for a while.
When someone is sick
When I have to move,
Or when I just need to get together
With family.
Yes, I have a sister.

One I can count on to be there
When I am troubled or in despair
She cheers me up when I am sad,
But she will scold if I've been bad.
Yes, I have a sister.

She's kind and gentle as can be
And yet as strong as an old Oak tree.
If of a problem she is aware,
Without you asking, she'll be there.
Yes, I have a sister. Her name is Colleen.

ODE TO OLD AGE

DOROTHY PATTON

Old Father Time laid a hand on my shoulder and said, "Now that you're older you needn't try anymore to save the world. Let the younger generation give it a whorl." So I took the weight off my shoulders and gave it to him. And he passed it on down and I saw that it was good. "And," he continued, "As for that sacred duty to judge and condemn those that stumble and go astray, well the Father is the judge, doesn't the good book say? He never did need the help you threw his way. Now isn't that a relief? We can leave all that self-righteous stuff to the young and the restless. "Now when it comes to your descendants," he said, "That bold and beautiful bunch, well, they're going to do what they're going to do. Won't do a bit of good to let it worry you" And I believed him and I saw that it was good. We can take a nap in the middle of the day if we feel like it. And there will be no dire consequences. We don't have to be slaves to custom or to time. I don't even have to make all these sentences rhyme. We do things our way; just like Frank Sinatra. So what if they don't always turn out just like maybe they should. We can put the blame for a lot of things on being senile And Mark Twain said that after you reach the age of seventy you don't have to behave yourself anymore. And I believed him and I saw that it was good. When a child asks us those embarrassing questions that nobody wants to hear or deal with we don't have to come up with an answer to that. We can plead ignorance. If they're skeptical we can remind them that when you get old you forget a lot of things. They know that's true. Bur your parents probably know the answers to your questions. Their memory is still good. You can ask your parents anything. They're smart; they have the answers. God bless America and old age.

LITTLE TREE

SUSAN AUBERT

I wish to bring you beauty,
In this little gift.

I wish to bring you thoughtfulness,
to give your heart a lift.

I wish to bring you hope and joy,
with every morning sun.

I wish to bring you peace and love
before each day is done.

I wish to bring you all the things
to set your spirit free.

And all of this was in my heart,
when I made this little tree.

This is a gift from Susan. A friend of hers set the poem
to music. I have a tape recording of it.

THE WISH

JERRY PHILLIP

I often wish upon a star
I send my hopes and dreams so far.
But I never wish for things that cannot be
like could I fly or uproot a tree.
I only wish for things that may someday come true.
Like that time I wished for a friend like you.

TRUST ME

J ERRY P HILLIPS

If I could be a horse I would run ore hill and dale and have such fun.
But that is silly of course. I cannot be a horse.
If I could be a bird I would fly. I'd sail and soar all over the sky.
But that is absurd. I cannot be a bird.
But I can put my heart at rest. For what I am is really the best.
For it is such fun, you see, to be….just me!

THE UNICORN

JERRY PHILLIPS

I spoke to the wind of a yonder land
where dragons feed from the pixies hand.
Where Syntars blow on a golden horn
when they call the Unicorn.

The wind just laughed said with scorn,
there is no such thing as a Unicorn.
Nor can there be a yonder land where
dragons and pixies eat hand in hand.

But I just smiled in my secret way,
for who is the wind to know or say,
if sometimes in my dreams I flee
to a land beyond the mystic sea,

where dragons play and dragons dine
by the pixie tree at supper time.
And who's the wind to know or care
if sometimes I can plainly hear
the silver notes of a golden horn
and touch the spike of the Unicorn.

STILL DANCING

JERRY PHILLIPS

It' time now, for me to dance to a new tune.
Oh, I've had my good times, but far too few,
And those memories are like campfires
Burning along the back trail.

The shadows so deep, no light ahead.
Ah, so beautiful, and yet, so sad.
For I was born to have so much,
and wind up with so little.

But through rack and ruin
and trial and stress
Oh, I'll still be strong.

Though the thunder rolls out
and the heavens fall in,
and friends betray me, I'll still be one of
the most solid son of a gun on God's green Earth.

When the dust has settled, hey! I'll still be dancing.
Yeah, but I'll be dancing to a new tune.
Perhaps a slower tune as the sap slows and
bark grows harder, around the greenwood.

THE RENDEZVOUS

JERRY PHILLIPS

Upon a starlight rendezvous,
mid vespers posed in diamond dew,
I chase elusive whispers in the wind.

Of what I seek I cannot tell.
I cannot rest, I cannot quell.

This mystery calling something deep within.
Siren voices call to me,
incants a yearning to be free
And sets atremble my enchanted soul.

The hours flee in frantic quest,
I cannot pause I cannot rest,
Lest the dawning steals my fervid goal
The darkness fades into the west.
From nights blind frenzy
I now must rest
and free myself from
slumbers troubled brew.
But at the waning of the day in vespers hush,
when voices play,
Once again, I seek my rendezvous.

COLLEEN

JERRY PHILLIPS

She sat there among Roses and Narcissus,
Natures beauty abounding.
The sun was just rising and off in the distance
morning bells were sounding.
She bowed her head and breathed a soft sigh.
The morning light glinted from a tear in her eye.
But she was not crying for loves withholding.
She cried for the wonders of the day unfolding.
She sat up easel, her brushes and oil,
ready to capture this moment, less it might spoil.

I LIVE

JERRY PHILLIPS

Do not stand at my grave and weep.
I am not there, I do not sleep.
I am the desert wind that blows.
I am the diamond glints of sun on snow.

I am the dawn that heralds the day.
I am the joy in children's play.
I am the rain that brings the flowers.
I am the peace in quiet hours.

So do not stand at my grave and cry.
I am not there, I did not die.
So as the sun and stars shine bright,
So I am here both day and night.
Forever.

WITH THE OLD APRON ON

LOREN CHAPMAN

In the twilight hours
Just before dawn
Mom's in the kitchen
With her old apron on.

Frying them taters,
Putting bacon on.
Got the morning coffee going
With her old apron on.

The bell rings out,
She yells out "come on y'all
Foods on the table!"
With the old apron on.

All day long
Chores to be done
floors to be scrubbed
With the old apron on.

Up with the sun,
No rest since dawn
Planting to be done.
With the old apron on.

Old man on the plow,
Kids chasing the dog.
Moms out in the garden
With the old apron on.

Now comes the sunset
The day finally gone.
Mom falls asleep by the fire
With the old apron on.

YOU ARE GONE

L O R E N   C H A P M A N

My heart still so sad
That you are gone,
But I know you would want us to carry on.
Life without you
Will never be the same.
To my friends and loved ones,
It's hard to explain.

They understand and help deal with the pain
And with love for each other
We will remain.
To remember the good
Along with the bad.

Just give a smile,
And don't be so sad.
Just remember they loved us
One and all.
But they had to go.
It was God's call.

THE PATH YOU FOLLOW

Loren Chapman

The path you follow,
The road you take
The life's decisions you must make.
For when life gets tough
Do not run.

Be with yourself, be as one.
Trust your soul deep inside.
Do not run, do not hide.

Stay true to your values,
Stand for your pride.
For you will succeed
If you have it inside.

AN ODE TO MY MORNING WOODY

LOREN CHAPMAN

My morning woody stands up-right
My morning woody I hold very tight.
It greats me each morning,
Usually up before I.
If I look down it, it might spit in my eye.
I caress and fondle, I play with pride
For my morning woody is nothing to hide.
The sixe is awesome, big and bold.
It's so big takes to hands to hold.
But all will end soon enough
When I make the trip to do my stuff.
I try to aim, I do my best but all
That happens is I make a mess.
Splatter the tank, piss on the floor.
Try to stop, but need to pee some more.
Seems like hours, longer than days.
And then my morning woody slowly goes away.
As I watch it shrivel and watch it shrink
I grab a towel off the sink.
I have a mess. Quite a chore
Before I turn and walk out the door.
And my morning woody, it is no more.

THE ROAD TO NOWHERE

L o r e n C h a p m a n

Please, do not follow me
For I am the road to nowhere.
My paths have been empty
All have dead ends.
Until I met you, I had no friends.
If you will help, I just might find
It's never too late to ease my mind.
Help me choose, find a direction
For I can make the connection.

The road to nowhere
I will no longer be.
If I have you and you have me.

THE DARKNESS OF NIGHT

LOREN CHAPMAN

In the darkness of night
Try not to fear
Not to fright
If you believe,
You will be alright.

In the brightness of day
Keep a smile on your face
And a quick pace.
Keep one step ahead,
Hope to win the race.

In the darkness of night,
The bright of day
You will survive
Through the way.

WHEN YOU SAY GOOD-BY

LOREN CHAPMAN

The tears I no longer cry
For I know you will say good-by.
It still may hurt
But that's ok
Just let me know when
you'll go away.
Over my shoulder
I will not look back.
I must go on
When you day so-long.
Good-by is forever
Just remember that.
When you leave
You can't turn back.

THE DAY AFTER CHRISTMAS

LOREN CHAPMAN

T'was the day after Christmas
I saw such a sight
Mr. and Mrs. Clause
Were in a big fight.
"you come home smelling
Of hookers and beer,
And you claim it's all
To spread Christmas cheer.
You sit in the Mall, you're
Lazy and fat.
Come here little boy,
is that your Mom?
I'd like to tap that.
You work one day a year
And what have I got?
Well don't look for your deer.
They are in the stew pot!"

THE INS AND THE OUTS

COLLEEN CHAPMAN

Once upon a time
There were the in people
And the out people.

The in people did in things
And the out people
did out things.

But one day
The out people found
What the in people were doing.

And started to copy them.

As a consequence
What the in people were doing
Was no longer in.

For the out people were doing it.

These were the bad years,
The lean years,
The out years when nothing was in.

But the in people rallied.

And started doing other things
That were in.
Because they were secret as yet

If you see people doing things
You don't understand,
Just copy them.

And they'll quit.

For what is in, is in
And what is out, is out.
And what is in may be in
Because it is out.

But what is out
Even if it seems in.

To be really in
it cannot be done by the out.
Or it has to be very far out.

And if it is in, it is in
Even if it seems out.
In, out,
In again,
Out again
And on and on.

THE HANDLE

While looking at my land today,
At what I am not sure,
I saw a lonely pitchfork
Stuck deeply in manure.

A sparrow saw the same as I
As he winged his way through space.
There was no doubt as to his goal
As he swooped with downward grace

He lit upon the handle there.
With style so swift and sure,
He worked his way down to his goal,
The large pile of manure.

He ate in quiet repose thereon
Until he claimed his fill.
Then climbed back up the handle
And cleaned his little bill.

He pulled his meager preflight check
Took one remaining peck
Then jumped off into outer space.
And broke his little neck!

The moral of this story is
To use as you see fit.
Don't fly off the handle
When you know you're full of shit!

JUST A LITTLE MIXED UP

Or
Retirees lament

Just a line to say I'm living,
That I'm not among the dead.
Tho' I'm getting more forgetful
And more mixed up in my head.

For sometimes I can't remember
As I stand at the foot of the stairs
If I must go up for something
Or if I've just come down from up there.

And before the 'fridge so often
My poor mind is filled with doubt.
Have I just put food away
Or have I come to take something out?

So if it is my turn to write you
There is no need for getting sore.
I may think I have written
And don't want to be a bore.

There I stood before the mailbox
With a face so very red.
Instead of mailing you my letter
I had opened it instead!

Today being my 75th birthday, (2009) it seems like a good time to post this.
Colleen Chapman

HOW TO STAY YOUNG

1. Throw out nonessential numbers. Like age, weight and height. Let the doctors worry about them. That's what they get paid for, isn't it?
2. Keep only cheerful friends. The grouches and whiners pull you down faster than you can lift them up.
3. Keep learning. Learn more about the computer, crafts, gardening, whatever. Never let the brain idle. "An idle mind is the Devil's workshop." And the Devil's name is Alzheimer's.
4. Enjoy the simple things.
5. Laugh often, long and loud. Laugh until you gasp for breath. Learn to laugh at yourself.
6. The tears happen. Endure grieve and move on. The only person who is with us our entire life is ourselves. Be ALIVE while you are alive. Be the kind of person YOU want to spend your time with.
7. Surround yourself with what you love, whether it's family, pets, keepsakes, music, plants, hobbies, whatever. Your home is your refuge. Be sure to invite in whatever Supreme Being your religion leads you to believe in.
8. Cherish your health. If it's good, preserve it. If it is unstable, improve it. If it is beyond what you can improve, get help. If it is beyond help, accept it and "let go and let God."
9. Don't take guilt trips. Take a trip to the mall, to the next county; to a foreign country but not to where your guilt lives. But do, if you haven't already, do whatever you can to make amends for whatever makes you feel guilty. Ask for forgiveness, forgive yourself, and move on.
10. Tell the people you love, that you love them. Don't take it for granted that they know. And even if they do, it's nice to hear.

And remember...life is not measured by the breaths we take, but by the moments that take our breaths away.

MY CHILDREN

Colleen Chapman

My children are adults now, and some I seldom see.
I wonder...do they know, where ever they go,
they take a part of me?
And do they know...where ever they go,
they are still here with me?
In their own spot in my heart,
where they will always be.

I hope people say I am like my Mom in a lot of ways. I have so many happy memories to bring to "Bits And Pieces", but the first one would be the one from when I turned 24. She wrote me a poem. This is how it goes.

Suzi

There is a young lady called Suzi,
who is very sweet and quite pretty.
On this day as she turns 24,
my memories turn to days of yore.

I can still see her wiggle as she learned to walk,
and hear her giggle long before she could talk.
With big smiling eyes and hair all a curl,
she was darn near perfect, that little girl.

There was a magic cure only Mom could do.
It was known known to be true a hug and a kiss
could cure any old booboo.
As she became a teenager, was often filled
with anger at her over protective Mother.

Both joy and tears were shared o'er the years
as the little girl became a woman.
Hearts were near broken by words
that were spoken by us to each other.
Bad times we did weather, grew closer together,
a new understanding to find.
'Twas hard to loosen the strings, but found that I must.
To try to keep her a safe little girl was unfair and unjust.

Knowing the mistakes she would probably make,
how I did worry and fret for my little girls fate.
For mistakes we all make as we learn and grow,
but down the right path I knew she would finally go.

She's all grown up now and has her own life.
Memories of good times far outnumber the strife.
Of the woman she has become I am very proud.
She is ready for real life, but still has her cloud.

313

For the silver lining she will always look
whenever life gives her a mean left hook.
Among my memories there will always be
a three year old Suzi running to me
for a "hub ana kith ana skeeze."

And from my heart I say, thank you,
God, for sending her my way,
to be my friend, my Suzi, my daughter.

I would like to add a postscript to this. Every once in a while, I take out this poem and I look at the cuter than cute oil painting cover she did of a little girl in a white dress and bonnet, holding and smelling some blue flowers, and then I read the poem. I can never get through it with dry eyes. I am sure your eyes are not dry and are having trouble reading this. What more can one ask for a birthday gift. At the time this was written, we were living far apart and this gift was and still is very precious to me. As a matter of fact, I must go dry my eyes and blow my nose, so this is the end of this "Bits And Pieces."

Mom wrote this on a birthday card.

SUZI

She is very special. I wonder why.
Is it because she was born on the Fourth of July?
Is that where she got the sparkle in her eyes?
She was born with a pop, a sizzle, zing and zang.
Yep that little girl was born with a bang.
She is still sizzling, singing and banging...
No wait! That doesn't sound right!
So I'll shut my mouth up tight.

All our yesterdays are called the past. That's what it is. Past. Gone. It can't be changed. Hang on to the good memories and let the rest go. Tomorrow is the future. Not quite here yet, just out of reach. Today is called the present. That's what it is. A present. Every morning we wake up to a whole new present. Be grateful. Use it wisely. Be happy. At bedtime ask yourself if Our Heavenly Father approves of how we have used his present to us.

WISHES

wish I had words of wisdom to pass along on this New Year's Day.
I wish I was so smart I'd know exactly what to say.
I wish people would stop killing each other,
and claim they are doing it in God's name!
God said we should love one another,
so I know He's not to blame.
I wish we would all learn to really live as Jesus would have us do.
I wish we really did care
when we ask "How are you?"
I wish we would not pass judgment on of our fellow man.
I wish we could give and get a smile
and lend a helping hand.
I wish, I wish I wish....the list goes on and on.
So I'll just say good luck to you all
in the year ahead.

THE TEENAGE YEARS

ACT YOUR AGE

COLLEEN CHAPMAN

My daughter Diane was taller than I am by the time she was 13. While at Disneyland, the kids and I were going to our car to get our picnic lunch and to rest a while. Walking beside me, Diane asked if I would let her be on her own when we went back in. My answer was no. "I am 16 and you ought to let me go on my own." she demanded. "No! I will not!" Some women walking behind us heard my reply. One of them, thinking Diane was the mother and I the child, grabbed the tail end of my sweater, and said, "How dare you talk to your mother like that!" Diane saw no humor in that.

A week or so later I was watering the flower beds in the front yard when Diane's date arrived. He was a little early and I was embarrassed at being caught in cut off jeans, barefoot and my hair in pig tails. He stopped to chat a few minutes as usual.

The next time he came to pick her up, he told me his older brother was coming home on leave from the Army, and he asked if I would go out with his brother, him and Diane. I said, "Sure, if my husband and kids don't mind." He looked very surprised and embarrassed. He explained he thought I was Diane's older sister and had felt sorry for me, being in charge of all the kids. Diane didn't think that was funny either.

The next morning she was still mad at me. She said if I would act and dress my age, (32), things like that wouldn't happen. That afternoon we were going shopping for school cloths for her. I pulled my hair back in a severe bun, put on a skirt someone had given me that needed to be shortened. It came a little past mid-calf. I chose the most matronly blouse I owned, and a pair of low heeled shoes to complete the outfit. She refused to leave the house with me until I changed my clothes.

Miniskirts were in style. My girls' skirts had to pass a test. The girls had to show me they could bend, stoop, and sit without showing something that should not be shown. It was not fair to the guys, I told them, to advertise unless they were giving away or selling what they were showing. Diane and her girlfriend had bought very short, tight skirts. She insisted she be allowed to wear it. Again, we were going shopping for school cloths, her senior year. I was prepared for this situation. I had bought a tight skirt at a Goodwill store. I shortened it. When she saw me in it, she was not pleased. She said she would change if I would. There was just no pleasing that girl!

BECOMING A LADY

COLLEEN CHAPMAN

When my oldest daughter Diane was about 12 years old, I made sure she knew what to expect as she left childhood and began her journey into womanhood. She was not at all sure she wanted to be a lady. Being a tomboy was soooo much fun! Want to or not, the signs were there. She would not be a little girl much longer. Therefore she was given the information and necessities for what would surely happen soon.

One Saturday she, her brothers and cousins were playing football. She came into the house, went into the bathroom, then into her bedroom, back to the bathroom, and in a few minutes, stood in the doorway between the kitchen and living room. Just stood there. I looked up from whatever I was doing, wondering what was wrong. She was wearing a pair of Howard old ragged pants which were several sizes too large. One leg was rolled up to her knee. The other was unrolled and rested on the floor, covering her foot. The old baggy shirt went very well with the pants. One pocket hung by a few threads. One sleeve hung at half-mast. What should have been on her shoulder was now closer to her elbow. One of her long braids was undone. The ribbon was gone, but various other things decorated her hair. Mud, grass, foxtails, and those seedpods with corkscrew tails, a lady bug or two, and I swear I heard a cricket! Mud decorated her in spots, from head to toe! Well, this vision of loveliness saw she had my undivided attention. She put one hand on her hip, the other to the side of her head, (fingers getting stuck in the muddy mess.) striking a glamour girl pose, she announced in a very good Marilyn Monroe type voice, "I" she said breathlessly, "HAVE BECOME, (pause, a little wiggle of the hips,) A LADY!"

THE GIRL UP THE ROAD

COLLEEN CHAPMAN

One day I was weeding my garden when I heard a voice behind me say, "Hi, my name is Emily. Oh! Sorry I scared you. I live in the new yellow house down the road. Can I help you?" Before I could say a word, she dropped to her knees and started pulling weeds. "What's your name?" she asked. In the next half hour I learned that she was 14, had two sisters and a brother, all home schooled except her older sister who was away at college. What church she went to, she loved to "hang out" at the library and would like to come and help me once in a while, and asked if she did a good job, could she get paid for it. That girl sure could talk!

"Yes, I can pay you for helping me, but I won't pay by the hour. I will show you what I want you to do, and we will make an agreement as to how much that job is worth. OK?" "Sure. The kids call me retard." she said, "Even my brother and sister. I am not retarded. I have a muscle skills problem, but I'm not a retard!" she said forcefully. "Do you do exercises to improve your muscle skills?" I asked. She shook her head. "If you would like, I can teach you some exercises. It will take time, but it will help." "Yes, I would like that." "I will have to get permission from your parents first. I'll give you a note to take to them. If it is OK, we can start tomorrow afternoon, and do it three times a week."

About a week after we started the exercises, I asked her if she was doing them every morning and night like she was supposed to. She wasn't. I told her that I could teach her the exercises, but it was her job to do them. (I had also been trying to teach her to think things through, use logic, etc.) She thought for a minute then said, "My job, huh. Well, people get paid for doing a job. How much do I get paid for that?" "How about fifty cents for each session?" "I think it's worth more than that. If I promise to do them every night and morning and pay attention to the new ones at our sessions, I think it is worth at least $1.00 each session." I agreed. I was so glad that she was thinking things through, using logic, becoming surer of herself, etc. After she left, I had to laugh. I was spending six hours a week working with her and had just agreed to pay her for it. So who was the "retard?" Her or me?

One day I was feeling irritable and didn't feel like having her around with her constant chatter and questions. I was hoping she wouldn't call to see if I had anything for her to do, but she did. I told her I couldn't afford to pay her to work that day. I have a rule, never lie to a child. I wiggled out of it this time by telling myself that my nerves couldn't afford her that day. "That's ok," she said cheerfully, "I'll help you for nothing. That's what Christians do. That's what friends do too." Well, I tell you, I felt very, very small. Since then there is always something for her to do! One day about a year later, Emily was not her usual talkative self. She looked sad and dawdled instead of working. When I asked her what was wrong she said she thought she was suffering from PMS. I told her I thought it was more than that, and when she was ready to talk, I was ready to listen. She sat crossed legged looking at the ground for a long time. Then the tears started. "I think I will run away or kill myself. My mom got really mad at me and called me names." "Do you sometimes get mad at your mom and would you call her names if you dared to?" "Well...yeah." "That doesn't mean that you don't love her, does it. Maybe you don't like her very much right then, but you still love her. Parents lose their tempers, they make mistakes, but they still love their kids."

"That isn't the only problem. My little brother and little sister call me retard all the time. So do all the kids around here. All the kids my age at our church are getting summer jobs. The girls have boyfriends. I will never have a boyfriend. I'm fat and ugly. And who is going to hire a retard?" "To start with, you are not ugly. You are no beauty, but you are not ugly. Yes, you are overweight. You can do something about that. And I will hire you. As it is now, you come up to help whenever you want to. If I hire you I will expect you to be here on certain days, certain hours and to do certain jobs. You can't just come and go as you please." "How come?" "Because that is the way it works. What if you went to Burger King and no one was there to take your order or cook your food because they decided to go home early?" "OK. That takes care of that problem, but what about my sister and brother? They are really mean sometimes."

"What do you do when they call you names?" "I call them names and say mean things to them too!" "That's a natural reaction, but it doesn't make things any better, does it. What do you think would happen if instead of calling them names, you say something like... pretend you are your sister or brother. I am you. Now call me names." "I can't do that?" "Yes you can. Do it." After some hesitation she called me a fat retard. "God loves you and so do I." I said. "My brother would say I don't love you!" "Then you should say that's all right, I know you don't. But God loves me and you, and I love you." "Then he would say shut up you fat retard." "Then you should say –yes, I am fat and a retard, but God loves me. God loves you and I am trying to!" She laughed and promised to try it. "As for the boyfriend, all in good time. Don't be in a hurry to be a grown up. You are a kid for a short time. Enjoy it. If there is someone out there for you, he will come your way when it is time for it to happen."

One day Emily noticed I have small feet. "Your feet are so little. Have they always been that small?" she asked. "No. When I was young they were big but the older I get the smaller they get." "My gosh! Why?" "I'm joking. You have to get used to being teased and know when someone is teasing or kidding you." Another time she was helping me place some pots. I used a yard stick to get the pots evenly spaced. After I had placed a pot it didn't look right, so I laid the yardstick on the ground again. The pot was an inch or two out of place. I said "Well, I must have used the other side of the yardstick when I measured the first time, and it must be longer on the other side than it is on this side." Emily thought that over, and said "You're kidding, right? That was funny. But if I said something like that people wouldn't know I was kidding. They would think I said it because I am a retard."

Poor girl. Last year when the Dahlias had died and had been cut back, I asked Emily to take the ones that needed to be divided out of the pots and put them into boxes. Each pot had a marker in it with the color and type of the plant. Each box was labeled with the color and type of plant that was to be put in them. Emily was supposed to gather all the pots of one kind, take care of them, them go on to the next kind. I went about doing something else and didn't notice that Emily was not doing as she was supposed to. Instead of going down the row of plants, she had taken them from one end of the bed, from all five rows, which were five different types and colors, and had done about 1/3 of the bed.

When it was time to stop for lunch, she was very proud of working so hard and getting so much done. I went to look and admire her work. When I saw what she had done, I was irritated to say the least. She saw the look on my face and asked what was wrong. I pointed out what she had done, and what she had been told to do. "I understand the mistake I made. I'm sorry. It won't happen again." she said. Then looking sad and defiant at the same time she said," You think I'm not very smart, don't you!" Dear Lord, I thought, please help me to say the right thing to her. "Emily, I don't know what your IQ is. Do you know what that is?" "Yes, it is intelligence quotient or something like that." "I know you well enough to know what your HQ is." "HQ? What is that?" "It is your heart quotient or something like that. You have a very good and kind heart. That is just as important." "Yes I do. But how far is that going to get me when I need to earn a living? How far will that get me when it's time to get married? Is it going to make me pretty? I don't think so!" Sometimes life just doesn't seem fair. We are not all born equal. Some people are born to a poor family, are ugly and dumb or crippled. Some are born to a rich family, are good looking and smart, and seem to flit through life with no worries, problems, or sorrows. Others must struggle, have all kinds of bad things happen to them. Who do you think learns the most and gets stronger every time they overcome difficulty? When we get to Heaven, who is God going to prize the most? The one who flitted through life on a breeze or the one who grew and learned and got stronger? I believe you are one of Gods special children. He gave you an extra burden for a reason. I think you are supposed to use your burden to do his work. You can show that people who are not quite as bright as others can do good in this world. You told me once that you would like to be a missionary but didn't think you could because you are not smart enough. How smart do you have to be to give a kid a bath, or comfort them, rock them to sleep? Or clean up after them. You get the idea. You don't have to wait until you are an adult to do good things. You could go to a nursing home and do things for the people there. Comb the women's hair. Play games with them. Just talk to them. You will think of other things to do. End of sermon." After giving this some thought Emily said, "I would like to serve God in that way. But how am I going to get to the nursing home?" UH OH! No, I didn't take on that task!

She doesn't come around very much now. She is 16 and met a guy at a party and dance for special needs people. She seems to be quite smitten with him and said he likes her.

A FUGITIVE FROM JUSTICE

DOROTHY PATTON

Ada had a big heart. I guess a lot of people considered her a refuge of sorts. I went over there one day and two high school girls were there. One of them, Yolanda, was a former neighbor of Ada's, but that was before I had come to Phoenix and I had never met either of the girls. But as soon as I came in they started pleading with me, "Can you get us into Patterdale?" Ada had told them that I worked part time as a relief counselor at the Patterdale School for wayward girls. The girls had skipped school and gone to the park where they had run into a neighbor who was tight with Yolanda's mother, Charlene. Of course she would tell, the girls reasoned, therefore it was not safe to go home. I told the girls that you don't check into Patterdale like checking into a hotel. You have to go through the courts. And besides, most of the girls that were there wanted desperately to go home. They were homesick, but once there you had to stay for a while whether you wanted to or not. But the girls insisted that they couldn't go home. They told of terrible beatings in the past and Yolanda said that her step-father had told her he would kill her if she messed up again and she believed him. Since I worked at Patterdale and also worked with young people at church, I was considered an expert and it seemed that I was expected to come up with a solution. So I called in another expert, Helen, the director of the young people's department at church. She came right over and we talked to the girls for some time but couldn't change their minds. Finally she called the pastor of the church and he told us to bring the girls to his office. But the girls were afraid to get in the car, they were afraid we were going to take them home.

So Helen made a promise to them that we wouldn't take them home till they were ready to go. We decided to take both our cars and Yolanda rode with me and the other girl with Helen. The pastor was soon able to talk the other girl into going home and Helen led her triumphantly out to her car and drove her home. Yolanda, however, would not relent. The pastor finally gave up and called child protective services. They were closing but made an appointment for Yolanda and her parents to come at nine the next morning. In the meantime, they said, Yolanda had no choice but to go home. Yolanda said nothing till we got out to the car. She wouldn't get in. "I really can't go home," she said. "I'll have to run away." I grabbed her hand as she started to go. "Let's go back over to Ada's," I said. "Maybe we can figure out something." Ada called Charlene and told her about the appointment the next morning and asked her to let Yolanda spend the night with her. But Charlene had talked to the girl that Helen drove home and knew that Yolanda was with me and what had been going on. She was furious. She said she would not keep the appointment the next day and demanded that I bring Yolanda home immediately or she would call the police. I could see how terrified Yolanda was. And I felt bound by the promise that Helen had made. I couldn't bring myself to take her home even if I could have gotten her into the car, which I doubt that I could have done. So when Ada suggested that I take her out to my mothers to spend the night I was all for it. Mother lived a few miles out of Phoenix and hadn't been there long. They wouldn't know to look there and I could have Yolanda to child protective services in the morning before they could get their hands on her. We got into Phoenix a little early the next morning and I stopped at a donut place. I left Yolanda in the car and when I came out a police car was sitting right beside mine. I almost dropped the coffee. I knew I was busted. But the only thing on the minds of those policemen was donuts and coffee. They walked right past me. We got out of there and ate the donuts in the parking lot of child protective services. As soon as they opened we went in and Yolanda was interviewed. But she had no bruises and no witness to the beatings. She had to go home and should come back when she had proof. Back to Ada's for a solution. Ada called Charlene and asked her to come over and talk. But Charlene was more furious than ever. Said the police was looking for me and demanded that I bring Yolanda home immediately. "No," I said. "I'll call the police and give myself up and try to convince them that she needs protection." So I called the police and Yolanda went into Ada's bedroom and fell over on the bed and started having a seizure of some kind. Her face was contorted and her body jerking. I looked out the window and saw a police car stop in front of the house. I ran out and told them we needed to get her to a hospital. They came in and Ada and George were rubbing Yolanda's arms and legs. One of the policemen started working with her and the other one took me into another room and asked if Yolanda had said anything about sexual abuse. No, I said, she had only talked about the beatings. "There is more here than a child afraid of normal punishment," he said. He got on the phone to Charlene and demanded that she come over immediately. When she got there he met her outside and they talked for a few minutes then came on in. Charlene was no longer furious and was very concerned about Yolanda. They were all in the bedroom with Yolanda for a while and I waited in the living room for the handcuffs. But when they came out nobody even mentioned the kidnapping. Yolanda was much better and the police escorted them home and talked to the step father. Yolanda had left her glasses and came by Ada's to pick them up the next morning on the way to school while Charlene waited in the car. Her mother was being real sweet to her, she said, and her step father hadn't said a word to her. I saw Yolanda a few years later at Ada's house. She was married and seemed happy.

327

GO DIG A HOLE

Sue Aubert

When Debbie and I were both in Jr. High (early 1970's) we were two years apart. We both had trouble with the local Mexican kids because our last name was Silva, but we didn't have dark skin or speak the language. Those kids loved to tease Debbie. One day after school, the poor girl got so frustrated over the teasing and tormenting, she whirled around with her arms by her side and fists clinched as tight as they could be, and yelled at the kids, "Why don't you just—just go climb a tree and dig a hole in it!" She then whirled around and continued walking home. She was so cute, but sooooo mad, that I didn't dare laugh. She was my sister and I had to take up for her. So I turned to the kids, who didn't know what to think about what they had been told to do, and said, "Yeah!" and then walked on home with Debbie.

PUT ON A HAPPY FACE

SUE AUBERT

When Debbie was in the 7th grade and I was in the 9th, (1971) she was in the chorus and I was in the orchestra. Our spring Concert was songs from musicals. The chorus was singing, the orchestra was playing, and there was Debbie in the front row, feet apart, arms by her side, brow furrowed and singing really hard. Unless you were deaf and lip reading, there is no way you would believe she was singing Put on a Happy Face.

INNOCENT GIRLS

COLLEEN CHAPMAN

Betty and a bunch of other teen-agers went to the movies in Salinas. She was telling all of us about the movie, and how they had run into some other kids who lived in Chualar and needed a ride home. They all piled into the car, and Betty had to sit on Jitter's lap and Laura sat on Arthur's lap. Louon shook his head and said, "You had better not be doing that. The first thing you know, you'll be pregnant."

One night Betty woke me up. She was almost in tears. She said, "I had to sit on Jitter's lap again tonight and I'm afraid I'm going to be pregnant! I'm afraid to tell Mother and Daddy! I don't know what to do!"

I said, "Betty, you're a good girl. God isn't going to make you have a baby for sitting on a guy's lap. You have to steal or do something real bad for that to happen."

JUST WHERE HAVE YOU BEEN?

COLLEEN CHAPMAN

All the kids had left the nest except for Loren, who was in high school. Howard had not retired yet, so most of the time it was just Loren and me at home. I had always made it a point to be at home when my kids got home from school. One day my errands took longer than expected, and I got home about an hour after Loren did. "And just where have you been?" he asked. "If you were going to be late you could have called." After explaining where I had been, and there isn't a phone on the country road my car stalled on, I thought, hey! Who does he think he is, my father? We discussed the situation. Now that he was a teen-ager, he had more freedom than he did when he was younger. So did I. That meant I did not have to be home when he got home. If I did plan to be gone, I would tell him ahead of time or leave him a note out of courtesy, telling him when I expected to be home. He was still my child. He was expected to continue following the rules. The car I was driving at the time ran fine except when I stopped and idled. Like at a signal light or stop sign. The engine would often die and wouldn't start again until it cooled off some. One day that happened several times. When I got home, Loren did his father act again. This time I made up a story no one could be expected to believe. This became the normal occurrence. Loren would listen, trying to keep a straight face and saying thing like…Uh huh, sure. One day when I came home late, the grandson of our next-door neighbor was there. This is the story I told:

My car died at the stop sign by Strathmore. I managed to coast to the side of the road and park. A man came out of the olive orchard and pulled me out of the car. He drug me into orchard. We struggled. When he went back to the car, it had cooled off enough to start. I knew it would die at the next stop sign, so I ran down the road and sure enough, there it was. I was hoping the man had abandoned it. I went into the orchard and approached the car carefully, but the man saw me. He came after me. (I described the fight blow by blow. Jeff was very excited and said things like…OH NO! HE DIDN'T…YOU DIDN'T! OH MY GOSH!) I stopped talking, got a drink of water, and sat down. Jeff said, "What did you do then? Are you OK? Are you going to call the police? ARE YOU ALL RIGHT?" He didn't stop to think that I should be covered with dirt and blood, my cloths should be torn and I should be cut and bruised if what I described really happened. I said, "He killed me." Poor Jeff said, "OH MY GOD!!!!....what?????" he stared at me for a second or two, and then turned to look at Loren. He said, "Last month she was swallowed whole by an alligator, kicked her way out, and then made a purse and shoes out of him"

MARY AND ED

COLLEEN CHAPMAN

My high school kids came home one day very upset. A friend had run away from home, and was at her boyfriend's house. I had to do something, they said. I didn't know this girl or her parents. Didn't matter they said, do something. I went with them to the boyfriend's apartment. Mary and Ed were there, as well as Ed's roommate. I told Mary she could come home with us. Of course, she didn't want to. I told her that since she was under age and Ed was not, he could be arrested for contributing to the delinquency of a minor. He could go to jail. To Ed's relief, she agreed to go home with us.

When we got home I told her to call her mother and tell her where she was. Then I would talk to her mother. We would work something out. Mary refused. I informed her that since she was a run away, I was breaking the law if I didn't let her parents or the Police Department know where she was. She made the call. We went to see her mother.

I could not believe the petty issues this family had. Mary had been sent from the dinner table by her father for wearing a tank top to the table. That is the reason she ran away. Her mother said she worked full time in order to afford the extra luxuries they all enjoyed. She was upset because she had talked about her working less hours, and her kids objected. She wouldn't be able to buy as much stuff for them if she earned less money.

Mary's sister made it known that her biggest concern was that Mary had taken her new color pencils with her, and she wanted them back. All I could think of to say to her mother was; these kids had to have learned their values and priorities from her and her husband. They had some work to do to get things straightened out, starting with themselves. Mary stayed with us several months. This "Nice, strictly raised Catholic girl" taught my kids some really raunchy songs. This was one kid I didn't mind not seeing any more after she returned to her family.

Ed arrived one evening during dinnertime. There was not enough room at the table for Howard and me. We sat in our living room chairs with a tray. We were all in the same room, since there was no wall between the living room and dining area. For some reason, Ed was uncomfortable around Howard. Instead of sitting down, he moved around nervously.

He bumped Howard's tray. The salad bowl fell on Howard's lap, upside down. Howard sat looking down at the mess, not saying a word. "I'm sorry, Mr. Chapman" Ed said. Howard didn't look up or answer. "Mr. Chapman, I am soooo sorry!" Still no reply from Howard. Ed bent forward, trying to see Howard's face. "Mr. Chapman? Mr. Chapman? Mr. Chapman?" Ed bent over more with each Mr. Chapman as he tried to see Howard's face. "You don't like me very much, do you Mr. Chapman." Still no response. I opened the front door and said, "Goodbye, Ed" Ed made a hasty retreat.

SECRETLY ENGAGED

COLLEEN CHAPMAN

Jack finished boot camp and had a two week leave. He and Susan were "secretly engaged." Taking a big chance, I invited him to spend his two weeks leave with us. We lived in Van Nuys, and were going to spend some time at the cabin on Tule River. If thing worked out as I thought they would, Sue would be sick of him by the end of the first week. Of course, it could be dangerous, throwing them together like that. But I thought having Jack there day in and day out wouldn't be as romantic as being engaged to a soldier who was far from home. Jack was in Junior high when he first started hanging around. Even when none of my kids were at home, or busy, he hung around waiting. I felt sorry for him; he wanted so very much to be a part of our family. I'm not sure just when he and Sue fell in love. Sue was only 16, and such a romantic, I worried about her.

It didn't take long for Sue to discover that Jack was a poor sport. If he lost a hand of card or any other game they played, he pouted. She didn't like that. He expected her to wait on him, and didn't ask, he ordered. She didn't like that, either. Our source of drinking water while waiting for our well to be dug was a stand with a large clay pot with a spigot. We had four five-gallon glass Sparklets water bottles which went upside down on top. Our water came from an Artisan spring. Jack offered to fill the bottles. He started to pick up two of the bottles at the same time. I suggested he do one at a time.

They may be light when they are empty but weren't when they were full. He said he could handle it, and before anyone could stop him, he picked up the two empty bottles and with a mighty swing, put them on his shoulders. The bottles crashed together behind his head and fell to the floor in many, many pieces. He looked funny, standing there with the necks of the bottles in his hands. He wasn't hurt by the glass, but our laughter cut him to the core. The poor guy. I wonder if he ever learned to laugh at himself.

I was right about Sue being sick of him by the end of the first week. On the fourth day she pleaded with me to get him out of there. He decided he would go spend the rest of his leave with his family. Guess what! The engagement was off!

SHUT THE DOOR

TAKEN FROM THE FAMILY SITE

Colleen, here is a story Mom told me, for the book. Sandi

It was a cold and windy day. Raining off and on. Ruby was expecting her boyfriend, and he was late. She went to the door, opened it and stood looking down the road. She then Sat in the open doorway. Daddy said, "Ruby, shut the door." She ignored him. After a few minutes Daddy again said, "Ruby, shut the door." Again, she ignored him. Then this patient, mild mannered man said, "Ruby, if you don't get out of that door and shut it, I am going to kick you out of it and shut it myself!" Ruby said, "Well, just kick me out and see who cares!" Daddy put down his coffee cup, calmly folded his paper and laid it on the table. He got up, walked calmly to the door, and kicked Ruby on the fanny and sent her flying down three step, and flat on her tummy in a mud puddle. I ran through the house and out another door, ran around the house and squatted down next to Ruby, who was still stunned. "Kicked ya out. huh." She giggled. "Well, I didn't think he would do it" Ruby answered, undecided if she wanted to laugh or cry.

Ruby... This is how I remembers the same story.

One evening Mother and I were having one of our arguments. Mother was getting really upset. I was standing in the kitchen doorway, which opened to the outside. Daddy had had enough of my rebelliousness and decided to do something about it. (I was 16 at the time) Daddy said "Ruby, if you don't shut up, I'm going to kick you out that door." I almost never talked back to Daddy, but this time I said "Well, kick me out then." The next thing I knew, I was sitting on the ground at the bottom of the steps! I was not hurt, just stunned. But that certainly ended the argument.

Colleen...Daddy was a very mild mannered man. He almost never showed anger. I cannot remember him striking one of us. When he was really mad or upset, he would walk back and forth with his hands in his pockets and say Dad blame the dad blame luck to the dad blame devil anyhow. **DAD BLAME IT!!!!** Sometimes there would be a few dadgumits thrown in

Dorothy…I remember watching Daddy walk toward Ruby. I didn't really think that he would kick her out. Actually, he didn't really kick, he just placed his foot on her fanny and gave a big push. I don't remember Ruby ever talking that way to Daddy again.

Ruby…I didn't see it coming. I just found myself on the ground very surprise and very shocked. I was not hurt, but I wanted to cry. I also wanted to laugh. I don't remember ever sassing daddy any other time. I had a lot of love and respect for him. He always treated me with respect. I don't know why I sassed him that time. I guess I could say "the devil made me do it."

Colleen…No, the devil didn't make you do it. The devil can make you WANT to do it, but he can't make you do anything. The choice is ours. I would say you made a baaaaad choice.

DRAWING BY SANDRA

SUSAN'S FIT

C O L L E E N   C H A P M A N

I don't know if I can do justice to her fit in print but I will try. The last time I tried to demonstrate it, I hurt myself. It went like this: Simultaneously raise arms, bent at elbows, raise hands slightly above head, palms facing outward, bend right leg at knee, bring it up as high as possible, while back forms an S shape and move like a flag whipping in the wind, as the leg is lowered, with the arms and hands flapping like a pair of wings, and the left leg repeats the actions of the right leg. This all took place as she progressed across the floor. Her movements were not fast but were emphasized by a high pitched stifled scream. We all stared in amazement. I said, "Clear the runway! I think she's taking off!" I don't know what she was so mad about. She did this only one other time. Good thing, too. I don't think her back could take much of that.

THE FIRST AND THE LAST

SUE AUBERT

First let me explain who I am talking about. This man I call Howard is the only father I have ever known. We call him Howard instead of Dad, because he is only seventeen years older than my oldest sibling, and when any of us called him Dad in public, we got funny looks and lots of questions. It was just easier to call him by his name. Because we did, so do his biological sons, my two younger brothers. Howard came into our lives when I was quite young, but not too young to remember the first spanking I ever got. Don't get me wrong, spankings weren't something that happened very often. There are times when a child needs one. This first one came out of love and fear. Here is the deal. Robert and I could not have been more than four and six years old. But we were tall enough to reach the burner on the kitchen stove. Just as we were about to insert a piece of paper into the open flame, I heard a noise behind me. As I turned to look, there was a big hand headed for my behind. That incident made a big impression on me. I tell ya, I never played with fire again.

Now here is second and last time my dad ever spanked me. It was one of those days most parents dread. The day when a strong-headed teen-age daughter feels she needs to take a stand. A stand against the horrible task of doing the dishes. Well, there I sat, on a little worktable in the kitchen, across from Mom's fairly new refrigerator, rebelling against the fact that I had to do the dishes yet again. Mom had had just about enough of my attitude and called in the troops. I guess I got a little too flippant with my dad and the events that occurred are as follows: he pulled me off the table, went down on one knee, laid me over the other, and spanked me. I don't know if he knows this, but I felt no pain. All I felt was defiance. I remember the stare I tried to work up, the defiance I tried to show, and I remember the look of pain on his face. Was this one of those times "It hurt me more than it did you?" I was and am a big girl. It couldn't have been easy for him, either physically or emotionally, but love for Mom and us kids was enough for him to do the right thing for us all. Teaching respect isn't an easy thing to do. I learned much more than that from Howard. He taught me about honesty, integrity and----how does one phrase this---if you are not going to do a good job, don't do it at all.

And the rest of the story is:

I very seldom "called in the troops", but when I did, Howard knew it was time for him to take over, and he did it very well. I told him I just could not deal with Susan any more that day. His reply was, "All it takes is a little common sense and patience." Yeah, sure! We are talking about a teen-age girl here! I told him I was fresh out of both, so how about him going in the kitchen and using his common sense and patience with her.

He had no intention of spanking her, but just as he got to the door, Sue kicked the fridge. BAD TIMING! So much for patience. That really was a look of pain on his face. His knee hit the floor rather hard; he banged his elbow on the doorjamb and twisted his back a little. Yes, it truly did hurt him worse than it did her. He said that being pissed off got the best of common sense and patience.

At the time of the first spanking, I had to take Debra to the Doctor. Howard got off work early and came over to baby sit. We were not married at that time. Diane's home teacher was there also. Diane was confined to bed because she had hepatitis. A few days before, Robert had gone into the street again. I had done everything I could think of to get him to stay out of the street. He would always say he forgot. I told him I loved him a lot, and I just could not allow him to get hit and maybe killed by a car. If he couldn't remember to stay in the yard, I would have to spank him so hard his bottom would hurt if he even thought about going in the street.

When I got home it was obvious the kids had been crying. Before I could ask what was wrong, Robert pointed at me with his pinkie finger, (he has a habit of making a point by pointing with his pinkie in a poking or jabbing motion.) and said, "Boy, Maw, Howard sure does like me and Suzi!" No, he didn't grow up thinking that the way to show affection is with violence. He learned that we would do whatever it takes to teach an important lesson or to keep our kids safe.

THE HAUNTED THEATER

COLLEEN CHAPMAN

Grandma Sullivan once owned a boarding house in Safford, Arizona. It was a big two-story house next to an old theater. The theater had been closed for a long time and was all boarded up. It was long and narrow and had two or three floors. We were told that it was haunted and at night you could hear the actors, long dead of course, putting on a play. Betty, our cousin Verda and I use to go creeping up the stairs on the outside of the building. The stairs went from ground level to the top floor. We always intended to go in through a window on the second floor, which had a few boards missing, or so we said. We would almost get to the window, then get scared and run down the stairs as fast as we could.

One day I told Betty and Verda they were ole scardey cats. I crossed my fingers behind my back and told them that I had gone in the day before. They were older than I was, and if I could do it, so could they. I dared them and double dared them to go in. And you know that anybody worth anything simply will not pass up a dare. Especially not a double dare. The three of us started up the stairs. Betty and Verda side by side with me following. They said they were really going to do it this time. Had to or they would never hear the end of it from that little pest. Yes sir, really going in this time. Uh hu, gonna do it. I began to worry when we got closer to the window than we had ever been, although Betty and Verda were going slower and slower, they were still saying they were going in. Me and my big mouth! What had I done!

I began to regret telling that fib. I didn't want to go in and had to find a way to stop them without letting them know I was afraid. I thought hard while they inched closer and closer. Then I had a brilliant idea. It would work. Both were filling out and were very self-conscious of the changes taking place in their bodies. I said, "Verda, did you know that when you walk your butt wiggles? And it *really* wiggles when you climb stairs. Betty, did you know your boobs bounce when you walk? And you should see how they bounce when you come down the stairs fast." I could out run them easily enough. The ghosts were forgotten. For now.

THE SUNDOWNER

COLLEEN CHAPMAN

Vince had some work to do on the engine of his car. He parked it in front of the cabin at the Tule River. Experience had taught me that things did not always go as planned when it came to car work. I did not want a puddle of oil in the middle of the yard, close to the front door. I told him to move the car before he did anything to it. He was in the Army and considered himself an adult and resented being told what to do by his mother. He insisted the car was O.K. where it was, and anyway he would be finished by sundown and there would not be any oil or grease on the ground. I did not argue or put up a fuss, just listened quietly. About an hour later he came in and got cleaned up and changed his cloths. He had permission to use my car to go get the needed parts. As he was going out the door, I told him if he left his car where it was, I would move it myself. He grinned and said, "I took some parts of already and it won't start." I smiled back and said, "That's OK. I have a tractor."

The grin vanished. He went out to move the car. Since it was not running, he had to push it out of the front yard. He couldn't push it very easily in the soft dirt. All he could manage was to push it forward and to one side. Before he could do that, he had to move a pile of lumber to make room for the car. All the kids were in school, so he had no help. By the time he had finished, it was too late to go into town. The kids got home before he was finished and helped. He came into the cabin, got cleaned up, and sat down. He was still very angry. He grumbled his displeasure. I told him if he had driven the car to the place I had asked him to, he would have saved himself a lot of time and work. He sat fuming and grumbling. I swear I could see smoke coming out of his ears. It was clear that there was a lot he would like to say to me but didn't dare. After a while he asked, "Did you wash any clean sheets today?" "No," I replied, "I washed 14 dirty ones. I really didn't see any reason to wash clean ones."

Everyone laughed. He was angrier than ever. The next day he went to get the car parts. They had to be ordered. It was close to a week before the car was on the road again. And there was a huge oily spot where the car had been. That car was forever after called The Sundowner.

THERE IS A BETTER WAY

C OLLEEN C HAPMAN

My kids were good kids. If I told them to do or not to do something, they usually obeyed without question. On school days I had no trouble getting them out of bed. They knew I would wake them once. If they didn't get up and get ready for school in time, they were going anyway. If they were late, I would not only take them to school, I would walk them to their classroom to make sure they got there. What could be more embarrassing than that, especially for a high school kid? I didn't make them do anything. They had choices to make. They could choose to get to school on time. If they didn't, that meant they chose to have me escort them to school late.

One summer it was a battle to get the older ones out of bed. After a week of morning battles, I thought there had to be a better way. I did not like to start the day out like that. I was not going to have kids dragging in all hours of the morning for breakfast. I told them they could choose to be at the table when breakfast was served, and if they were not, it meant they chose to do without food until lunch time.

The next morning I told everyone it was time to rise and shine. They didn't. I waited half an hour. I went into the hall, screamed as loud as I could, and hid in my closet. The kids came running. They searched the house and yard, got dressed and were planning what to do next. Three would go to the neighbors' houses to see if I was there. One would stay home with the younger ones in case I showed up. I came out of my bedroom and said, "Oh, I'm glad to see you're all up and dressed. I can fix breakfast now."

The next morning I went into their rooms, woke them and whispered, "You're missing it. This is the only time this will ever happen, and you're missing it." They hurried in and asked what they were missing. The answer was...today, of course.

The third day, they all got up as soon as I woke them, except for Diane. I sat on the edge of her bed and bounced while singing Oh What a Beautiful Morning. I cannot carry a tune. She couldn't stand the torture and got up. The morning after that, she didn't. I told her in ten minutes she was going to get a pitcher of ice water poured on her. She didn't get up. Two of the boys and I tip toed into her bedroom. They jerked the covers off, and she yelled, "I'm getting

343

up!" just in time. Good. I really didn't want to soak the bed. Later I told her if she had so much trouble getting up, she must be over tired. I would have to insist she got to bed earlier. That would mean no staying out after nine on the week-ends. No more problems.

One day I got to thinking about all the things I did that Mother or whoever I was living with, didn't know about. What were my kids doing I didn't know about? There must be a way to find out. After giving it some thought, I found a way. When they came in for lunch, I acted like I was very sad. They kept looking at me and at each other. While eating lunch, I would sigh and shake my head. They finished lunch and went outside. I watched out the window. They were standing in a circle talking. They came back in and sat in a row on the couch. Dave being the oldest was the spokesman. "Mom, is something wrong?" I sat down and hid my face and pretended to cry. I said, "Yes! I'm sorry I'm such a bad mother. I thought I taught you kids better than that! I'm so sorry. I promise I will do better." They said, "Mom! You're a good mother! You did teach us better." They apologized for the following.

Robert didn't mean to get the sheets on the neighbor's line dirty. Vince didn't mean to hit the boy next door quite so hard, Susan didn't mean to call the girl next door a poop head, but she was just sooooo mad. Dave didn't mean to throw the baseball over the fence and conk Mr. Anderson on the head, Steven didn't mean to run into the flower bed, Diane didn't mean to ruin my panty hose she borrowed to play dress up with. Well, at least they weren't doing anything dangerous!

When Loren had been driving about six months I pulled a similar trick on him. We were living at the river, and he drove his car to school. After school one day I said, "Loren, why would a Highway Patrolman come here looking for you?" He said he didn't know, and I went on about my business in the kitchen. Loren got a glass of milk and a sandwich. As he sat eating, he was obviously thinking hard. About thirty minutes later he said, "I did drive a little fast to school this morning, and then there's the red light I ran yesterday morning, but I didn't see a Highway Patrolman or anyone else. When was he here?" "When was who here?" "The Highway Patrolman." "A Highway Patrolman was here?" "You said there was." "No I didn't. I asked if you knew why one WOULD come here looking for you. Don't go anywhere until we have a talk about your driving habits."

Vince was home on leave from the Army. We were on our way from Van Nuys to the river. The car was crowded and he was irritable. He and one of the other kids got into an argument. Or as they called it, a debate. Whatever it was, I was tired of listening to it. What I usually did when that kind of thing started, was pull off of the road and park the car. We didn't move until there was silence. But this time we were just a few miles from the river, it was a very hot day, I was tired, and didn't want to stop. I slowed down and looked out the window, looking at the mountain top. When the kids asked what I was looking at, I said, "Do you guys see an eagle on a rock near the top of that mountain? There are Bald Eagles around here, or so I've heard." The kids were still looking for the eagle as I pulled into the driveway. I went on into the cabin and most of them stayed outside, still looking for the eagle. Vince came in and asked exactly where I saw it. I said, "I didn't say I saw an eagle, I asked if you guys did." He was not amused.

YOU JUST NEVER KNOW

C O L L E E N   C H A P M A N

Suddenly I was wide awake. I sprang from the recliner alert, listening, looking. Why had I allowed myself to doze off? I knew better! No telling what he might have done while I, who was on guard duty, had slept. There was a dim light coming from the kitchen. Holding my breath and on tip toe, I crept toward the light. There he was, standing in front of the open refrigerator. Just standing there, looking into the fridge. Then he yawned, scratched, and started groping for something. This guy had to be watched every minute when he was in this condition. You just never knew what he might do when he had a fever. A high temp made him weird. Yes, time had taught me that he was unpredictable. Trying not to startle him, I slowly approached. He had never gotten violent, but you just never know.

I watched as he fumbled and groped. What is he doing, I wondered. Softly, I said 'Loren?" "Can I have some privacy?" he said with a scowl. "Of course." I said, backing up a little. I watched as he continued to grope and fumble. It seemed he couldn't find what he was looking for. Or if he did find it, it somehow eluded him, escaping his searching hand. He grew more impatient and desperate. Like a mother I felt sorry for him and wanted to help. But I couldn't do that.

At sixteen, he would resent my help. And on second thought, I really did not want to help him. As the youngest of my six sons shifted from one foot to the other, impatient, desperate, an old memory began to emerge. I had seen this behavior before. OH NO! He wouldn't! Would he? But WHY? I found no answer. I had to act quickly. "Loren, you are standing in front of the refrigerator with the door open. Since when does that require privacy?" No answer.

LOREN! WHAT ARE YOU DOING?"

"I've got ta piss. OK?"

"IN THE FRIDGE?"

Then came the gesture that must be universal with teenagers. The one that conveys their impatience, disdain and contempt for the fact that parents are so dull minded, so out of touch with reality, and just do not understand anything at all. You know; the long slow intake of breath while rolling the eyes upward, and a tusk of the tongue. He said, "Well, the milk is in there."

PEARL AND LOUON

PEARL AND LOUON

COLLEEN CHAPMAN

Pearl and Louon were married when she was 15 and he was 18. It may not have been the great love story of the century, but they stayed together through thick and thin until his death in 1976. They were, and Pearl still is, very caring, honest, descent people. They were always there for everyone in our very large family. If they were aware of a need, they didn't wait to be asked. They offered. They were not well off, but shared what they had, asking nothing in return. When I was a kid what I appreciated the most was, they shared themselves. It seemed like one or two of us kids were with them most of the time. They came to my rescue several times during the ten years of my very bad first marriage. When I was pregnant with my seventh child, I had sued for a divorce. We became homeless, and they took us in.

Both Pearl and Louon wanted several kids. Someone asked Pearl how many kids she wanted. As many as she could have, she said. It was discovered too late that she couldn't give birth as nature intended. The baby died and she almost did. After Larry and Sandra were born by C section she couldn't have more. I'm sure no children were more wanted, loved, and spoiled than those two! Everything was for them or because of them. In spite of that, they grew up to be good people. Sandra and Larry, it couldn't have been easy, sharing your parents, and putting up with me and my kids, several times. Thank you!

Pearl and Louon were also comical. Pearl was full of mischief and all too often up to something. After she pulled something on Louon he would sigh and say, "Pearl, I swear you are going to cause me to have a nervous breakdown someday." Or "Damn it Pearl, no wander I have an ulcer." Or something similar. Several times, after he had bawled her out for one of her pranks, I heard him laughing and telling someone about it, but never in her presents. The following are some of the favorite stories about them. They are not in chronological order.

BAD TIMING!

Louon was taking a nap on the couch. Pearl was doing the laundry. She found a little firecracker in a pants pocket. Going quietly into the kitchen, she got a match. Giggling, she tiptoed into the living room. She held the firecracker with her long fingernail, lit it, and waited for it to be just right to explode at the same time it hit the floor next to the couch. Her timing was not good. It explodes in her hand! She screamed. Louon rolled onto the floor and scrambled to his feet. Looking at the firecracker on the floor and Pearl's burned fingernails, he said, "You know I already have an ulcer. Are you trying to give me a heart attack?"

drawing by Sandra Johnson

MAYBE NOT

Louon's car had a dead battery. He got a chained and told Pearl to put her car in front of his. He would chain the cars together, He told her to pull his car down the road around the fields. When it started, she was to stop so he could unhook the chain. She merrily drove around the fields, singing all the way. As she turned the last corner and headed toward home, she wandered why the car had not started. Uh oh! There was Louon leaning against his car, "Oh boy. I'm gonna catch it now. He's gonna be mad and bawl me out good. Huuuuum. Maybe not." She parked in front of Louon's car, got out and slammed the door. "I thought you wanted me to pull you. I went all the way around the field and here you are, just sitting here. If you want to be pulled, stay behind me for heaven's sake." Louon said, "It works if both ends of the chain are attached to cars. We will try it again, but this time, wait until I have this end attached to my car. Oh, my stomach is killing me"

Drawing by Sandra Johnson

BAD ADVICE

When Pearl and Louon were newlyweds his father told him "Pearl will make a good wife if you show her who is boss and kept her in line. A whipping once in a while should do it." The first (and only) time he slapped her; she took a broom and lit into him. It ended up with him lying on the bed bawling while she taught him his daddy had given him bad advice.

THE BOTTLE

Louon found a job on a farm way out in the country. A lonely life for a 15-year-old bride. She became acquainted with the only family for miles around. One day Louon threw a soda pop bottle on the floor in a fit of anger. Probably because Pearl was acting like a bored little girl, which she was. He ordered Pearl to pick it up. Pearl said she didn't put it there and was not going to pick it up. That bottle stayed there for months. When Pearl cleaned the floor, she carefully cleaned around it. The mother of the family down the road came to visit for the first time. She couldn't keep from looking at the bottle but didn't ask questions. Years later she remembered it and asked about it. Pearl explained and said she would never have picked it up. Louon picked it up one day while Pearl was out of the house. They never mentioned it to each.

GERRRRRRROWL

Pearl washed her long brown hair and was playing with three-year-old Larry while it dried. On her hands and knees, with her hair hanging down over her face, she growled as she chased Larry through the living room, the kitchen, and both bedrooms and back to the living room, around and around. Larry had just dashed through the living room when Dorothy answered a knock at the door. Pearl heard Dorothy's voice, and thinking Dorothy had said something to her, paused in the bedroom, and said, "What?" Dorothy was trying to talk to whoever was at the door. When she spoke again, Pearl said, "WHAT! Well, speak up or hush up!" Pearl came crawling and growling into the living room. The man at the door had started to say something but stopped and stared at Pearl. Dorothy said, "Pearl!" Pearl stopped, looked up and saw the man and saw Dorothy pointing to the kitchen. Pearl exited the room crawling and growling. Later, Dorothy said she would never answer the door for her again.

LET ME GIVE HIM A BATH

Pearl came by on her way to…. somewhere. She was all dressed up. Nice hairdo, dress and high heels. She looked very nice. When she arrived, I was getting ready to give Vincent a bath. Pearl said, "Oh let me do it. I love bathing babies." "No, you'll get wet," "I'm going to do it. You go do whatever else needs to be done. Get out of my way." "OK, but he isn't sitting alone very well, so you'll need to keep one hand on him. And remember I'm telling you that you will be sorry." "Oh don't be silly! Go on." She said, giving me a push. I took my time getting cloths off of the line. When I got back to the kitchen Pearl was standing as far away from Vince as possible, hanging onto his shoulder. Vince splashed what little water remained in the baby tub with glee. Pearl's hair hung wet and straight, her wet dress clung to her legs. What a contrast those two were. A look of pure joy on his face and a look of misery on her wet one

CANASTA

Pearl was going to teach me to play canasta. She told me to cut the cards while she put on some coffee. Thinking she didn't have enough cards, I asked where her scissors were. She explained what she meant and told me how to do it. Louon was sitting on the couch and couldn't see us. His broken leg was in a heavy cast and it was driving him nuts. It kept getting an itch where he couldn't scratch. When he heard us laughing and having fun in the kitchen he said, "Here I am with a broken leg, can't work, I just turned 30 and have a wife and two kids to support. I'm worrying myself to death and you two are laughing like a couple of idiots without a care in the world! You don't even care that I'm in here worrying all by myself."

Pearl and I put down our cards and went into the living room. We paced the floor, wrung our hands, bit our knuckles, pulled our hair and moaned. Louon said, "What the hell are you doing!" Pearl said, "Louon, we are pacing the floor, wringing our hands and…." "I can see what you're doing. Why the hell are you doing it?" "Why Louon, we are helping you worry." "Dam it Pearl, I already have an ulcer…."

SLEEP WALKING, TALKING, DRIVING AND PEEING

COLLEEN CHAPMAN

Daddy used to sleep walk and talk. I guess my kids take after him. One time Daddy got up in the middle of the night, took hold of the bedstead and began shaking it violently. Mother was awakened from a sound sleep. She jumped out of bed, scared half to death. She asked Daddy, "What in the world are you doing?" "I'm shucking corn." he replied.

Loren was sick with the flu. I had been giving him water and lots of juice. I got him up about two in the morning and guided him to the bathroom. When he tried to put his foot in the toilet stool, I knew he was not awake. I pulled down his Pajamas and sat him on the stool. He sat there with an unhappy frown. He started to get up. I put my hands on his shoulders and held him down. He said, "What do you want me to do?!" "I want you to pee, Loren." He did. I gave him his medicine and took him to the hallway and faced him toward his room. I put his medicine away and turned to leave the bathroom. There was Loren, sitting in the bath tub. Laughing, I pulled him to his feet. "What do you want me to do?" he asked. "I want you to get out of the bath tub and go to bed." "Well, I wish you would make up your mind!" He got out of the tub and started down the hall toward the kitchen. I grabbed him, turned him around and led him to his room. With a deep sigh he got in bed, and as I tucked him in, he said, "It sure would be a big help if I knew what the heck you want!"

I was in the shower about eleven o'clock one night. I heard Rusty say, "Bye, Mom, I'm leaving for school. Gotta hurry or I'll be late." I grabbed a big bath towel and wrapped it around myself as I ran to the living room. He was already gone. I took off after him, thinking I could catch him before he got to the end of the block. He was still running when he got to the end of the third block. If the traffic light had not been red, I might have had to run all the way to the school. I couldn't take my car for the chase. It was in the driveway with Dave's car blocking it in. The four older boys slept in a trailer/bunkhouse in a far corner of the back yard. No time for that. No telling what would happen to him, or where he might go. I didn't think about how it looked, soaking wet, wearing nothing but a flapping towel, and running down the street! Didn't matter, I had to do it.

Susan hated to do dishes, even after we got a dishwasher. She would have all kinds of excuses; go to any length to keep from doing dishes. One day she kept going into the bath room, claiming she had to pee every ten minutes. I followed her into the bathroom and handed her a jar. "You had better pee in this." I said, thinking she might have a bladder infection or something. The Dr. would want a urine sample. I had already called to make an appointment. Sue had convinced me she really did have a problem. Sue thought I wanted to see if she really did have to pee and wanted to see how much. Sure enough, she had a problem. The cure was very simple. She was drinking too much Cool-Aid. I stopped keeping a pitcher of it in the fridge.

O.K., to be fair, I guess I'll tell a tale or two about myself, before someone else tells them. This way you'll get MY version!

We were traveling from Salinas to Van Nuys one hot summer night. I was eight months pregnant and had to go often. It was miles to the next restroom, and I had waited as long as I could. Howard pulled the car off of the highway as far as he could. I saw a big bush and went behind it and squatted. A big truck and trailer came by, pushing the fog up and away. In the glare of his head lights, I could see I was in the SHADOW of the bush. What could I do but wave as he passed, honking his horn.

Sue belonged to the Girl Scouts and missed out on a lot of trips because she would faint if she got too hot or excited. I would have to go get her. She would be alright in a few minutes, but they insisted I come for her. Debra joined the scouts too. Her troop was a little sister troop to Susan's troop. Debra's troop lost their leader, so I volunteered to give it a try. I didn't know the first thing about it. I attended a few classes for leaders but didn't learn nearly as much as I needed to know. This way both girls could go on the summer camp out, since the troops would camp close to each other.

One very dark night, I had to go. I had loaned my flashlight to a girl who had forgotten hers. Shouldn't be a problem, even though I have night blindness, I thought, the bathrooms were straight ahead, slightly down hill. I missed them and found myself in the stream. After groping around and not finding them, I gave up and tried to find my way back to the tent. There were some bushes nearby. I would go there. After bumping into trees, tents, garbage cans and heaven only knows what else, I made my way to the bushes close to the tents. With great relief, I squatted. I heard giggling. Debra turned on her flashlight. I was doing my business on the corner of a tent. It belonged to the father of one of the scouts. That was a fun week. I had been afraid I would not be able to keep up with my troop, and especially worried about keeping up with Sue's teen age troop when we did activities together. As it turned out, most of them had trouble keeping up with me. My troop said we all had to choose an Indian name. They named me Chief Huff N' Puff. And believe me, I did!

Pearl, Dorothy, Ruby and I arrived at the Bob Cat Den an hour early, where we were to meet George Page and others for breakfast the day before the Family reunion. We sat and drank coffee. Too much coffee! A couple of hours later, Pearl and I rushed to the bathroom. It was occupied. We waited more than five minutes. I could wait no longer. The men's restroom was right next to the women's and was not occupied. I told Pearl, "Cover me. I'm going in!" while I was in there, a man started to go in. Pearl said, "You can't go in there." The man looked at the door, looked at her and said, "This is the men's." "I know, but you can't go in right now. My sister is in there."

Betty and Larry were taking Pearl, Dorothy, Sue, and me to Sparks Nevada where they have a time share at a resort. We stopped at a service station, and Larry said he wanted to rest for 30 minutes. We headed to the rest rooms before taking a walk. Betty was in a hurry. As she reached for the restroom door, I said, "Betty, you don't want to go in there." She said, "Oh yes I do!" I said, "Well, alright." She opened the door and gasped and shut the door. "There's a man in there!" she exclaimed. "That's because it's the men's rest room. I told you you didn't want to go in there."

Sue, Dorothy and I stopped for lunch before going to a movie. The key to the rest room was kept on a hook at the end of the Deli bar. As we left the rest room, Dorothy wanted to go in. Sue held the door for her and I put the key back on the hook. We stood at the end of the deli Bar, deciding what we would have for lunch. A man asked if we knew where the key was. I pointed it out to him. He took the key and unlocked the door. I knew by this time Dorothy would be washing her hands, but she squealed anyway.

Our preacher was visiting us for the first time. I was in the kitchen when Dorothy came through the kitchen, headed for the bathroom, carrying Debra's potty with a newspaper over it. OH no, I thought, I had heard Debra saying, "See I did!" several times. I had no idea she was showing the preacher and his wife what she had done in the potty. They had all looked and admired what was in it and told her what a good girl she was. She was so proud of herself. She had done it all with no help for the first time.

Howard was spending the summer with his sister. One-night Sierra was having a bridge game with some friends. Howard had been asleep for a couple of hours. He got up, wearing his tee-shirt and shorts. He went around the table, behind Sierra's chair, and stopped facing the corner. Sierra said, "Howard, what are you doing?" "Oh, just pissen'" he said.

I awoke sitting on the stool. I had been dreaming I was hunting and hunting for a place to go. After I sat on the stool, I remember in my dream, I wasn't sure if I was awake, or if I was dreaming I had finally found the bathroom, so was afraid to go. Even after I really was awake, I wasn't sure I was.

Shortly after we put a new white carpet in the bedroom, I dreamed I was working in the Dahlia bed. It suddenly got dark. I was trying to find my way to the house. Couldn't find it. I started back to the shed to get a flashlight I keep there. I felt something, and said to myself, "This is the pole of my bedside lamp. What is my lamp doing out here?" Groping around some more, I found what I thought was one of my hiding places where I keep coffee cans to use instead of going all the way up to the house. So I used it. Then I bumped into my bed. "What the heck is my bed doing out here? Oh well, I'm cold and tired! I'm going to bed and figure it out in the morning." The next morning there was a big wet spot on my new carpet!

In my dream, Howard did something that really ticked me off. I am not a violent person, but I was going to slap him. I woke up, on my knees, facing him. I was tempted to go ahead and slap him and pretend to do it in my sleep. It probably isn't a good idea to slap a sleeping man.

In the middle of the night I heard Diane and Susan talking. I got up to see what was going on. Moonlight lit up the room well enough for me to see they were both asleep. The conversation went something like this:

"You did too."

"I did not."

"Yes you did."

"No I didn't"

"I know you did."

"No you don't 'cause I didn't"

"Yes you did. I'm gonna get you, too."

"You better not. I'll tell Mom. Anyway, I didn't."

"No you won't tell, and you did too."

"Yes I will"

"No you won't".......

I decided to have some fun with Diane. I asked her who George was. She thought and thought and couldn't think of anyone she knew named George. "I don't know any George. Why do you ask?" "Don't tell me that. I heard you talking in your sleep last night." "You did? What did I say?" "You started out—Don't, George. George, don't. Quit, George. Oh, George, don't. George, don't, stop. That went on for quite a while. You ended up saying.... OH GEORGE, DON'T STOP! Now Diane, I want to know who this George is, and just what was going on!" She swore she didn't know a George. Then she got on the phone and called her girlfriends to ask them if they knew a guy named George. The kids accused her of wanting to find that guy named George.

Pearl and louon went dancing. For the first time in her life, Pearl had a little too much to drink. Put that together with sleep walking, and you've got a problem. Or Louon did. He woke up to see Pearl peeing in her shoe. He said, "Pearl, what are you doing?" She said, "Louon, just hush and hand me your boot."

Pearl woke Louon in the wee (no pun intended) hours of the morning and probably anybody within a mile, with screams. She went into the closet instead of the bathroom and ran into her new fake fur coat. She thought she had encountered a hairy monster.

I dreamed Paul, our neighbor who was elderly and not well, was in trouble and needed me. I had been helping to take care of him and his wife Evie for a couple of years. I had driven them to the Hospital and Dr. many times. I was knocking on their door when I woke up. Evie opened the door and said she was just going to call me. Paul needed to go to the hospital.

My niece Sharon drives in her sleep. Her husband has always heard you should not wake a person who is sleep walking, so he goes with her. She drives around town and goes back home. He says she drives better in her sleep than she does when she is awake!

STRANGE BUT TRUE

A STRING OF EMAILS ABOUT THIS HOUSE

Colleen----When we moved back to this house it had been rented out for over 25 years. It was filled with...for lack of a better word... negative energy. It was not haunted, as people think of "haunted." I was told the negative energy had once been attached to one or more of the former tenants. It is gone now, but some strange things happened here before it left. Dorothy had some experiences with it when she was staying here, as did my son Rusty and his wife Kathy, and my daughter Sue. Maybe they will tell about them.

The first thing that happened to me was when I came here to get this place ready to move back into. I had gone to bed and was still wide awake when I felt three pushes on the bed. It felt like a child had pushed on the edge of the mattress. I thought it was my dog trying to get my attention. I told her to go lay down. It happened again the next night. This time I knew that Puddles was in the living room, and the door was closed. I turned on the light and saw no one. I turned off the light again. Felt the three pushes again. Well, it had worked the night before, so I said, "Go lay down" It never happen to me again.

The next time I saw Mother and Nila, who had lived in this house in the past, I asked them if anything odd had happened to them while they lived here. Nila said the whole family had felt the three pushes on their beds. Always three pushes. Mother said she had seen horrible looking faces in her room. I asked Nila if anything else had happened. She said there had been other things but refused to tell me about them.

Dorothy----I will tell what happened to me in the back bedroom. I was in bed reading when I started feeling little ripples in the mattress. I thought it felt like a large dog under the bed bumping it with his head. I got up and tried to look under the bed but it was a kind of platform with no openings. No way for a dog or anything else to get under there. After Colleen explained that it was this negative energy I would just say "God bless you" when the bed started acting crazy and it would stop. Before that, several times I had seen the scarf which covered a small bedside table swaying as if the wind was blowing it gently.

Colleen----When Dorothy told me about the bed, we striped it and examined the mattress for holes where a mouse or snake might have gotten through. There were none. We made up

361

the bed, and we were sitting on the bed talking. I was sitting with my knees bent and ankles crossed. I asked Dorothy if she had been dreaming and it didn't really happen. Just then I felt, and we both saw, in the space between my torso and my ankles, a lump come and go, as if the mattress had been punched from inside by a fist. I said, "Uh oh. Maybe not!" We didn't feel threatened or scared. I then told her about the negative energy.

Sue----I too, had a strange experience in that room. One morning as I was laying there thinking about whether or not I should get up, I heard footsteps coming down the hall. So I decided that since Howard was up, that I should go ahead and get up. Once I got dressed and went into the kitchen, there were my parents sitting at the table. Howard did not have his shoes on yet. I asked them if they had been down the hall and they both said no.

Oh ya, there was one other strange experience. One night shortly after going to bed, it happened. The bed shook three times. Like someone had their hand on the bed and gave it a good healthy shove 3 time. Boy did I say my prayer of protection. I think if the prayer was recorded on audio tape no one would have understand it because I said it so fast. Once I got into the habit of saying my protection prayer when I went to bed, there were no more incidents.

Dorothy----I also heard footsteps in the hall when there was no one there. And felt the bed move like someone was pushing on it. Things would disappear and then reappear too. I think we were all pretty brave about it but Colleen told me that Howard was gone over night one time and she decided that she didn't want to stay in the house alone so she slept in the van.

Colleen----Yes, I did spend the night in the van. I don't always go with Howard to the airplane events. If you are not flying yourself, it can be as exciting as watching the sap rise in a tall tree on a cold day. The van is a camper van. We no longer use it for long trips, but keep it stocked for short trips, for ONE of us. I had gone to bed and was almost asleep, then was suddenly wide awake and terrified. It seemed as if the room was filled with something evil. If I were a cat, I would have had an arched back, and every hair on my body would have been sticking straight out. With no hesitation or even thinking about what I was doing, I ran to the van, got in and locked the doors. Then I felt silly. I went back in the house, and it felt OK until I went into the bedroom. (not the same one that Dorothy and Sue had used) As soon as I stepped into the bed room, the sense of evil was so strong; it almost knocked me off my feet. This trip to the van took less time than the first one. I locked all the doors, closed the curtains, and felt silly again. Since when will locked doors keep something like that out? Only one thing could protect me, and I spent some time on my knees talking to God. I spent the night in the van. The next day everything was ok in the house. That was the only time anything like that happened.

Sue and I had started calling the mischievous little entity who liked to play tricks on us, George. Don't remember why, but maybe it came from the saying-let George do it. In this case we said George did it. The pushes on the bed felt like a small child or dog pushing on the edge of the bed to get your attention. That happened to me only twice. The footsteps in the hall seemed to come from the back of the house, down the hall and go into the bathroom. As far as I know that happened just a few times.

One day when Susan and I were doing the arts and craft stuff, a pattern I wanted to use disappeared from a box of patterns. It had been put on top of everything else in the box the night before. We spent a lot of time looking for it. Couldn't find it. I told George he had had his fun, I didn't have time for his non-sense, and I was going to put on a pot of coffee and when I came back, I wanted to see that pattern right where it was supposed to be. Believe it or not, it was.

All of you who have never experienced things like this probably think we are nuts. At the reunion, you might think oh! Here come the crazy cousins! But don't be afraid of us. We are harmless, and I promise to make George stay home. Just kidding about George. He and who ever or whatever else was here have gone on to where ever they were supposed to go in the first place.

The person who told me this house had negative energy from someone who had lived here, told me I could get them to leave. I did, like this: I relaxed in my recliner, and after asking for protection from evil energies, I told the negative energies they weren't supposed to be here. I asked them to go on to where ever they were meant to be, and asked God to bless them. After a few seconds it felt as if something was going away, like a breeze going out a window. Whatever was here is gone, but occasionally other odd thing happens, but not in this house.

My friend and neighbor Dona and I were in Costco. When we were leaving and had to show my receipt at the door, I couldn't find it. I thought maybe I had put it in my wallet with my Costco and ATM cards. It wasn't there and neither were my cards. We went to the customer service counter and they printed out a new receipt from the computer. A woman came hurrying up to me and handed me my Costco card. She said she had found it on top of some boxes stacked against the wall. We had not been near them. She had not seen my ATM card. We left the store, and I stopped to put my Costco card in my wallet. The original receipt and my ATM card were there. Dona was a little spooked. On the way home, we stopped for something else. When I opened my wallet, both cards were gone! I had some cash, so used it instead. To be on the safe side, as soon as I got home I had both cards canceled and got new ones. They never did show up. No one tried to use them. Can spooks use cards?

Rusty and Kathy were staying with us while he waited for a job at the Diablo Canyon Power Plant. He helped with things that needed to be done here, and Kathy signed up with a Temp. Agency. She went to bed earlier than the rest of us when she had a job the next day. I noticed that she would sometimes get up and stay up until Rusty went to be too. I asked her if something odd happened to cause her to get up. She said it did. Pushes on the bed and things swaying, and had seen a huge black spider, although the light was off, and the room was dark. I then told her and Rusty about George and the negative energy George was nothing to be afraid of, but the negative energy might be. A few nights later, shortly after they had gone to bed, Rusty came running into the living room with Kathy right behind him. He was laughing, but Kathy was not. She was angry. There was a stack of boxes containing their belongings between the bed and the wall. Kathy slept on her side, facing the boxes. Rusty had used some fluorescent paint and painted a skull on a box. After the light had been turned off, Kathy turned on her side, and was face to face with the skull.

After she calmed down and they went back to bed, Rusty came running again. This time dragging the sheet. He had also painted a skull on the ceiling, right above Kathy's side of the bed, knowing she would not face the boxes again, but lie on her back.

STRANGE EVENTS

C OLLEEN C HAPMAN

When I was very young I was always getting into trouble for telling lies. I was too young to understand what a lie was. I can remember Daddy trying to make me understand the difference between what is true or real and what is not. But how could it not be real if I knew it? I learned that I saw and heard things that other people did not. It became obvious to me that there were some things I should just keep to myself.

Over the years I learned to pay attention to…I don't know what to call it. Some things came in a dream, but not always. I would just know something and have no idea how or why I knew. I learned that if there was something happening or going to happen, and there was something I could do to prevent it, I was made aware of it, and knew what to do. And if something was meant to happen, and there was nothing I could do to prevent it, I was not made aware of it. Sometimes I knew something awful was going to happen, but not know what it was, and knew I could do nothing. That is not a good feeling, but it prepared me for whatever was to come.

Some of the things that have happened over the years are not in chronological order.

Howard and I were on our way home with three-month-old Loren. We had taken him to a specialist in L. A. Loren was born with a cleft lip and pallet. We were on a long, two lanes stretch of highway 101, when I began feeling jittery. I tried to relax but couldn't. I became very nervous and told Howard we needed to get off the road. He said I was overtired, and to get in the back seat and lay down. I did, but it didn't work. I was soon sitting up and almost screaming for Howard to get off the road. Just then we were approaching King City and he pulled off at a café. We had just received our coffee when I was suddenly calm. I told Howard we were OK now. Just then we heard sirens.

We finished our coffee and got back on the road. Just a few miles down the road, there was a wreck. A big truck, coming from the other direction, had come into our lane, and the vehicles we had been in-between for many miles, had been hit by the truck. A few other cars were involved too. If we had not stopped, we would have been in the middle of it.

365

Robert was winning all the races when he was in junior high, what is now called middle school. A group of boys tried to convince him that he should let the number two boy, who was their friend win. Robert didn't see things their way, and the group of boys decided to use physical persuasion instead of verbal persuasion. He wasn't worried, because he could outrun them. When I found out about it, I was worried. I talked to the principal, but nothing changed. I decided picking Robert up at school was the thing to do.

The second or third day I was busy sewing and forgot about the time. I heard Robert say, "Hey, MOM!" I looked up and said "What?" The other kids were sitting at the table with their after-school snack. They looked at me questioningly. I asked where Rob was. They said he wasn't home yet. I grabbed my keys and ran to the car. The car was parked in the driveway. Instead of going in the direction of the school, I went in the opposite direction to the end of the block and turned right. Down the street I saw a group of boys. I pulled alongside, stopped and grabbed a short 2x4 from the floorboard. I had seen it when getting in the car and had wondered why it was there. I pushed and pulled my way to the center, swinging the board, grabbed Rob and made it back to the car. Robert said the group had divided up and were waiting for him in different places along the way home. He had tried to avoid them by taking a different route home. They had caught up to him, three groups coming from different directions. How did I know where to go? I don't know. It was as if I had done it without really thinking about what I was doing.

I was in bed, but not yet asleep, laying on my right side. (This happened in Van Nuys, long before we moved back to this house.) It felt like our dog had gotten on the bed. Intending to push him off, I reached back, but nothing was there. Then the mattress in front of me felt like something heavy was there. From the light coming in the window, I could see nothing was there. I turned onto my back and started to get up but couldn't. Some unseen thing was on my chest. I couldn't breathe. I thought, "God, whatever I'm supposed to say, 'get thee behind me Satan or whatever, please consider it said." The weight was immediately gone. I got up and made it the few steps to the bathroom and turned on the light. I had purple lips and dark circles under my eyes.

I dreamed that Diane, Dave and Steven were with their friend Vickie. They had run out of gas, and they were pushing Vickie's car while she steered it, along the edge of the freeway. A car was coming up behind them, not slowing down. All three of my kids were about to be crushed.

A few days later the kids asked if they could go to the beach with Vickie. Although I didn't want to, I said yes. When they got home they were rather excited. They said the car had to be pushed, and they all three, at the same time, remembered me telling them about that dream. Without looking back, they all jumped out of the way. Vickie's car was rear ended. It didn't do much damage, but the kids would have been hurt, had they not gotten out of the way.

I dreamed I saw Loren's red and white Corvair on its side, skidding down a road. I didn't recognize the area and would not let him drive his car anyplace out of town. He borrowed Debra and Ken's pickup to attend a concert in Fresno. What I had seen did happen sometime later. He was just on the outskirts of Porterville, when he got T boned by a pickup. His car was skidding, on its side, headed for a fence and trees. Since the car was hit on the passenger side, and the driver's side was on the pavement, I don't know how he got out. He was bruised and very sore, but nothing was broken. It's a good thing no one was in the passenger seat. That side of the car was pushed in to about the center of the car.

I was in bed and almost asleep. Suddenly it felt as if the bed was moving very fast. I opened my eyes and saw a flash of light in front of me. The next night I was going to some event in Porterville. There seemed to be a power outage, because all the lights were out. The street I was on was not a very busy one at that time of the evening, and there was not another car in sight. But feeling uneasy, I slowed down. A truck and trailer, without lights on and unseen by me, was going slowly in the right-hand lane. I was in the left lane, approaching my left-hand turn. The truck suddenly made a left hand turn right in front of me. My headlights caught the silvery metal of the side of the trailer. I hit the brakes in time. That was the same silvery flash I had seen the night before.

I was working in my vegetable garden and found myself having a "conversation" for lack of a better word, with a being, or spirit, who was to be my grandson. When I realized what was happening, I thought, "Wow! I have been in the sun too long!" I don't remember the whole thing, but I was being told that this spirit was supposed to be born to Debra but couldn't until Ken wanted it too. If it didn't happen soon, it would be too late for him and he couldn't wait. He would have to be born by me. I said that was not possible, since my uterus had been removed. He said that with God, all things are possible. Then I remembered having read about a woman who had given birth after having her uterus removed. The next thing I knew, Debra was there, walking toward me. I suppose I looked strange because she was looking at me questioningly. Then it was her turn to look strange when I told her what had just happened.

A few months later I was on my way home from a trip to Salinas. I stopped for lunch, and while browsing a gift shop, I bought a little teddy bear. After getting back in the car, I wondered why I had done that. Then I knew. Debra was pregnant, and she would have a boy, and would name him Nicholas. Before going on home, I stopped at Debra's in Porterville. I gave her the toy and said it was for Nicholas. She and her friend, who was visiting, stared at me in surprise. Debra had just learned she was pregnant and had chosen names. I don't remember the name chosen if it was a girl, but if it was a boy, its name would be Nicholas Andrew.

Dorothy, Pearl and I attended a retreat, based on the teachings of Edgar Casey. At the time I knew little or nothing about him, but a week or so in the mountains with two of my sisters was just what I needed. We attended several classes, based on different interesting things. One was about Angles. After the class as we were walking to the dining hall for lunch, we saw some wild Irises with buds. Just then the English woman who had given the lecture came hurrying past us. I asked her if we asked the Bloomin Angles, could they make the Iris bloom before we had to leave. She did not see the humor in it. In another class, before we got there, objects had been gathered and put into small paper bags. We sat in circles of six or seven people. The person leading the class said we would each be given a closed bag. We were not to open it or feel it. It would be placed on our palms, and we were to try to see if we could get an impression of what was in our bag. While she was explaining this, I thought…. pine cone. So what was in my bag? A pine cone! Pearl was sitting in a circle next to ours, and we were back to back. Somehow I knew her bag contained a baby blanket.

Another exercise we did was to form two circles, standing, facing each other. My circle, the outer one, was to close their eyes. The person in the inner circle was to take our hands. As we held hands, the one with closed eyes, was to try to get an impression of the other person and tell what they got. The first person I held hands with puzzled me. All I could think of was ear rings. When I told her this, she laughed and said she had what had to be one of the largest ear ring collections in the USA. The second one had me puzzled too. I thought a trick was being played on me, and two different people were holding hands with me. I said "I sense two people here. One is male and has red hair." She was pregnant. She said her husband has red hair. She sent me a card after her baby was born. A boy with red hair.

Sue and I were on our way home from……I think it was the trip to Oklahoma when Dorothy's ashes were put at the foot of Jack's grave. We had spent the night in Porterville and were on our way to Rusty's and Kathy's near Atascadero. We were taking a shortcut Sue had not taken before. When it was time to make a turn, she was not sure which direction to turn. Since I had been that way only once, we wanted to consult the map. I reached into the pocket of my door, where the maps of all the states we had driven through were kept. The first map I pulled out was the one we needed, folded to the area we needed, with the rout marked with a see-through marker. We continued on our way, and I replaced the map. The map looked just like the one Rusty had shown me a few months before. Not the new one we had bought when we began our trip, but I thought nothing of it at the time. When it was time to make the next turn, Sue wanted to see the map again. We couldn't find it. She pulled over and stopped. We searched the whole car. The map was not there. When we stopped before, we had not gotten out of the car or even opened a door or window, but that darn map was gone. We made it to Rusty's with no problems. When we told Rusty about it, he walked over to a desk or table and picked up a map. THE MAP! He said he had not given it to me but had only shown it to me.

FRED

COLLEEN CHAPMAN

Pearl called and said Fred was in the Hospital and was running a high temp. The Dr. did not know what was wrong with him in spite of doing several tests. She was afraid he was dying. I was very worried and trying to figure out if I could arrange for someone to stay with the kids so I could go to see him. Then, in my head I heard Daddy say to my brother Donny (Daddy and Donny had passed several years before) "if they don't find what is wrong with Fred he will be here with us." I felt faint and laid on my bed. I had my eyes closed but I saw a large medical book opened to a page showing a bright red thing about the size and shape of my thumb. It was behind an organ, but I didn't know what that organ was. I called Pearl and told her about it. She was successful in getting the Dr. to listen to her. She called the next day and said they had found an abscess on something she didn't remember the name of, but they had taken care of it and Fred no longer had a fever, and was getting better.